COCKY

BY TONY BARNES, RICHARD ELIAS & PETER WALSH

*The Rise and Fall of Curtis Warren
Britain's Biggest Drug Baron*

ISBN 0 9530847 7 9

Typography and layout by Barron Hatchett Design, Manchester.

Printed and bound in Great Britain by Guernsey Press Co Ltd,
Guernsey.

Sold and distributed in Great Britain by Turnaround Publisher Services
Ltd,
Unit 3, Olympia Trading Estate, Coburg Road, London N22 6TZ.
Telephone 020 8829 3000

MILO BOOKS
PO Box 153, Bury, Lancashire BL0 9FX
info@milobooks.com

'Everyone's entitled to one bad habit'

Curtis Warren

Contents

ONCE UPON a time in the Nineties, the Home Office asked an eminent sociologist to carry out research into serious crime. Though a professor at an old and venerable red-brick university, he had been born and raised in a tough part of the East End of London and was one of the few British academics prepared to delve into the murk of the underworld.

His work led him to spend time in Liverpool, at the headquarters of Merseyside Police. During one visit, he happened to enquire about 'organised crime' in the presence of a high-ranking officer. The officer bristled.

'We do not have organised crime in Liverpool,' he thundered.

Later that day, a young but streetwise junior detective took the professor to one side.

'We do have organised crime,' he whispered. 'But we keep it in a box marked: *Do not open, too difficult to handle.*'

This is what happened when that box was opened.

PREFACE

Curtis Warren has been described as 'the most significant bust HM Customs and Excise have ever had' and as 'the richest and most successful British criminal who has ever been caught'. The story of how he reached those dizzy, dubious heights, and how he fell so spectacularly, is the subject of this book.

AN hour before daybreak on 24 October 1996, dozens of police officers armed with stun grenades, disabling gas, heat-seeking detectors and sub-machine guns burst into two homes and a warehouse in the Netherlands

Their targets were members of a dangerous gang of British criminals engaged in a global drug conspiracy. The co-ordinated raids followed an eight-month undercover probe by Dutch police. Ten men – nine Britons and a Colombian linked to a notorious cocaine cartel – were dragged from their beds and arrested.

The raid in Holland yielded approximately 400 kilograms of cocaine, sixty kilos of heroin, 1,500 kilos of cannabis and fifty kilos of Ecstasy. The haul was worth around £125 million on the street. Also discovered were 960 CS gas canisters, several grenades, a variety of handguns, false passports and £370,000-worth of Dutch guilders.

Simultaneously, British law enforcement officers executed search warrants in premises across north-west England to mop up some of the gang's cohorts. They had been working on the case for even longer than the Dutch: two and a half long years of exhaustive surveillance and intelligence-gathering, the biggest joint investigation ever mounted by police and customs officers, codenamed Operation Crayfish.

Newspaper headlines heralded the conclusion of a successful operation:

'MR BIG' HELD AS POLICE SMASH £100M DRUG RING

The Mister Big in question was Curtis Warren, a thirty-three-year-old Liverpudlian dubbed 'Target One' by the press. He has since been called the biggest scalp ever claimed by British law enforcement officers. He has been described as 'the most significant bust HM Customs and Excise have ever had' and as 'the richest and most successful British criminal who has ever been caught'. The story of how he reached those dizzy, dubious heights, and how he fell so spectacularly, is the subject of this book.

The backdrop to that narrative is an even more important – and hitherto untold – account of how one city came to dominate much of the drug importation into the United Kingdom. There are historical and economic reasons for the disproportionate influence of Liverpool criminals in the drug trade. Yet until now it has gone almost unnoticed. Three recent and otherwise admirable books about organised crime in the UK – *Gangland Britain* by Tony Thompson, *The Underworld* by Duncan Campbell and *Gangland Volume 2* by James Morton – fail to mention it. Morton, a criminal lawyer, reports a 'consensus of police, lawyers' and sociologists' opinion that on balance there has been no organised crime in Liverpool; certainly not on the scale seen in London'. About drugs, he adds, 'Officers maintain, almost certainly correctly, that the trade is minor compared with that of Manchester from where, in the main, the local dealers get their supplies.'

It is not easy to understand how such well-informed writers missed the story so completely. Perhaps it has something to do with the unspoken official secrecy which for so long shrouded the words 'organised crime' and forbade their mention by police officers outside the Met. Perhaps it is testimony to the success of the smugglers in maintaining relative anonymity. Perhaps it is the natural expectation of London-based commentators that the capital must dominate. Thompson points out that seventy per cent of crime takes place there. True. That leaves thirty per cent that doesn't, and that's a lot of crime.

The authors are deeply indebted to those who knew the truth and were prepared to tell it. We could not have written this book without the co-operation and help of many people. From Her Majesty's Customs and Excise they include Paul Acda, Colin Gurton, Steve Rowton and Ranald Macdonald and his team. Senior police officers who provided insight and help included Sir James Sharples, Mike Keogh, John Thompson, Phil Jones and, from Holland, Tom Driessen. Many other customs and police officers gave invaluable information on condition of anonymity. We offer our sincere thanks.

We are also grateful to Pat Ashworth, the former Press Attache at the British Embassy in The Hague, to Warren's solicitor Keith Dyson and Dutch lawyer Han Jahae, and to other barristers, solicitors and court officials, particularly the staff at Chur Cantonal Court in Switzerland. Reporters Jonathan Foster of the *Independent on Sunday*, Angus Hoy of the *Middlesbrough Evening Gazette*, John Sweeney of the *Observer*, John Mooney of the *Sunday Times* and Liz Allen of the *Sunday Independent* were especially helpful. We are grateful to Colin Hunt and Les Rawlinson at the library of the Liverpool *Daily Post and Echo* for background cuttings and pictures, to Steve Brauner, to Lynda Roughley and Colin Simpson at Liverpool Crown Court and to Nils Heithuis and Peter Elberse of the ANP news agency in the Netherlands. Bill Godber at Turnaround was a model of advice, encouragement and, above all, patience, as were the staff at Milo Books.

Numerous underworld sources also spoke to the authors in the course of our research. Not one was willing to go 'on the record', for understandable reasons. We can, however, vouch that every opinion or anecdote related in these pages can be sourced. In one or two places, where indicated, we have used pseudonyms and occasionally quotes from two people have been amalgamated into one. There were also legal barriers to complete openness. Certain people who could, and should, have been named in this book are at the time of writing facing serious criminal charges.

Curtis Warren turned down all requests, written and verbal, to be interviewed, as did members of his family. At the time of writing he is in prison in Holland, serving a twelve-year jail sentence and intending to pursue an appeal to the European Court of Human Rights against his conviction for drugs smuggling. He also faces a Dutch legal action to seize his criminal assets and a consecutive four-year term for the manslaughter of a fellow prisoner. His English lawyer says he 'blows hot and cold' about whether or not to tell his side of the story; he would like to but feels it is so earth-shattering that 'no-one would print it'.

Many of Warren's secrets are too well buried to be found. Partly for that reason, this is not a conventional biography. Rather it is an attempt to use one man's life-story to chart the development of a particularly active arm of the modern drugs trade and the official attempts to combat it. We hope it sheds some light on a dark world but would not pretend for a minute that this is anything like the full picture.

The drug debate is complex. Only recently have some senior police officers and doctors been able to discuss it rationally. The politicians are still catching up. By 1996, the United Nations estimated that illicit drugs accounted for eight per cent of all world trade, more than iron and steel and the motor industry. The annual turnover was put at £250 billion. Such a huge business necessarily involves a lot of people. This is the story of just one of them.

Curtis Warren's many friends talk well of him. Interestingly, so do his enemies – up to a point. He is, they say, personable, humorous, clever and fearless. That his considerable talents found an outlet in such an unsavoury arena is a tragedy, for him but more especially for the tens of thousands of unhappy souls who became addicted to the narcotics he peddled or the unknown number who died from an overdose of his heroin or a single tablet of his Ecstasy. However glamorous his life became, the sordid and miserable reality of hard drugs should never be forgotten.

1 TARGET ONE

'The black-clad Merseyside firearms team
materialised, pointing sub-machine guns at his
chest and ordering him to hit the dirt...'

UNDER a leaden pre-dawn sky, the lorry rumbled from the belly of the Holland sea ferry and onto Felixstowe docks. It crawled in low gear through a cloud of diesel fumes, joining a slow snake of vehicles heading towards the customs checkpoint. Turkish number plates betrayed its origin; otherwise its blue cab and soft curtain sides were typical of the hundreds of bonded TIR lorries that had passed through the East Anglian port every day since the 'container revolution' of the 1950s transformed a fading resort into the cargo capital of Britain.

Driver Hidayet Sucu, aged thirty-three, had risen early, slurped a quick black coffee and thrown his passport and papers onto the passenger seat before starting up. His documents indicated the truck was empty and after a cursory check he was waved through customs. Ahead of him lay a south-to-north, coast-to-coast drive across England. Sucu yawned; he had had a tiring few days and a restless night. At least his onward journey was all motorway. He tuned into a pop station and put his foot down, heading off into the brightening

November gloom. He never noticed he was being followed.

Unmarked cars scattered around the port area began to pull out. They worked as a team, their occupants keeping radio contact on secure wavebands, tailing Sucu as he headed towards London. At a steady sixty-five miles per hour, he made the long haul across to the M25, then turned north up the M1 to the M6. His escorts stayed with him, some in front and some behind. At Knutsford service station in Cheshire, more cars discreetly joined the secret cavalcade, shadowing Sucu as he turned onto the M62, heading west towards Liverpool. At the end of the motorway he passed the landmark Rocket pub before lumbering down the dual carriageway of Edge Lane and into the city.

Sucu was under close surveillance by both police and customs officers. They believed his lorry was carrying a large, hidden load of heroin. Trafficking 'smack' to Europe is a Turkish speciality: about 80 per cent of the drug entering the UK is refined there from opium grown in Afghanistan and Pakistan before travelling the well-established Balkan Route to Western Europe. The officer in charge of the operation was 'Fletch', a highly-experienced customs man. Small and bespectacled with a modest paunch and mildly lugubrious look, he was a veteran of many similar operations and had developed the useful knack of watching without appearing to. He also knew what to look for.

'The drug barons often put cars near the Rocket and run their loads past it; if they see a car they don't like, they follow it. They also put spotters on the footbridges over the motorway. It's known as a dry-cleaning run – a journey made for the sole purpose of checking if anyone is following. If there's anything at all they don't like, they abandon it. On this occasion the load was taken on a deliberately circuitous route and through several well-known choke points, where traffic congestion and the road system stops the tailing cars and makes them easier to spot.'

Customs had anticipated such manoeuvres. A helicopter monitored the lorry from the sky. Once into Liverpool city centre, the lorry stopped and parked on yellow lines outside the main Passport Office at India Buildings in Water Street. It was a Thursday and there was a queue of people outside waiting to apply for passports. The driver put on his hazard lights and remained there for the next three hours. 'We didn't really know what was going on,' says Fletch. 'The truck was in a very prominent position right in the heart of the city and he simply stayed there. I got on the radio and told the tailing cars to make themselves scarce.'

Shortly after three o'clock in the afternoon, Sucu flicked off the flashing lights and set off, re-tracing his route to the M62 towards Manchester. After half an hour, he indicated left and pulled into the service station at Burtonwood, a few miles from Warrington. Four cars followed him along the slip road. In the back of one was Fletch. He watched as the truck pulled around the service buildings into the HGV park and stopped.

One of Fletch's team was Mark [*author's note: not his real name*], a young officer highly-regarded for his skill on stakeouts. He was waiting in a car at the same service station but on the opposite, Liverpool-bound side of the motorway, to check for any suspicious vehicles or spotters. He watched as a silver, K-registration Honda Legend sharked up into the car park. As it drew closer to his hidden vantage point, he had a clear look at the driver's face.

'It was like an electric shock,' says Mark. 'There he was, large as life. He drove around the car park, had a good look around, and then took off.'

The face he saw was that of Curtis Warren, a stocky, thirty-year-old Liverpudlian with a sorrel complexion, razor-cropped hair and the shoulders of a wrestler. Mark knew all about Warren. A few months earlier he had walked free from the biggest drugs trial in British history. He was sharp, resourceful and could smell the Law a mile off. After scanning the parking bays, he brazenly drove onto the private service road that dips through an underpass and connects to the westbound service area. There Sucu's lorry was parked.

A few minutes later, Fletch, unaware of Warren's presence, saw him emerge from the shopping bay onto a raised area overlooking the car park. His heart jolted.

'I knew exactly who he was. He looked as if he was just stepping out for a breath of fresh air. However, from where he was standing you could get a good view of all the cars coming into the service area. He spent no more than a few moments looking at the car park and then he was gone, back inside the building. That was the last I saw of him. I got on the radio immediately and told everyone else that under no circumstances should they pull into Burtonwood.'

Warren made no attempt to approach the suspect lorry or its driver, but the officers were taking no chances. Some of the tailing cars – there were fourteen in total – pulled off at the previous motorway exit while others carried on to the next. A vehicle containing a Merseyside Police firearms team, dressed in body armour and carrying sub-machine guns, stayed on the motorway. The next few minutes were tense. Fletch knew Warren had violent friends and a record that included attacks on police officers. The investigators already in the car park dispersed into the shops, the toilets and the petrol station.

In the now super-charged atmosphere, Sucu jumped down from his cab and walked to the bank of phone kiosks, where he made a short call. Whoever it was to, and whatever was said, it had a dramatic effect on the Turk. Glancing furtively around, he trotted back to his cab, started up and pulled out once more onto the motorway. Warren, meanwhile, had gone; other officers reported seeing his Legend heading back to Liverpool.

Had they been sussed? Fletch tried to think. *What the hell was going on?*

Sucu drove east along the M62, past Leeds, and turned south onto the M1. He continued without stopping until he reached the Scratchwood service station just a few miles north of London. It was now late evening and the lorry had covered hundreds of miles in a loop around the country. Some of the tailing officers had been in their cars for more than eighteen hours. Sucu pulled to a halt and walked into the service area to use the toilet and grab a coffee. As he returned to his truck across the dark and virtually empty tarmac of the lorry park, the black-clad Merseyside firearms team materialised, pointing sub-machine guns at his chest and ordering him to hit the dirt. Scared witless, he complied instantly.

A search team dismantled the lorry the following morning. Behind a rear panel they discovered bolts which allowed them to remove a metal plate stretching the width of the trailer. Beneath it was a false floor filled with blue-grey steel drawers. The customs men tugged the nearest one and, with a hair-curling metal scrape, it slid out. Inside were large packets, each the size of a five-pound bag of potatoes, wrapped in transparent white plastic and containing brown powder. There were twenty drawers, each ten feet long, eight inches high and holding eight packets. It was 180 kilos of almost pure heroin. When cut and sold on the street, it would have been worth up to £40 million. It was the biggest heroin haul any of them had seen.

The record bust was in itself cause for celebration. But it was the sighting of Warren that generated most excitement. Other officers had already pulled the intelligence file on him:

Name:	CURTIS FRANCIS WARREN
Born:	Liverpool
Date of birth:	31 May 1963
Height:	5 ft 9 in
Weight:	190 lbs approx
Build:	Stocky
Eyes:	Brown
Hair:	Black/dark brown. Shaven. Thinning at crown.
Features:	Freckles. Thin scar on left temple
Address:	Wapping Dock, Liverpool
Nicknames:	Cocky Watchman, Cocky, the Cock
Occupation:	Unknown

His official criminal record stretched back to the age of twelve. There was more, much more: pages and pages detailing his associates, the cars he used, his haunts, past operations against him. Curtis Warren was regarded by British law enforcement officers as one of the most important drugs brokers in northern Europe, a man who had taken the modus operandi of the ghetto pusher – the glib tongue, the cellphone, the fast car – and applied it successfully to multi-million pound deals. The principles were the same, only the scale was different. 'You couldn't take the street out of Curtis,' says a customs investigator who tracked him for years.

His presence at Burtonwood service station at the same time as a lorryload of heroin could have been coincidence. There would never be any evidence to link him to the drugs and the arrested driver, Sucu, gave no indication of knowing him. But customs officers are a sceptical bunch. They believed he was there watching for something, and had been spooked. The police firearms team had not been using encrypted radios; perhaps their air traffic had been picked up by someone with a scanner. Mark, the surveillance officer, believed that Warren's appearance at the scene was typical of him.

'He always turned up when he had a load coming in. Sometimes he would be close by, sometimes three or four miles away, but he had to be around. It was his trademark. It was just pure curiosity. Sometimes he was very ostentatious, swanning up in his Legend, and other times he would be in an old Escort. It depended on his mood. In a way he was just protecting his investment. He never trusted anyone completely. If he didn't turn up, you knew it was a dummy run. He was like a shepherd coming to oversee his sheep. And if he didn't like the look of something, he would write off the load there and then. Although driven by greed, he had the ability to walk away no matter what was at stake. He was never there for the "slaughter".'

Curtis Warren was a priority for HM Customs and Excise. Sometimes they called him Target One. So when Fletch reported back to his boss Paul Acda, the top customs investigator in the north of England, he was delighted. He believed Warren to be 'a unique trafficker in UK terms' because of his contacts with all the main men in all the main centres of drug production: Colombia, Turkey, Africa, the Netherlands. Despite the lack of concrete evidence, this sighting – on 18 November

1993 – gave them the excuse they had been looking for to launch a fresh investigation into his activities.

'That's it,' said Paul Acda. 'He's back at it.'

CURTIS WARREN gunned his £30,000 silver Honda Legend down the motorway back to Liverpool. He was dressed cool and loose in designer-label sports top, tracksuit bottoms and clean new trainers. A cellphone lay on the passenger seat. He steered smoothly, the automatic gear stick – he preferred automatics – in Drive, his right hand on the wheel, elbow resting against the side window, no haste in his movements. His brown eyes took in everything. Only the regular flicker of his gaze towards the rear view mirror betrayed any tension.

They said that Yasser Arafat, that guy who ran the PLO, could tell by instinct when the Israelis were coming for him. He would leave a safehouse minutes before their hit squads came crashing through the windows. It saved his skin many times.

Warren had it too, a tingling unease when there was danger in the air. 'I've got the sixth sense, haven't I?' he would tell friends. Once alerted, he could vanish without trace: 'I can just go to ground, know what I mean? The little moonlight flit.'

He lived and travelled light. He never carried a wallet, flashed a credit card or signed a cheque. He changed cars and phones regularly, discouraged photographs and, on paper, owned very little. He had no qualifications and appeared to have no regular job. Yet he earned more than a top City trader, worked longer hours than a junior doctor and commanded the loyalty of a small army. He ran a global business spanning five continents and juggled orders, purchases and sales totalling hundreds of millions of pounds with clients who spoke a plethora of languages. *And he did it all in his head.*

All he needed was his portable phone, his 'portie'. It was as much the tool of his trade as a surgeon's scalpel or a reporter's ballpoint. His near-photographic memory retained scores of telephone numbers; he never had to write them down or store them in the phone's memory where others could find them. He moved in a world of subterfuge and deceit, where nicknames and aliases hid myriad sins. So there was the Werewolf and the Vampire, Cracker, Macker and Tacker, the Bell with No Stalk and the Egg on Legs. There was Lunty, Badger and Boo, Twit and Twat, Big Foot, the Big Fella, the J Fella, the L Fella and dozens more. His own streetname, the Cocky Watchman, was an obscure Scouse slang term for a nosey nighwatchman or park keeper and meant someone who was always vigilant. Usually it was abbreviated to Cocky.

He was used to being hunted and hounded and had learned not let setbacks get him down. He liked to lay back. That was why he liked the Honda: a classy car, tasteful not flash, its fuel-injected V6 engine powerful without seeming so. He cultivated the same understated strength. Even when he was pissed off, the surface was calm. He glanced at the mirror again. No tail. Still, take no chances. He eased the Legend towards the environs of Toxteth and his gaze drank in the ragged streets he knew so well. He nodded at a small knot of young men standing on a corner. They stared back coldly before recognising the coffee face and the shaven head. They grinned and raised a salute to the casually-dressed drug baron.

On he drove, back to his turf, back to the place where it all began.

THE RISE

Curtis Warren ran a global business spanning five continents and juggle orders, purchases and sales totalling hundreds of millions of pounds with clients who spoke a plethora of languages. And he did it all in his head.

2   'A BUCK'S A BUCK'

You can spot one a hundred yards off,

even before he turns round and speaks to

you. It's the way they behave...

LIVERPOOL is a city apart; a coastal statelet divided by accent and attitude from the English hinterland. Laid out haphazardly in a mosaic of redbrick streets, on a gentle slope where the River Mersey meets the salt of the Irish Sea, it has more in common with Dublin or Marseilles than Birmingham or Leeds. Waves of immigrants have spiced its unique flavour. Independence, verbal wit and physical toughness are prized, authority resented. The inner city especially has a raw, gritty feel; at times it seems to crackle with a special charge. The famous psychoanalyst Carl Jung called it 'the pool of life'.

Liverpool derived its identity from its role as the country's main transatlantic seaport. It was a modest fishing town until around 1700, the year the *Liverpool Merchant* sailed for West Africa to collect a new form of merchandise: 200 slaves, bound for Barbados. A wet dock opened soon after. The boom that followed saw Liverpool control five-sixths of the world slave trade. Guns, alcohol and textiles were bartered for captured African tribespeople who were then transported to America and the Caribbean. One side effect of that brutal commerce was the settlement of the first large black community anywhere outside Africa; from 1772, a slave was free once he or she had set foot on British soil. Some settled in a former Royal chase close to the seafront called Toxteth.

The abolition of slavery in 1807 was just a hiccup in the city's growth. An upsurge in trade with North America, the advent of the steamship and, above all, the emergence of textile mills in Lancashire and Yorkshire transformed it into the world's greatest cotton-port. Liverpool became the gateway to the Empire. Nine miles of dockyards served merchant ships trading with every corner of the globe, while the ocean-going liners of the Cunard and the White Star lines sent millions of people to a fresh start in the New World. 'The discoverer of America was the maker of Liverpool,' says the inscription below a statue of Christopher Columbus in Sefton Park. The men who prospered built fine civic buildings and ornate houses around lush parkland.

As the money came in, so did the immigrants: from Africa, the West Indies, China and especially Ireland, where hundreds of thousands packed the ports to flee poverty and the Great Famine, paying sixpence to cross the sea. Often they went no further than the city they saw through the fog as they arrived, finding lodgings in the rows of terracotta homes which began at the docks and spread up and inland. They found conditions as bad as those they had left: unspeakable slums, high infant mortality, crime and vice.

Liverpool responded by appointing Britain's first ever medical officer of health. It also had the first borough engineer, district nurse, slum-clearance scheme and public wash-house. Such measures had little noticeable effect on the squalor of a large part of the ever-rising population. Still, the city continued to thrive, dominating world shipping well into the 20th century. In 1934 the Mersey Tunnel opened, then one of the largest underwater road links anywhere.

Yet by the 1950s an air of decline had set in. Hitler's Luftwaffe had reduced much of the docks and many factories to rubble. The black market became the only reliable source of many items. At the same time, the city council embarked on a programme of slum clearance. Thousands of homes were bulldozed and the occupants moved out to new towns like Kirkby. Amid the brick dust, rubble and waste land, the remaining buildings seemed to age prematurely. The population began to fall. The docks were struggling: air travel was hitting the liner business and southern ports were better-placed for the increasing trade with Europe as the sun set on the Empire. Even Everton and Liverpool, the two professional football teams that are central to many Scousers' lives, suffered lean times.

Into this ailing but still vibrant melting bowl sailed Curtis Aloysius Warren, a seaman with the Norwegian Merchant Navy. His father, also called Curtis, was listed as a 'coffee manufacturer' in the Americas, but the sea had lured the son to chance his luck in the shipping lanes of the Atlantic. During one stop in Liverpool he met Sylvia Chantre, the daughter of a shipyard boiler attendant from St James's Gardens in Liverpool city centre. She too had an exotic background; her mother's maiden name was the Spanish Baptista.

On July 22, 1960, Curtis, then twenty-five, and Sylvia, twenty-one, were married at St Vincent of Paul's Roman Catholic Church. They took rooms in a Victorian townhouse at 238 Upper Parliament Street, the long, broad Toxteth thoroughfare that dissects the postal district of Liverpool 8 and runs down to the throat of the Mersey. A sailor's life meant long and frequent absences for the new husband; nonetheless their first son, Ramón, was born early in 1962.

Their second child was named after his father and grandfather. Curtis Francis Warren was born at home on 31 May 1963. It was the Whitsun holiday weekend. The weather was fine, the baby was healthy and the decade welcomed new possibilities. The Sixties were starting to twist and shout, inspired by four mop-topped young men who had just released their first album, *Please Please Me*, and embarked on a tour of Britain's concert halls and cinemas. The infectious brashness of the Beatles and Merseybeat blared from pub jukeboxes and the dark cellar of the Cavern Club in Mathew Street.

Despite the wrecking balls and the rubble, Toxteth retained much of its ebullience. In the Granby ward, where the Warrens lived, 'swarms of spidery-limbed, brown-skinned children were running everywhere, their ample mommas sitting on the steps of the towering, dilapidated old houses, chatting idly in the sun' (John Cornelius, *Liverpool 8*). It was a close-knit and self-supporting community where everyone knew everyone else. Down at the seaward end of Parliament Street, the dockyards were still busy, the alehouses overflowed and prostitutes lolled under the lamplights, offering cheap sex and gabbling in backslang, their own impenetrable dialect.

The streets were a bazaar. Granby Street had its Muslim butchers and its Arab, Pakistani, and Bangladeshi food stores displaying strange fruits, vegetables and spices. Old West Indians in Panama hats smoked ganja on their doorsteps, women in saris or coloured robes and head-dresses sashayed in and out of the stores, Hindus, Muslims, Rastafarians and Christians mingled together. There were faces and garbs of every shade, strange accents, dialects and lingoes.

At night it came alive. A clampdown on drinking dens in the city centre in 1957 to spruce up the city for an anniversary had pushed many shebeens into Toxteth. There was the Somali Club, with its giant doorman called 'Boss' because no-one knew his real name; the Gladray strip joint; the basement Alahram and its clientele of Arab deckhands, where Jamaican reggae or Yemeni folk records were intercut with commercial disco; the Olympus, frequented by crazy Greeks and card-slapping black elders; the Tudor Club, known as 'Dutch Eddy's'; the Caribbean, the Mediterranean, the Silver Sands, the Sierra Leone, the Nigeria, the Ibo and dozens of others.

Each was different yet all shared the unique flavour of Toxteth. The All Nations Club – the 'Lucky Bar' to its regulars – was open all night, every night, a joint where 'business girls' read the Journal of Commerce to see which ships were in. John Cornelius, a local artist who toured the clubs sketching customers, captured its ambience in his book *Liverpool 8*:

> It was a scruffy place: it was dirty, seedy. It smelt a bit, too. But it had an instant, exciting atmosphere like nowhere else. Small, it was just a parlour, the windows screened off so that no lights could be seen from the street. There were ships' lifebelts on the walls, Salvador Dali reproductions, bullfight posters, African masks, obscene postcards and dozens of quirky, blurred flashlight snapshots of drunken revellers. All the sort of things you'd expect to find in a sailor's cabin, in fact.

The place had a wild, party atmosphere. Party? No, the word is too mild: Mardi Gras would be better. The women, glossy and exotic, varied from ageing madames to bright-eyed girls in their late teens. The men were nearly all foreign seamen of various nationalities and colours... Norwegians, Danes, Swedes, Russians, Icelanders, Portuguese, Spaniards, Turks, Libyans, Americans, Canadians, Chileans, Argentinians, Malaysians, Japanese and Chinese, tough but generous seamen, out to have a good time, temporarily released from their floating prisons.

Looming above it all was Britain's largest Anglican cathedral, a brooding, mysterious presence that seemed to be watching wherever you went: 'Built in a modern Gothic style, its distinctive head-and-shoulders shape and the odd way in which it appears to alter its dimensions according to your viewpoint make it an eerie but inescapable fixture of the Liverpool skyline,' wrote Cornelius. 'Sometimes it appears to be way over in the distance; other times it looms suddenly huge as you turn a corner. But wherever you are in Liverpool 8, the Cathedral is only a mile away at most.'

Curtis junior followed his brother into the local Catholic primary school before enrolling at a comprehensive with a particularly tough reputation. Apparently he was rarely there beyond his early teens; though his mind was extremely acute, he did not take to the discipline of lessons. He was not alone: some schools regarded twenty per cent truancy as good. For Warren, the 'Triangle' – the Granby area bordered by Upper Parliament Street, Princes Road and Lodge Lane – was a microcosmic universe where the street was more exciting than indoors, more relevant than the classroom.

So Warren and others like him would 'sag' school. They had no money to go anywhere and no gardens to play in, so they spent the days hanging around: slouching under the *Christ On The Cross* sculpture at the corner of Mulgrave Street, prowling through the huge cathedral cemetery, playing footie in Princes Park. They also mastered backslang, a form of street patter peculiar to the area. Backslang is a linguistic trick that takes ordinary words and splits their syllables with meaningless sounds. Spoken with the nasal intonation and natural quick rhythms of Scouse, it is incomprehensible to the uninitiated. It became the language of criminals and, in particular, of whores who could talk about their customers without them knowing:

'Y'alright toni-igh-ghite, babe?'

'I don't nay-go yay-get: think he's a bit fry-ghitened of whimmer-ghimmen but he's got da mer-gunny so don't nay-go. Way-gate and see.'

Sport was a favourite pastime. A love of football is imbibed with mothers' milk in Liverpool and the weekly trip to Anfield or Goodison was a quasi-religious ritual for those who could afford it. Boxing was also popular and in 1974 the whole of Liverpool 8 gathered around TV and radio sets as locally-born John Conteh punched his way to the light-heavyweight championship of the world against Jorge Ahumada. There was also a craze for the martial arts, inspired by the chop-socky films of Bruce Lee and the TV series *Kung Fu*. Teenagers in shades and monstrous afros, with sharpened steel combs stuck in the back pocket of hip-hugging flared jeans, high-kicked and *hai-ya*-ed on street corners. The area was to produce a remarkable number of top-level martial artists over the next two decades.

Crime also beckoned. As unemployment began to rise from 1974, Toxteth was particularly hard hit. Jobs vanished; even casual work on the docks dried up. If you were black or mixed race, forget it. Few white employers wanted workers from what they called 'jungle town'. The area drew inwards, became alienated and bitter. By the latter part of the decade Granby Street was littered with broken glass, its dwindling number of shops encased in wire grilles to deter burglars. Outsiders once attracted by Toxteth's multiple cultures began to feel vaguely threatened by it. Local people began to complain about racism and police harassment. The young men who gathered in large groups at the Windsor Clock pub on Kingsley Road suddenly seemed menacing.

In an increasingly tense environment, innocent childhood pastimes paled. Nicking cars and joy-riding – being chased by the 'jam butty' prowl cars of the traffic police – became a fad. Car thefts were particularly prevalent in the summer months when there were more out-of-town visitors to the Anglican Cathedral and to the new Catholic Metropolitan Cathedral half a mile away. Local youths became expert at opening a vehicle within seconds, sometimes to sell or strip for parts, often just for 'the buzz'.

Curtis Warren had just turned twelve when the police stopped him in a stolen car. Though barely big enough to see over the steering wheel, he was charged with the unauthorised taking of a motor vehicle. He was taken to the local police station, where towering officers gave him a very stern talking-to before summoning his mother to take him home. Such offences were usually dealt with by a caution but this was deemed serious enough to put before Liverpool Juvenile Court. Warren was placed under a supervision order for two years. It had little effect.

A year later, he graduated to the magistrates court, this time for burglary. He was ordered to spend twenty-four hours at an attendance centre.

Young Curtis was caught on a spiral of petty offending. It seemed to be the thing to do. Youth crime was becoming a burning issue in the city. In 1975, a quarter of all people prosecuted in Liverpool were juveniles, while the same number again received cautions. The Chief Constable saw problems ahead; if things did not improve, he said, the city centre might need an 'army of occupation' by 1980.

The contemporary mood was expertly captured by a South African-born writer, James McClure, who spent months following the men and women of the Merseyside Police 'A' Division, which includes Liverpool 8. His book, *Spike Island*, revealed the feelings of officers towards Toxteth and its inhabitants and provided eye-witness accounts of how a new breed of young criminal was emerging by the late 1970s. One inspector said:

> The original Liverpool coloured person was never involved in crime. Those who are involved tend to be largely Lagos Nigerians and Kingston Jamaicans, although I'd imagine they're the type who would be criminals back in their own country, so that's not all of them. We get West Islanders who're noisy and cause trouble, only mainly among themselves and usually over women. I don't find them a bad type at all; they're hardworking, very happy and cheerful people.

It was the next generation, especially from the forbidding Myrtle Gardens tenement a half-brick throw from the Warren's home, that caused most concern: 'Its young half-caste kids – nine, ten, eleven – are wilder than any kids I know, and I'm anticipating trouble in a few years time…'

Young men of mixed race – like Warren – aroused particular unease in an almost-exclusively white police force.

'If you come across a bad white, he's bad; if you come across a bad black, he's bad; if you come across a bad half-caste, he's evil,' another officer told McClure. 'I know some half-castes, great guys, but they always carry a weapon for some reason, or they'll use anything to hand.'

A detective concurred. 'You see, the problem with the half-caste is that he's got this big chip on his shoulder; you don't know whether you come from A or B, so you find your own level with the villains. Their choice of identification is wrong; that's where they're falling down.'

Any incorrigible, regardless of colour, was known to the police as a 'buck'. The term, derived from the Irish 'bucko', is rarely heard outside Liverpool. It describes a young man, strong and lawless, who lives for the day and hangs the consequences. A buck trades on wild masculinity, gratuitous violence and contempt for social mores.

'A buck's a buck – no matter what bloody colour he is – in Liverpool,' said one copper. 'I think most bobbies draw that line: a buck's a buck and it's the first thing you notice about him. You can spot one a hundred yards off, even before he turns round and speaks to you. It's the way they behave – and that stands out more than colour.'

The teenage Curtis Warren was well on the way to buckhood. His freckled face and stocky frame were becoming all too familiar to the local beat bobbies, to whom he showed none of the normal childhood deference and certainly no fear. While still only thirteen, he returned to the attendance centre for twenty-four hours for stealing and was put under another two-year supervision order for 'allowing himself to be carried in a motor vehicle knowing it had been taken away without lawful authority'. At fourteen he appeared at the juvenile court for his most serious offence to date, robbery. He was fined £10. Five months later he received a one-year driving ban and was back at the attendance centre for taking another car without authority. And a week after that he was fined a fiver for offensive behaviour. A series of petty convictions followed – going equipped for theft, taking a car without consent, allowing himself to be carried in a car taken without consent. On 20 July 1978, the magistrates sent him to a detention centre for the first time, for three months.

The centres, known as 'DCs,' were a school for crime. Across the north-west a generation of young men who would lead the crime gangs of the 1980s and 90s was passing through the same system. The centres were also failing: a few years later Tory Home Secretary Willie Whitelaw would replace some of them with boot camps to administer 'short, sharp shocks' to youth offenders, though that would fail too. Warren treated the place as a joke and came out worse than he went in.

In June 1979, while other sixteen-year-olds were looking forward to the end of school and their final-year exam results, Warren was back before the magistrates. The charges were breach of the peace and assaulting two cops: he had punched one and headbutted the other. He was fined £5 plus £10 for each assault. With no qualifications and a growing criminal record, he was heading straight for the dole queue – and a life beyond the Law.

The city's young offenders were monitored by the juvenile liaison team. Taped on a wall of their 'A'

Division office was a sheet of paper with a typed quotation from the poet TS Eliot. It could have been written for the young Curtis Warren: 'What kind of peace may grow between the hammer and the anvil?'

MARGARET SCHWARTZ had been so looking forward to the cathedrals. The seventy-eight-year-old spinster had made the long trip from genteel Kingston-on-Thames in Surrey especially to visit Liverpool's two great churches. She was particularly keen to view the Metropolitan, an extraordinary conical structure dubbed 'Paddy's Wigwam' by locals. It was a Sunday evening. Mass had finished and the dark, hangar-like interior with its pervading odour of incense echoed to every cough and footstep.

Miss Schwartz left her two travelling companions to use the toilet beside the basement café. As she returned up the stone steps, gripping the bannister, three youths confronted her. One grabbed her handbag. Caught in a vortex of confusion and fear, she struggled to keep hold of the strap and was dragged roughly off her feet, tumbling down the stairway like a rag doll. Her face hit the concrete, fracturing her right cheek and shattering her spectacles, causing glass fragments to lodge in her eye. 'Her face was so badly cut that she was a horrifying sight,' her friend Anne Downey later testified. She moaned in agony as her attackers fled.

Miss Schwartz was rushed to St Paul's Eye Hospital where surgeons operated to save her sight. The attack on such a frail and elderly victim, at a cathedral, caused outrage. It made the front page of the next day's *Liverpool Echo* under the headline, 'City Mugging Victim May Lose An Eye.' Police appealed for help in tracking the muggers.

'A BUCK'S A BUCK'

Curtis Warren, then sixteen, was arrested six days later and charged with robbing Miss Schwartz of her handbag and its contents. He denied the offence but was sent for trial at Liverpool Crown Court on 12 February 1980. The case again attracted newspaper interest, with Warren's name withheld because he was still legally a juvenile. Whatever the reason for his arrest, the case against him was weak and several days into the trial the judge directed the jurors to acquit Warren because of insufficient evidence for a conviction. However, he had also been committed for sentence from the city magistrates court on two separate charges: assault occasioning actual bodily harm and assaulting the police. The details of these crimes have not survived but attacking the police was clearly a serious offence. Warren was sent to Borstal.

He was in there for eleven months. When he finally emerged, on 6 January 1981, his stock with his mates was sky-high. He had battered the 'bizzies' [*busybodies* = *police*], been to Borstal, even made the active criminal index, the card file collated by the police to keep tabs on their local villains. He was the Cocky Watchman.

IT STARTED with a young man on a motorbike. The son of a prominent local West Indian, he was spotted at 9.45 PM on Friday, July 3, 1981, by a Merseyside Police traffic unit. They thought the bike was stolen and gave chase. The rider crashed in Selborne Street, a stone's throw from the Warren family home. As the officers jumped out of their vehicle and grabbed him, he pleaded, truthfully, that the bike was his; they arrested him anyway. He tried to struggle free, shouting for help as a crowd began to gather.

Suddenly one of them ran forward and a punch broke Sergeant Gerald Evans's nose; PC Michael Evans was hit, kicked and bitten on the ear; PC Brian Harrison, who went to help, was also attacked. The mob managed to wrestle away the motorcyclist but a voluble local man, Leroy Cooper, was held. Officers drove him away as stones bounced off their vehicles.

Less than three months earlier, a ferocious race riot had torn through Brixton in south London. Toxteth had been simmering ever since. Now it boiled over. The next night a telephone call falsely reporting a stolen car drew police into the depths of Granby, where a mob of 200 young men was waiting. 'There they were ambushed and set upon by a crowd of black youths,' reported the *Daily Telegraph*. 'As violence spread, more rioters, black and white, joined in. Shops were looted, cars overturned and buildings set alight. The police became targets of petrol bombs and bricks and formed lines behind plastic shields. During the first night, seventy policemen were injured, but only three rioters arrested.'

Senior officers were unprepared. They adopted a tactic of containment, lining their men up behind shields and even bin lids to hold back the rioters. It failed. 'On the first night of the riot I stood in the front line for about twelve hours with seven other officers. At the end of that night, one was in hospital with a fractured skull, one was in for about two weeks with complications to his spleen after being hit by a brick and two other officers were in for two or three days each. It was only myself and two others who returned to duty the next day. It was a bloody disaster,' one policeman later told the film-maker Roger Graef.

As word spread, families poured out of their houses to clear out local stores. Elderly couples hurriedly pushed shopping trolleys of loot along pavements carpeted with glass. Flames shot above the skyline as the inferno leapt from building to building. Wailing sirens, breaking windows and the thud of brick on plastic merged in a sinister cacophony. Rage filled the air. 'I realised, standing there with a shield, that people wanted me dead. Now that's a frightening thought,' recalled one PC.

Sunday night was even worse. Troublemakers from all over the city came for the thrill. Hundreds of police officers were drafted in from neighbouring forces yet did little but hold back the tide. 'When I was in Northern Ireland, a riot like the one we had in Toxteth would have been dealt with by no more than 100 men,' said one. 'On the Sunday night at Toxteth, there were over 4000 police officers deployed and we still lost. Half of the Toxteth area was burnt to the ground. Now we lost not because of the skill and the courage of the bobbies but because you just stood there for most of that night and waited your turn to become injured.'

By the early hours of Monday morning, more than 700 officers had been hurt. There was little left in Toxteth to steal or burn, so some of the rioters now attempted to break out of the area ringed off by police lines and make their way towards the city centre. On the first floor of Hope Street police station, the mood was as grim as the outlook. The man in charge, Chief Constable Kenneth Oxford, was a fifty-seven-year-old former bomber pilot with twenty-five years police service in London and Liverpool. In a distinguished career he had arrested James Hanratty, infamously hanged for the murder of a man on the A6, and Christine Keeler, the call girl who brought down a Cabinet minister. 'He was a professional of the old school,' says a former colleague. 'A very strong character, very respected by his officers.'

Oxford felt his men might be over-run. He considered the unprecedented step of calling the Army.

Just as he was about to phone the Ministry of Defence, a junior colleague volunteered another option. The force had a number of CS gas guns, though they had never been used anywhere on the mainland to quell a civil disturbance. It was a high-risk call but at 2.15 AM, Oxford gave the order to break out the gas.

The first salvoes were fired soon after, the gas spitting out in a fizzing white spiral as the canisters landed in the crowd. Bodies hit the deck. By mistake, some officers had been issued with guns and cartridges designed to penetrate doors and windows but not for dealing with general civil disorder. They injured several rioters and some bystanders. It had the desired effect. The mob scattered and the city moved back from the abyss.

Daylight revealed the devastation. Much of the district smouldered. Thick smoke rose in ominous plumes above the rooftops. Hardly a soul stirred on the streets. The remains of burned out buildings stood like charred ghosts in the gloom. The shells of torched cars blocked the streets. Scorch marks from petrol bombs scarred the tarmac and walls. A smell of burning wood and foam furniture hung in the air.

The following weekend, riots were reported in virtually every English city with a substantial immigrant population, as well as many with none: Manchester, Birmingham, Blackburn, Bradford, Leeds, Leicester, Wolverhampton and two dozen others. Toxteth saw isolated outbreaks of unrest for the rest of the month. The sight of a police vehicle often drew an instant response of rocks and the occasional petrol bomb. On the night of July 28, boiling water and old TV sets were hurled at the police and a disabled man died after he was hit by a police Range Rover. The following day, Prince Charles married Lady Diana Spencer. There was no further trouble; many would-be rioters took advantage of special licensing laws allowing all-day pub opening to get drunk.

A total of 244 people were arrested in the Toxteth riots, most of them white. One hundred and seventy two would eventually be convicted, including many of Curtis Warren's friends and neighbours. Yet Oxford's use of CS gas brought him bitter criticism from the Liverpool Labour Party, which demanded his resignation. Lady Simey, the chairman of Merseyside Police Authority, said conditions in Toxteth were so bad that residents 'ought to riot'. Relations between the police and the people would never be the same.

'The riots put paid to the notion that the uniform could maintain law and order,' wrote Roger Graef. 'The riots erupted on television, shocking the nation, most especially the police. They saw what looked like a mini-civil war. Its effect was much like that of Vietnam – television cast the police in a wholly new role: anonymous adversaries. And they lost.'

For Curtis Warren and the street youths of Granby, things would never be the same again. They had fought the Law… and won. The bitter brew of unemployment, crime, poverty, resentment, racism and social exclusion had for a while been sweetened by the thrill of fighting back and the power of 'victory'. While a new television soap opera, *Brookside*, conveyed one view of suburban Merseyside, Alan Bleasdale's coruscating *Boys From The Blackstuff* showed the reality of trying to keep your dignity and family together without a job or hope. Some of the young men who had burned Toxteth would now take their new-found self-confidence and adopt the city's entrepreneurial spirit to criminal, perverted ends.

Carl Jung's pool of life was in danger of becoming a cesspool.

> *'There are a number of people in Merseyside*
> *who fifteen to twenty years ago were*
> *dockers or merchant seamen and are*
> *now millionaires'*
>
> A National Crime Squad detective

BY THE AGE of eighteen, Curtis Warren was a fully-fledged buck. His broad, five-foot-nine-inch frame had filled out with muscle, his head was a bullet on a boxer's neck. He was the tough product of a tough neighbourhood. Fighting, sticking up for yourself, was as natural and as necessary as breathing or sex. 'I think violence for him was a very common thing,' says a Dutch detective who would later arrest him. 'He didn't think much about using it. When he discussed it, it was just like he was talking about the weather.'

Violence was endemic in the rougher parts of Liverpool. 'I was appalled by the amount and extent of it when I first came to work on Merseyside,' said then-Chief Constable Ken Oxford. 'Mythology has it – and I exclude nobody from this – that the area is tough. It has the unfortunate effect that people feel they must react to this and be tough.' And more than half of all violent offences in the county were concentrated in one district – Toxteth.

Among his contemporaries, there was one youth who could give even Cocky lessons in mayhem. Johnny Phillips, two years older than Warren, was a powerful young man with a volatile temperament. He had been hauled in for throwing petrol bombs at police lines during the riots and his antics raised eyebrows even among the seen-it-all denizens of the Triangle. Johnny, they said, was a timebomb. He and Cocky made a formidable combination.

One speciality of the city's young hoodlums was 'rolling'. If prostitution was the oldest profession, rolling was probably the second. Gangs of youths would persuade – or force – the local hookers to lure their clients to isolated spots, where they would be waylaid, beaten and robbed. Sometimes they were trapped in the act of sex, caught in a car down a darkened street, the doors wrenched open and their belongings rifled.

So when Warren and Phillips saw a girl standing alone under the streetlight, they saw a victim. She was young and pretty and sold herself to men, clicking out in sharp heels and tight skirt each night, through the rubble and broken glass, to pose in the sodium glare of a street lamp and watch the cars cruise by. Fewer and fewer stopped now. The riots had scared the punters away. Many of the clubs had shut their doors and there were no more laughing, generous seamen out on a spree. Only a few thrill-seekers and her smattering of regulars dared venture into the no-go zone of Toxteth. The air was bitter and no-one was safe.

Warren and Phillips cornered her and ordered her to pick up a customer and steal his money. 'We'll be back,' they said.

It was three days before she saw them again, looking mean and demanding their 'share'. She didn't have it.

'If you don't get our money we'll slit your throat,' she was told.

Warren and Phillips were driving through Toxteth shortly afterwards when they saw the girl in a car with a man. They leapt out, smashed one of the car windows and hit the startled punter with a wrench. As he tried to drive away with the terrified girl beside him, Phillips and Warren set off in pursuit and rammed his car. The man and the prostitute made it to a police station and, unusually, told officers what had happened. Their attackers were picked up and in March 1982 appeared before Liverpool Crown Court on charges of blackmail, criminal damage and theft. Phillips claimed it was case of mistaken identity. Warren did not give evidence but also denied the charge. Both were convicted. Phillips, who was said to be the prime mover, was jailed for three years, Warren for two. 'Men like you blackmail people they think will not go to the police. This unfortunate girl did. But for your youth, your sentence would have been much longer.' said the judge.

It was Warren's first spell in adult jail. He soon became aware of how low down the criminal pecking order he was. Here were real villains: conmen, forgers, burglars, bank robbers, fraudsters and enforcers, full-time, never-worked-a-day recalcitrants who could not live a straight life if they tried. Few of them were hostile to the young bull from Granby. In Liverpool, older criminals often acted as mentors, welcoming new recruits to the fraternity, teaching them 'the score'. Warren was exposed to the kind of men who were making the city a byword for lawlessness. He found there were some very big players indeed.

ON THE VERY DAY that Cocky was jailed, Chief Constable Ken Oxford faced a phalanx of journalists in a small conference room at the Lancashire Police headquarters near Preston. The Merseyside Police boss was quietly relieved that, for once, there would be no questions about the riots. For the previous three days he had presided over the annual drugs forum of the Association of Chief Police Officers, held behind closed doors and attended by Home Office mandarins, senior customs officers and international experts on crime. Now was the traditional final-day news conference.

Like most police officers of high rank, Oxford knew how to grab a headline. His theme was dirty money and the new 'barons' who were starting to amass fortunes from the burgeoning trade in drugs. Oxford was a believer in the principle that had brought down Chicago gangster Al Capone: Follow the money. Freeze and seize their cash and you would neuter the bad guys. He pulled up his chair, leaned on the table in front of him and enunciated his message for the benefit of the microphones.

'We are talking about millions of pounds. It is essential that that money does not go back into the international syndicates because as one gang is busted there is always someone to take its place. There is no diminution of supply and the key to the supply is the exchange of large sums of money. It is important that these people do not gain from their criminal activities.'

It was all about money. Suddenly a tidal wave of cash was washing through the British underworld and the rush to jump in was reaching Klondike proportions. Illegal drugs had become as available as lager or crisps in most inner cities and could be bought, with a little persistence, in every town and many villages. And the more that was sold, the more demand grew.

There was LSD, lysergic acid, which came in tiny squares of impregnated paper and changed people's perceptions of sight and sound, inducing illusions and hallucinations known as 'trips', sometimes of a paranoid nature. There was amphetamine, or speed, usually taken as a laboratory-produced powder that powered a buzz of abundant energy and garrulousness. There was cocaine, the crystalline white powder from South and Central America, known as the champagne of drugs, that produced euphoria and alertness and increased the pulse rate and blood pressure. There was heroin, or smack, the scourge of Britain's sink estates, a brown or white powder that was smoked or injected to produced an addictive mixture of euphoria and drowsiness.

Most of all there was cannabis – pot, grass, dope, hash, ganja, blow, weed – smoked as resin, oil or leaves. Grown in many areas of Asia, North Africa, the Near and Middle East and the Americas, it was cheap and increasingly ubiquitous. Its effects were signalled by fits of irrelevant giggling followed by a fuggy, pleasurable 'high'.

Though some of these substances had been used for millennia, industrial production methods were now churning out unforeseen quantities. Societies both advanced and backward were fighting a rearguard action against increased crop yields, the use of vastly-improved international transport and communications and a formidable market created by European and North American populations with more spending power than ever. Profits were huge. The product of just £500-worth of coca leaves sold by a Peruvian hill farmer could fetch around half a million pounds on the streets of any western city, a mark-up of 1000 per cent, making cocaine the most valuable commodity on the planet. Neither the lawmen nor the criminals had seen anything like it.

Liverpool gangs excelled in the new trade; so much so that one leading customs investigator refers to the city as 'the number one UK centre of excellence for drug smuggling'. At the heart of its pre-eminence was a unique collaboration between older, well-established white criminals, sometimes known as the Liverpool mafia, and their black or mixed-race counterparts, labelled the 'Black Caucus' by senior police officers. Police have used the term 'Black Caucus' in at least two court cases to refer to a group of violent criminals based in and around Toxteth. However, they must not be confused with an entirely legitimate and law-abiding group, The Liverpool 8 or Merseyside Black Caucus, which campaigned against racism and produced pamphlets. Any further reference in this book will apply to the criminal gang. In time this unprecedented alliance was to launch a young buck called Curtis Warren on an extraordinary journey: from a street scally who nicked cars to a position as one of the major drugs brokers in Europe.

Even as Ken Oxford spoke, those of his officers with their ears closest to the ground knew the truth: the stable door was open and the horse was gone.

THE LIVERPOOL MAFIA is not a rigid hierarchy like its Italian namesake or the US Cosa Nostra. It is loose, flexible and, in the seaport tradition, trade-based. It is also something of a catch-all term for a large number of white males, most now aged in their fifties or sixties, who have engaged separately or together in on-going criminal conspiracies over many decades. Not all of them work together and some are deadly rivals, but they all inhabit the same milieu. Whether or not it is 'organised crime' on the classic Mafia model, it is organised and it is most definitely crime.

The key figures were born in the 1930s, at around the same time as the infamous Kray and Richardson brothers in London. While just as tough as their Cockney counterparts, they were to establish an empire of a different sort. The traditional crime gang is territorial; it controls an area or 'manor' and runs a variety of rackets there. The Krays' power base was their Bethnal Green stronghold, from which they gradually extended their grip throughout the East End and to the fringes of the West. The Richardsons parcelled up parts of South London with others such as Freddie Foreman and also ran protection and slot machines in the West End. When boundaries were crossed – as when the Richardson gang and the Haward brothers clashed over a club in Catford – bloodshed followed.

The Liverpool mafia men largely eschewed strong-arm gangsterism to pursue economic crime. In doing so they established a form of loose syndicate unlike anything seen before in Britain. Above all, they exploited the waterfront. Many had strong links with the city's miles of docks, working there or mixing with those who did. Always a trove of plunder and smuggling, the dockland came into its own during World War Two, when black marketeering was rife. US forces stationed in the area were obliged to organise a special corps of soldiers to stop the ransacking of their stores, mainly for cigarettes. At the end of 1945 the *Report on the Police Establishment and the State of Crime* stated:

Crime had increased 68.9 per cent since 1938. The raids on the city [*the Blitz*] left many premises very easy to break into and premises made unfit for occupation provided cover from which to attack adjoining premises and also for hiding stolen goods. The shortages of all kinds of food and clothing made it easy for thieves to dispose of stolen property and also made it worthwhile to steal what before the war would not have repaid the trouble and risk. Crimes on a large scale were often instigated by operators on the black market and on many occasions a whole lorry load of goods was stolen. Many such large scale operations were detected by the police and successful prosecutions resulted but it was seldom possible to obtain the evidence necessary to establish the guilt of the principal offender.

By the 1950s, one extremely capable criminal had risen to prominence in the city's underworld. He was a figurehead to many younger hoodlums, in particular a gang based in the notorious Scotland Road area who 'had all grown up together and who ran together as a team in later life', according to an underworld source. They would later be leading lights in the Liverpool mafia.

According to legend, some of their number faced down the Kray twins, who were trying to muscle into Liverpool. The tale should be treated with caution; every major British city has its 'Kray story', which usually goes like this: the fearsome twins arrive at the train station, only to be met by the local hardmen, warned that they are not wanted, and put back on the next train out. In the Liverpool version, the two sides clashed at a pub on the East Lancs Road. It was related to the authors by a knowledgeable underworld source: 'The police in Liverpool followed the Krays round wherever they went and wherever they parked their cars but at the same time the city's underworld were doing exactly the same thing. The meeting at the pub did not involve shooters, just baseball bats and blades. It was a bit of a chat really.'

One of the main figures was an enterprising wideboy who, for legal reasons, we shall refer to as 'the Main Man'. He became a main organiser of robberies, fencing and other crimes. 'He would solve problems,' says the source. 'He was associated with a family of brothers and he would point them in the right direction, let them do the job and take his cut later. He also used to do a lot of work with the cheque-kiters. But he never got his hands dirty or his collar felt. He was the paymaster.'

Though never collared, the Main Man did get bitten. 'Once he let some people down very badly. They thought he had grassed them up, so two brothers walked into a pub which he ran. He was sat at the bar. One of the brothers grabbed his arm and put it on the bar and the other chopped it with a machete or meat cleaver. He needed a number of stitches for a very deep wound. People who climbed on board with him tended to end up either very upset or locked up at the end of the day.'

Another man who was rarely locked up was to become the major figure in the Liverpool mafia. He cannot currently be named for legal reasons but we shall give him the sobriquet of the Banker. Though not a nickname used by himself or his associates, for the purposes of this book it is as good as any. The Banker was raised in Kirkdale, north Liverpool, and worked on the docks as a young man. He and his gang used it as an opportunity to pilfer on a huge scale. By the Sixties he had enough money to move away from stevedoring and open a succession of small businesses. He also specialised in hi-jacking lorry-loads of spirits or cigarettes. One tale relates how he and others stole a consignment parked up for the night at a depot in Bootle. They drove brazenly into the lot in their own tractor cab, unhitched the wagon, hooked it to their unit and drove out, waving to the nightwatchman. On another occasion, while burgling a warehouse 'over the water' – south of the Mersey – one of his team crashed through an asbestos roof and was killed. 'To this day he has never set foot back on the Wirral or gone through the Mersey tunnel,' says the gangland source. 'He thinks it is an unlucky place.'

The Banker recycled his loot into pubs and clubs. He also ran a tight ship, rarely allowing the police to get their hooks into him. He spoke softly, looked ordinary, but wore an air of subdued menace.

'He seems innocuous, like your uncle stepped straight off the golf course,' says a customs officer who has twice questioned him about serious crimes. 'He wears woollen jumpers and slacks. But he is without doubt the most unnerving person I have ever interviewed. We questioned him at a police station in the presence of his solicitor for a total of about an hour. And for that whole sixty minutes he just stared at whoever was asking the questions. Right into their eyes. He didn't give a single answer, not so much as a "yes," a "no" or even a "no comment." Nothing. I have seen other criminals do this but they tend to look away and get distracted when you really start putting the pressure on. He just stared at the corner of the room for a few seconds, then turned his eyes back on the interviewer.'

But even the Main Man and the Banker took a back seat to the most flamboyant Liverpool crook of his era: Tommy 'Tacker' Comerford. 'You can chart the entire development of drug smuggling in Britain through Tommy Comerford,' says Ranald McDonald of HM Customs National Investigations Service. 'He was probably the first major criminal to import every kind of illegal drug.'

Comerford, also known as 'Top Cat' after the quick-witted children's cartoon character, was a big, fleshy man with long strands of hair swept across a bald crown, twinkling eyes and a ready grin. He became a legend in an underworld where a glib tongue, lavish spending and incorrigible criminality are much admired. Here was an unreformed scallywag who cruised the Caribbean on the *Queen Elizabeth II* while on the dole, jetted to the best hotels while applying for a council flat and snorted coke with rock stars while claiming housing benefit. 'Even today his notoriety brings a wry smile to the faces of the most experienced Liverpool detectives,' reported the Liverpool *Daily Post* in 1996. 'Comerford was affable, approachable and good-humoured, mixing with the stars and lapping up the limelight. He was the first high-profile drugs dealer to emerge on Merseyside. The Hollywood image of flash cars, cute women and lines of white powder on a glass coffee table had finally arrived.'

He was born in 1931 and began a career of dishonesty in the Fifties. Within ten years he was renowned enough to figure in yet another version of the Kray story: this one had Comerford on the platform at Lime Street station politely telling the twins to clear off. Like the Banker, he bought into pubs and clubs. There the similarity ended. The Banker was quieter, hard-headed, more stubborn; ice to Tacker's fire.

Comerford's leap to criminal stardom came in 1969 with the 'Water Street Job'. He and his gang spent two days of the August Bank Holiday weekend tunnelling into a bank in Liverpool city centre from an adjacent bakery. They used thermal lances to cut into the steel doors of the strong room – the first British criminals ever to do so – and made off with £140,000. Comerford was later jailed for ten years for masterminding the raid. The judge, sentencing him for the offence of 'burglary at a counting house', said, 'This was top level, professional, organised crime, carried out with the most-modern sophisticated equipment and with all the planning and precision of a commando raid.'

His period of incarceration coincided with the early rumblings of a tectonic shift in the crime landscape. And the cause was drugs.

UNTIL 1916, there was no specific anti-drugs law in the UK. Then came the Defence of the Realm Act, which outlawed the possession of cocaine and opium without a prescription, and, in 1920, the Dangerous Drugs Act. Even so, drugs both hard and soft remained a fringe problem in British society, despite the occasional scare stories in the more racy Sunday newspapers. Cannabis, or hemp, was portrayed as a sense-numbing peril used by black sailors and immigrants to tempt innocent white girls. Cocaine enjoyed something of a vogue in society circles in the Twenties and Thirties, while opium and its derivatives, morphine and heroin, were associated with inscrutable Chinamen, a faint air of mysticism, and Sherlock Holmes.

As late as the 1950s, most natives of the UK still associated drugs with black people: either the new immigrants arriving from the West Indies and Africa or the artists of American jazz. Many of the top musicians, men like Charlie Parker, were hooked on heroin. Even the avuncular Louis Armstrong smoked cannabis for almost all his adult life. Blues singers too had always had their drug songs, reflecting the realities of life in the ghettoes of the urban United States.

The crossover into mainstream culture came, paradoxically, through the counter-culture. The 'beat' movement of the 1950s and the permissive hippie scene a decade later coincided with the opening up of foreign travel, an unprecedentedly wealthy population, and the exposure of many American servicemen to cannabis and heroin in the Vietnam War. Drugs became a staple of the white rock scene. The Beatles experimented with them, the Rolling Stones took them, Jim Morrison and Jimi Hendrix died from them. While Lou Reed sang of buying heroin on a New York street corner in *Waiting for the Man*, England's working-class Mods had their pills and reefers. The psychedelic drugs of the California counter-culture added a new and mind-expanding horizon.

Britain's response was to set up regional drugs squads in 1967 and to introduce a new Dangerous Drugs Act banning doctors from prescribing heroin and cocaine. 'They also had to notify the Home Office of anyone known or suspected of being addicted,' according to Ron Clarke, a former police inspector who has done extensive research into drug use. 'Overnight, treatment for people with drug problems was removed. We started to get an increase in burglaries at chemists and drug stores. That led to a hue and cry by the police and drug enforcement agencies. We weren't skilled to deal with drug addicts. That led to the Misuse of Drugs Act of 1971. That was when we really started policing drugs in this country.' The effect was that, almost overnight, Britain developed a heroin problem, as illicit dealers met the demand previously satisfied by prescription. The first major seizures came in 1971, mostly sourced to the Golden Triangle, a wild, mountainous region where the borders of Burma, Laos and Thailand meet.

British gangsters moved into the market in the mid-1970s. They found only a few hippies and chancers as competition. Soon underworld figures in London, Glasgow, Liverpool, Manchester and Birmingham were putting down their sawn-offs and reaching for their snap-bags and scales. Free-wheeling charmers like the Oxford-educated cannabis king Howard Marks were roughly elbowed aside as 'the headbands gave way to the headcases', in Guardian crime reporter Duncan Campbell's phrase. In 1979 the unthinkable happened:

a customs officer, Peter Bennett, was shot dead in London Docklands while working on a cannabis case. It came to symbolise the darker mood.

Drugs were nothing new to the streets of Liverpool. In the 1950s it accounted for one-third of all dangerous drugs prosecutions. It was believed to be the biggest port of entry for marijuana because of its Caribbean and West African links. Local newspapers dubbed it the 'Cannabis Capital'. By the late seventies, the city's senior white criminals were perfectly placed to take over and expand the trade. They had the nerve, the contacts, the savvy and the lack of morals. 'The heavy white criminals saw what was going on,' says a former Liverpool detective. 'They were well ahead of the game. Previously the top-notch robbers and burglars would have thought anyone who dabbled in drugs was unreliable, a bit flaky. But Liverpool already had that tradition of smuggling stuff in through the docks and they caught on very quickly.'

One gang imported hash hidden in cocoa beans from Nigeria. Another flew first-class to five-star hotels in Miami, the Bahamas and Jamaica to organise shipments of cannabis; on one occasion, two of its members jetted into Heathrow and then paid £225 for a taxi home to Merseyside rather than wait two hours for a connecting flight. When ten of the gang were trapped unloading cannabis from a container at Seaforth Docks in 1981, most turned out to be unemployed dockers. In another court case the Main Man was identified as a central figure in the city's drug scene, though he was not himself on trial.

Tommy Comerford emerged from prison to find opportunity thumping at his door. He was soon in the thick of it. He recruited four dock workers to pick up a cannabis consignment from north Africa but they were arrested as they went to collect the drugs from a Liverpool quayside. Comerford and seven others were flush enough to post sureties totaling £120,000 to get bail, on condition they surrendered their passports and reported to a police station twice a day.

Their trial at Liverpool Crown Court was the best show in town. Every morning Comerford held impromptu Press conferences at which he would swop quips with reporters, opine on legal issues and muse about life. He revelled in the attention, taking a particular shine to one short-skirted female journalist whom he dubbed 'Legs'. Asked what sentence he thought he would get if found guilty, he cracked, 'I've had a word with the judge and told him there's no way I'm going to accept a community service order'. In the event he pulled seven years, later reduced to four on appeal.

This time, his spell inside coincided with a boom in the use of heroin, which started to pump into the country from a new cultivation zone, the so-called Golden Crescent region of Iran, Iraq and Afghanistan. It soon became more available than cocaine and the street price dropped by more than one-fifth. Heroin was regarded even by the people who sold it as a 'vermin' drug, hooking addicts in a prison of despair. Usually sold as a brown powder, it starts life as the milky sap of the opium poppy. The sap is collected and dried to form a gum; the gum is washed and becomes opium. Opium contains two painkilling alkaloids, codeine and morphine. The latter is further refined to create diamorphine, or heroin. Initially, most heroin users feel nauseous and often vomit. Those who persevere experience feelings of relaxation, warmth and well-being. Nothing matters; they feel wrapped in cotton wool. Once this has passed the user is able to interact normally with other people, although reality will have a dream-like quality. There are two main risks: overdose and dependence.

The Liverpool barons did not give a toss. One of the first indications that they had moved into the trade came in September 1983 when customs officers, after six months of surveillance, broke up a crew running loads through the docks at Liverpool and Dover. They found cannabis and heroin hidden in a container of cocoa beans. The leader, a haulage contractor from Kirkby, was jailed for twelve years.

From the day he was released from his cannabis smuggling sentence, Tacker raised the stakes to a new level. He was soon organising supplies of heroin, cocaine, cannabis, amphetamines and LSD in a web stretching from his Liverpool council flat to Colombia, the USA, Pakistan, the United Arab Emirates, Germany, Italy and Holland. Something unheard-of had been going on: for the first time, a British criminal had forged links with almost all of the major sources of drug cultivation and manufacture around the world. Clearly Comerford could not have established all of those links alone; he had been in prison. Someone had been very busy.

Using the city centre Holiday Inn as his 'office' – without the knowledge of staff – Tacker put together a team including his daughter's boyfriend, Dean Yardi, and Michael Wilding, a slim thirty-four-year-old Liverpudlian with a drooping moustache and seventeen previous convictions. Their base was a second-floor flat in south Liverpool; the council paid the £27-a-week rent. Less than a mile away was 'Treetops,' the luxurious bungalow where Comerford really lived with his wife, Theresa.

Regular visitors to the council flat included a US Army sergeant who ordered large quantities of drugs to sell to fellow servicemen stationed in West Germany. One run consisted of 1000 dots of LSD, enough to trip out an entire garrison. Comerford's heroin came from his links with Pakistan and was cut and mixed at the flat before distribution. Some was sold in London by a fifty-year-old Jamaican. Wilding and Yardi did much of the dirty work. 'One of Tacker's greatest abilities was to avoid the high-risk areas and pass them onto other people,' said a detective who worked on the case. 'Whenever he went through customs he would always go first and get someone else to carry the drugs.'

Comerford's taste for the good life increased. Using aliases like 'Parker' and 'Hawkeye', he stayed in five-star hotels around the world, charmed fellow guests and staff alike, mixed with celebrities and flaunted his wealth. At the same time, he was claiming rent rebates from the Department of Health and Social Security and a local authority decorating allowance as well as his dole. For Christmas 1983 he took his wife on a £5,000 cruise to the Caribbean and New York on the QEII. True to form, he submitted an insurance claim on his return for £11,500 for suitcases he had 'lost' while at JFK airport.

In May 1984 Comerford was placed under surveillance by members of the number one Regional Crime Squad, based in the north-west. Officers arrested one of his runners with a package of cannabis after a high-speed chase through Liverpool. Six weeks later, police were tipped off that Comerford would be flying from Stuttgart to Heathrow. They staked out the airport. Tacker loomed into view as he strolled through the green 'nothing to declare' channel, carrying two suitcases and a duty free bag. Yardi was there to meet him. As they walked to a car, they were arrested. Inside one case was half a kilo of heroin. In the other was £20,000-worth of sterling, US dollars, Swiss francs, German marks and Portuguese escudos. Wilding was arrested three weeks later, in possession of heroin and a gun. Resentful at the way he had been treated by Comerford, he spilt the beans about the entire operation.

'Micky was simply a dogsbody to them,' said the detective. 'He was never given any credit and was, in his eyes, treated very badly. He took all the risks and got very little in return. While he received just small amounts of cash, despite taking all the risks, Tacker received all the riches. Once, he carried out a sting on a dealer from Stoke-on-Trent whom he met in a Liverpool wine bar. This netted £22,000-worth of cannabis resin for Comerford but all Micky got was £900.'

Comerford, fifty-three, and Yardi, thirty, were charged with possessing heroin worth one million pounds and conspiracy to import drugs. Comerford was also accused of trying to bribe one of the arresting officers by offering him £15,000. Shortly before the trial began, police were warned that there was a £20,000 underworld bounty on Wilding's head. The case was moved to the Old Bailey in London for greater security and the star prosecution witness was kept at various police stations and safe houses, being moved regularly and giving evidence during specially-arranged early morning hearings.

'Thomas Comerford was a man with two faces,' said Paul Purnell QC, opening the Crown's case in November 1985. 'To the local authority, he was a high-priority council house applicant. On the other hand, he was a man with a Bank of Ireland account in the false name of Thomas Curry through which nearly £200,000 passed in a year. The syndicate was international.'

Wilding told how he would travel to Europe and strap bags of heroin to his body using crepe bandages and sticking plaster before flying back to England. He admitted conspiracy to supply heroin and other drugs and possession of a firearm and ammunition and was jailed for five years. 'I take into consideration that your actions have placed you at considerable risk for years to come,' said the judge.

Neither Comerford nor Yardi gave evidence. They were found guilty of the drugs offences, though Comerford was acquitted of bribery. Judge Francis Petre sentenced him to the maximum fourteen-year term. Yardi was given ten years and Bartlett four. Tacker's good cheer did not desert him. As he was being led to the cells, he turned to the judge and said, 'Merry Christmas, your honour.'

The Liverpool mafia learned a lesson from Comerford's downfall. He had exposed himself too much, got his own hands dirty. They were mistakes the Banker would not repeat. Many believe he and his associates were now setting up one of the most comprehensive and successful smuggling syndicates ever seen in this country. They would be assisted by a remarkable alliance with a network of black drug traffickers from Toxteth, labelled by police the 'Black Caucus'. In time this unique black-white collaboration would be headed by Curtis Warren.'

'Before the riots, each group would keep to their own little section but afterwards they realised there was more money to be made by joining forces,' says a Liverpool solicitor who has represented many major criminals. 'Initially it was the blags [*armed robberies*] that they worked on but then they moved into drugs. Liverpool 8, for the right reasons or not, has always been associated with drugs and there has always been a market for them there. The white lads realised this and teamed up with the blacks who were already established. The whites were able to provide the money to fund bigger and more regular deals. A brighter, more ruthless type of criminal emerged.'

4 STREET SURRENDER?

*They're miles ahead of us, while we
were fighting over territory, they were doing
multi-million-pound deals*

A Manchester villain

CURTIS WARREN emerged from prison to the dole queue. A world economic recession and upheaval in the British economy had brought the highest levels of unemployment since the Depression. One in four Liverpool adults was without a job, four out of every five in Toxteth. The fortnightly Giro cheque was often spent before it arrived. The unemployment exchanges had been renamed job centres but there were still scores of applicants for every small white vacancy card. Cocky faced a crossroads and every route was a dead end.

A hardening of the Merseyside criminal class became evident. In 1983 the use of firearms in robberies almost doubled in the county. Following a similar rise in armed robberies the previous year, it must have left Chief Constable Oxford wondering why he had ever taken the job. 'Crime and violent anti-social behaviour, together with unemployment, social conditions and political conflict, were the dominant features of life in Merseyside in 1983,' he concluded grimly in his annual report.

Every crime had its victims. On a spring day in 1983, a petite, thirty-seven-year-old housewife named Pamela Walsh was shopping in Smithdown Road, the extension of Upper Parliament Street that runs out of the city, through parkland and on to the suburbs. Her four children were in school and she was enjoying the chance to get out and have a natter after a recent stay in hospital. She knew the area well; perhaps that was why she sensed something odd about the behaviour of a man standing near the Post Office. She watched him out of the corner of her eye as a Securicor van pulled up and its driver started unloading cash bags.

Suddenly the strange man was joined by two accomplices. One produced a pistol, another a sawn-off shotgun. As they yelled at the security guard to lie on the floor, passers-by froze. All except Mrs Walsh. Although small and slight, she was a fiery lady with a strong sense of injustice.

'I was livid when I saw the man with the shotgun, although to be honest I thought it was an iron bar at first,' she would later recall. 'There must have been around thirty people standing around watching and there were plenty of men there but they didn't do anything. I think that made me angry as well. I just couldn't let these yobs think they could go round on the streets with guns so I waded in. I've always had a fairly short temper.'

She attacked one of the robbers. The shotgun man lashed back with the stock of his weapon. Mrs Walsh fell to the ground with a fractured skull. The raiders fled with £8,193. Two of them, however, were eventually caught: Curtis Francis Warren, aged nineteen, now living at Sir Howard Way, and Liam Anthony Tierney, twenty-three, of Croxteth Grove, both Toxteth.

They were tried that July at Bromborough Crown Court on the Wirral. The fearless Mrs Walsh had made a complete recovery, having refused to stay in hospital for more than a few days, and was there to give evidence. Her testimony and that of a teenage girl who had closely observed the crime sealed the robbers' fate. Warren denied being the man with the shotgun but was found guilty of robbery and was jailed for five years. Tierney pleaded guilty and also admitted a previous robbery. He was jailed for six years. The teenage witness and two detectives were praised by the bench, while Mrs Walsh was awarded £100 from public funds. 'I think she acted in an extremely courageous and determined way,' said Judge Alan Booth. 'She showed spirit which other members of the public may envy. I do not wish to say others who do not act as she did should be condemned because we are all different and some of us are more timid.' (The redoubtable Mrs Walsh was awarded the Provincial Police Gold Medal Award, the highest police honour for civilians. A year later, she helped to chase and detain a suspected burglar.)

Five years was more than twice as long as Warren's previous longest stretch. Yet paradoxically, incarceration broadened his horizons. Granby had been a prison in its own right, as a local councillor described at the time:

> The stress of life in a deprived area was given a new dimension by a rising sense of claustrophobia. To those of the Black community who lived there, the walls of the ghetto were felt

to be closing in. With the continuing rise in unemployment, fewer and fewer had any cause to move outside that limited area; young Blacks do not often go to football matches. Such as could be identified by the colour of their skin ceased to venture into town lest they be turned back by the police and told to go back 'where they belonged'.

Margaret Simey, Democracy Rediscovered

Jail removed Cocky from a beleagured enclave and introduced him to villains from all over the city and beyond. Contacts were forged with kindred spirits from the crime gangs of the region's two great cities. From Greater Manchester came members of the fledgling Salford firm, scared of no-one, into thieving and fighting; the Cheetham Hillbillies, young armed robbers with access to considerable firepower; and various gangbangers from Moss Side, the notorious Manchester ghetto which had suffered dreadful riots soon after Toxteth and was fast becoming the biggest drugs market in the country. They were joined by Merseyside mobs from Toxteth, Dingle, Kirkdale, Huyton and Kirkby. In an adult jail the traditional Liverpool-Manchester rivalry tended to be forgotten. The phrase 'college of crime' was rarely more apt.

These gangs and others like them were to change the nature of organised and semi-organised crime in Britain. Their most striking features were their readiness to use weapons and their immersion in the drugs business, two things that marked them out from their predecessors. The Manchester gangs were particularly wild, settling disputes with the trigger rather than the fist. They in turn admired the Scousers' criminal nous and money-making abilities. 'They're miles ahead of us,' one Manchester villain told the present authors. 'While we were fighting over territory, they were doing multi-million-pound deals.'

Warren also took a growing interest in the wider world. He started to read, something he rarely did outside, and to follow current affairs. His home city was rarely out of the news, for these were the Militant years. The Labour Party had taken over Liverpool City Council from an ineffectual Liberal-Tory alliance. Its new ruling group was dominated by the secretive, hard-Left Militant Tendency, which embarked on a policy of direct confrontation with Margaret Thatcher's Tory Government. The Left also attacked the Chief Constable, who fell into a state of almost permanent conflict with the Labour-dominated Merseyside Police Authority. The city became synonymous with political strife.

> It fed off grievance; and there was plenty to grieve about... it seemed possible that Liverpool could be read as a portent for Britain as a whole, that we would all, outside the shires and a few cathedral towns, end up like this. Impoverished, sometimes funny, often drunk, without a meaning or a role in the world... Unemployment in the United Kingdom reached three million, imports in manufactured goods overtook exports for the first time in British history, crime and poverty grew.
>
> *Ian Jack, Liverpool looking out to sea*

It had a corrosive effect on Liverpool's image. Thousands deserted the city to look for work, only to encounter a wall of prejudice. Liverpudlians had become tarred as thieves and whingers. The city of a million comedians itself became the butt of crude jokes: *What do you call a Scouser in a suit? – The accused.* 'Gizza job', became a mocking catchphrase. Football fans taunted, 'You'll never get a job,' to the tune of the Scouse anthem *You'll Never Walk Alone.* The Heysel disaster of May 1985, when the storming of a terrace by Liverpool supporters led to the death of thirty-nine people at the European Cup final in Brussels, gave further ammunition to the city's critics.

None of this would directly affect Warren as he passed the hours reading and listening to music in a shared, cramped cell. More important for his future were events on the ground in Granby.

CANNABIS has a long tradition in Toxteth. During the Fifties, the supply was reportedly run by Rudolph 'Bull' Gardner, a Jamaican immigrant who arrived with less than £15 in his pocket and started selling grass to fellow blacks and to US servicemen stationed in the city. Gardner was eventually jailed for two years after police raided a shebeen he ran; this was followed by a drugs conviction. But he had highlighted a lucrative market with a regular clientele, including many students from the nearby university.

By the time Curtis Warren was a teenager, two brothers had risen to the top of the Toxteth street hierarchy. Michael and Delroy Showers were the Liverpool-born sons of a Nigerian merchant seaman who claimed to be a tribal chief. Michael was born in 1945, the older sibling by six years. Athletic and articulate, he played chess, enjoyed classical music and was always immaculately groomed. His exaggeratedly cultured air hid an evil streak. At seventeen he went to Borstal for wounding. Three years later he was jailed for robbery. He went to jail again for trying to run down a police constable with a car. In 1970, while working as a debt collector, he was charged with attempting to murder Ahmed Aldi Saleh, an African seaman, by blasting him with a shotgun as he stood in the doorway of the Somali Social Club on Upper Parliament Street. Showers was jailed for seven years for wounding.

Delroy was shorter than Michael, at about five feet eight inches, but worked out relentlessly and was built like a small tank. 'He's short, and looks nothing much in clothing, but when he strips off you can't believe your eyes,' wrote his close friend Paul Sykes, once a highly-rated heavyweight boxer, in his auto-biography *Sweet Agony*. 'He's massive, with masses of thick, hard muscle. He's handsome too, a dead ringer for Ken Norton [*the American boxing contender*]. He doesn't smoke, doesn't drink, and trains almost every day.'

'Delroy is a real gentleman,' says another friend. 'He is well-spoken, polite, holds doors open for ladies. But if you cross him, get out of town.' Like his brother, he had a penchant for flashy dress and affected the speech and manner of an English gent. He lived in expensive flats and hotels and hired top-of-the-range cars. He also, between 1977 and 1979, controlled a complex syndicate importing cannabis from Africa. Using a series of passports, he travelled to and from Kenya, bribing officials to allow drugs to be smuggled in suitcases by sea to Liverpool and by air to Heathrow. Consignments were also sent in the post during the Christmas rush, when parcels were less likely to be checked.

Delroy was arrested in London in 1980 after a huge police operation. Intriguingly, he was in the company of Charlie Richardson, head of the eponymous south London gang, who was on the run from prison. It revealed a link between London and Liverpool gangsters which would dramatically resurface several years later. Described as 'the ringleader and the manipulator' of a large drugs conspiracy, Delroy was jailed for nine years at Chester Crown Court. 'You profited vastly from your crime,' said the judge. 'In this class of case, ringleaders are very seldom caught and when they are they must expect a sentence of the utmost severity.'

There was no evidence that Michael was involved in Delroy's scheme. On the surface, at least, he had decided to move in a different direction. In the immediate post-riot years, he emerged as the public champion of Toxteth. 'He discovered a new weapon – the politics of the Hard Left,' reported the *Daily Mail*. 'He became a leading light in the Liverpool 8 Defence Committee set up to help rioters from that district. He oozed self-confidence – whether preaching his anti-police gospel on Sir Robin Day's *Question Time* programme or parading behind a butchered pig's head demanding the sacking of Merseyside's chief constable.'

Though he lived in Childwall, south Liverpool, with his Russian-German wife Hassie and their five children, Michael Showers daily cruised the Granby streets in a white Rolls-Royce, rolling down the window to gauge the pulse and dispense advice. Many people looked up to him. The police despised him. Privately, they called him a dangerous criminal and claimed his community-champion image was a sham. He said they were out to get him. 'I think they have created so many scars that the best thing they can ever hope for is to be able to walk along Granby Street and be ignored,' he told a BBC *Panorama* documentary.

A series of successful brushes with the Law reinforced his 'flameproof' image. In 1982, he won an acquittal from firearms and drugs charges after claiming he had been framed. Three months later, he was back in court after police found cannabis and a Walther pistol in a Toxteth flat he admitted using 'occasionally for adultery'; he said he had no idea they were there and was cleared again. In 1985, he was named at Tommy Comerford's trial as being involved in cannabis distribution but was never charged. He even landed a £16,000-a-year job, paid for by the city council, with the Merseyside Immigration Advice Unit. It was a two-finger salute to the cops.

At around this time, the eminent liberal jurist Lord Scarman had been commissioned to make a report into the causes of the riots. His recommendations included sensitive 'community policing' in areas of high racial tension to restore public confidence in the boys and girls in blue. 'It meant that instead of patrolling the area insulated in patrol cars, officers would be on foot and usually in pairs,' reported the BBC's *Panorama*. 'Most of the officers involved were volunteers and early observers thought the scheme was working well.'

The beat bobbies made a point of chatting to people in the street, visiting schools and dealing sympathetically with routine complaints. They turned a blind eye to certain petty offences; anyone caught with ganja was liable to a warning rather than arrest. But as the months went by the policy became more and more controversial. The belief – part-myth, part-true – grew that Granby was somewhere criminals could operate with little interference. There were rumours that villains being chased would drive into the Triangle knowing that the cops would be unlikely to follow and risk sparking public disorder. In the popular mythology of the area, the police had surrendered the streets and what happened next was a direct consequence.

The amount of hard drugs shipped in by the Liverpool mafia had been growing year-on-year. Heroin gripped the region's many run-down housing estates, where networks of walkways and derelict buildings provided safe places from which to deal and a warren of escape routes. Smoking heroin – chasing the dragon – became a vogue in parts of Birkenhead and city dumping grounds like the Radcliffe Estate on Everton Brow, where huge derelict warehouses known as 'bondies' became magnets for junkies. The high-rise blocks in the concrete nightmare of Croxteth, on the city outskirts, were known as Smack Heights.

'We'd go in looking for our main man, up in the lift and to his door,' says an ex-junkie who frequented Croxteth. 'It was a heavily defended flat with a big iron door and a cage built behind it for security. He'd only deal through the letterbox. You had to post the cash through first and then the gear would be pushed out afterwards, wrapped in newspaper or in a ripped magazine page. If he was out we knew we could go up a couple of floors and go to another door where the same thing would happen. On any day we could go to any of eight or nine doors in those flats to get what we needed.' Insurance premiums in Liverpool became the highest in the country. One survey found that half of the people in the inner-city were too scared to venture out after dark.

Granby had never been noted for smack. But the soft-policing strategy served to entice dealers into the area, believing they would be able to operate with impunity. They were resisted. Graffiti appeared on walls in Granby:

NEWSFLASH! THIS IS TOXTETH NOT CROXTETH. STRICTLY GANJA

It was a warning that heroin would not be tolerated, only cannabis. When some smack dealers set up shop in several flats in the Triangle in the summer of 1985, a 150-strong vigilante mob attacked them and broke a pusher's kneecaps with a hammer. A black market economy had become a black market society, with its own law and punishments. How much this vigilantism was a front to keep out rival dealers is unclear. Backing the campaign was Michael Showers, who spoke out at anti-drug meetings. The police, who privately referred to him as the 'Godfather of Toxteth', were sceptical.

Tensions rose again in the summer of 1985. There was a fight at a Caribbean carnival and a visitor from Brixton was stabbed to death. When a local man was arrested, a 200-strong mob laid siege to Admiral Street police station. Four youths later appeared in court for affray; that night there was serious rioting. The operational support unit drove directly at the crowd. Community policing was dead. Michael Showers put on an Oscar-winning performance for a Press conference the next day, tears welling up in his eyes as he vilified the police before storming out of the door, apparently overcome with emotion.

A few days later he told a television reporter, 'At present I feel very bitter about what happened but possibly in the future I may well sit round the table with police officers and discuss other matters.' How right he was. Showers was arrested soon after, accused of assaulting a young woman. Despite his protestations, he was jailed for four months.

A GENERATION divided Showers and the young bucks of Granby. Though they respected his reputation and authority, they had their own niche to carve. By the mid-Eighties Warren, fresh out of prison, had a tough circle of associates, some of whom were involved in crime. They included the frightening Johnny Phillips, his physique pumped up by weights and workouts; Paul Uchegbu, a hard-looking, cool-headed robber; Mark 'Sonny Boy' Osu, a reckless young car thief; Andrew 'AJ' John, six feet three inches tall and supremely fit, the Midlands and North West karate champion and a member of the British team by his early twenties but jailed in 1984 for robbing a security guard at the Polytechnic College; burglar Andrew Kaseem; and others who cannot currently be named for legal reasons.

Then there was the one-boy crime-wave called Stephen Lunt. A white youth with an infectious grin and a Jimmy Osmond mop, Lunt made national newspaper headlines at the age of fourteen when he drove a stolen car at two policeman in an attempt to run them down. A crown court judge called him 'a very serious menace to the community' and sent him to a detention centre for four years. His driving skills were highly-valued for getaways. 'Lunt would drive at night at 120 miles an hour with no lights on. That takes some bottle,' says an officer.

Their hang-out was the International Café, a Granby Street landmark. A visiting reporter from the *Independent* recorded the atmosphere:

All but one of the black youths standing at the fruit machines or at the pool table had a criminal record. Many had been in Risley Remand Centre. A 24-year-old said: 'If you don't have a criminal record here by the age of 15, you're strange. All you have to do is break a window and they charge you instead of cautioning you – just to give you a criminal record, they want us all to be criminals. It makes no difference who you are as long as you live in Toxteth – if you're white you're treated just the same, you're just a nigger-lover, which to them is just as bad.'

The community does not welcome strangers in Granby Street. 'If you're a stranger, you're a threat out there on the street. You may not be police, but you're a pig to us all the same,' one man in the cafe said. There are police they accept – or tolerate – and there are police that they do not. The community bobby is OK: 'They accept what's going on.' But there are the outsiders, the drugs squad for example, who will not drive into the area in daylight.

While Warren was one of the sullen young men who frequented the International, little is known of what he was up to. At some stage, he moved into the drug business. Perhaps he was propelled by an episode that revealed to him what was already obvious to others: he was never cut out to be a thief.

CHUR IS THE OLDEST CITY in Switzerland, the sleepy 5000-year-old capital of a canton that includes the famous ski resorts of St Moritz, Davos and Klosters. A fortnight before Christmas 1987, it was a picture of Alpine romance. By early evening the street decorations were twinkling against a greeting-card backdrop of frosted mountains and snow-covered pines. Along the main Hartbert-strasse, couples wrapped in coats and furs window-shopped at expensive gift stores. The female assistant at the exclusive Waro shoe shop busied herself with the display.

In through the door burst Curtis Warren and an accomplice. They knocked her to the floor and emptied the till of 3208 francs – about £1300. Then they were gone. What Cocky was doing in Switzerland is one of the many secrets of his life at this time. The Swiss crime rate was low and businesses were far less security conscious than England but a mixed-race Scouser in a snooty Swiss town was hardly inconspicuous. The shoe shop raid may well have been an opportunism; if so, it was a miserable failure. Warren was followed to the train station and arrested. His accomplice escaped. In April 1988, Warren was jailed for thirty days for theft at Chur Cantonal Court.

On his release, he returned to England. He found the drug trade in full swing. 'Basically, the police had pulled out of doing anything significant in Toxteth and the kids took over,' says a Liverpool city councillor who asked not to be named. 'Not that the police would admit that, but that's exactly what happened.' It seems that Warren joined in.

We identified Curtis Warren as a street level dealer during one operation. He was just one of many dealing in small amounts of stuff on street corners at that time. He wasn't a big fish.

A senior Liverpool police officer

Warren was not a stand-out player at that time. If you asked me to name the people who caused us most problems, he wasn't really one of them. There were others who were much more active. Either he was up to things we didn't know about or he wasn't that big. It makes what he became later seem all the more remarkable.

A detective who worked in Toxteth

I first went there in the late Eighties and he wasn't very well known. He was a nobody really, probably on the first rung of the ladder. He was living in Toxteth in a mews house. It was a hovel. He and his mates all used to hang out at the International Café, as it was then, on Granby Street.

A former Toxteth WPC

Curtis had always been one of the kids around Toxteth, there were loads of them, all the same. Half-caste, black and white, it made no difference. They were all tearaways who you could see were going in one direction only. It was about 1989 when I think his name started to come up more frequently as being one of the top lads. You'll not get many people talking about him. People are very afraid of that whole scene and they have to live there, you know, get on with their lives. People are very afraid.

A long-time Toxteth resident

Despite its supposed 'ban' on heroin, Granby had succumbed. The vigilantes who had once routed smack dealers were either cowed or converted, according to one well-informed resident. 'I think Warren and some of his friends basically gave them an ultimatum. Either knuckle under or face the consequences. Nobody was able to stop him from selling his gear. Toxteth is full of hotheads and so-called hardmen but nobody messed with Warren. Looking back now, I also think he was a lot brighter than most of the other lads.'

Granby Street became infested with vigilant young pushers, most in their teens or early twenties, selling 'wraps' at £10–30 a time. They employed young lookouts on mountain bikes and eavesdropped police radio messages on scanners. Vicious dogs were kept for protection: one of the crew had a Doberman and another a pit bull terrier. Dealing was done from car windows, doorways and alleys, as one officer recalls:

> You could see the stuff being bought on Granby every day. We didn't know what to do. We didn't have a helicopter then and we couldn't get near the place. We heard they were bringing the stuff in from Bradford or Wakefield in Yorkshire. Michael Showers had connections there although we could not pin anything on him. Curtis Warren was never about. They sometimes used a Bedford Dormobile camper van to sell from and had kids as spotters.
>
> We decided that the only way we could get near them was to use two empty shipping containers to observe the comings and goings. The bottom one was lined with polystyrene for soundproofing and the top one was so we could see what was going on. There were about five or six officers in there at any time. They used to go

in at three in the morning, for seventy-two hours at a stretch. It was risky. The locals were very suspicious and would climb on top of it. They once poured petrol over it and tried to set it alight.

We also put a camera in the Post Office in Granby and used microwaves to beam the pictures into a flat and then into Admiral Street police stastion. We had to stop because we were interfering with the frequencies of NATO, which was operating in the North Sea. We then put a camera into a piece of breeze block which was set into the upstairs window of a building. It was great until we got a phone call to say, 'Have you got a camera in Granby?' We said 'no' but were then told, 'Well, someone has because it's lying in the middle of the street smashed up.'

Operation Eagle was ultimately a success, resulting in the conviction of a string of heroin dealers. But the Mr Bigs remained untouched. 'It is said that the real disciplining of the streets is in the hands of an unspecified mafia. Rumour has it that the international drug trade has found it useful to have a base in a supposedly no-go area... The fear of crime exceeds the reality. People are hag-ridden by apprehension to such an extent that they impose a voluntary curfew on themselves,' wrote councillor Margaret (now Lady) Simey. The names of Michael and Delroy Showers were often whispered. 'The Showers brothers would almost certainly have been mentors to Warren and his boys,' says a former detective. 'They were the big men of the area.'

Curtis Warren was not picked up in Operation Eagle. He was, police believe, already one rung above the street pushers and learning, finally, to use his remarkable mind.

His encyclopaedic memory meant he could remember the faces of every officer he had ever come up against. His previous blanket hostility to the uniform was replaced by a sarcastic surface friendliness. 'He was respectful. If he knew an officer's name he would address him as Mr So-and-So,' says one ex-bobby. 'If he spotted a policeman in plain clothes or out socially in a bar, he would delight in going up to him, addressing him by name and enquiring, "How are you?" It was his way of showing that he had them logged. He was a weird character.'

Not all of Warren's friends were involved in drugs. Some were pioneers of ram-raiding, a late-Eighties phenomenon that was to spread across the country. They would steal pairs of high-powered cars and drive one of them through the display windows of electrical goods stores, boutiques, jewellery stores, anywhere they could smash and grab. Once inside the team would leap out, pick up as much as they could carry, hurl it into the back of the waiting getaway car and burn off at high speed. They favoured heavy BMWs and Rovers, preferably with sun roofs: they would load up the cars with bricks, broken paving slabs and golf balls and throw them out at pursuing police. On one occasion a gun was allegedly waved at chasing officers. In the autumn of 1988, they raided at least fourteen shops. Paul Uchegbu was the organiser. He made so much money that by that Christmas he was able to pay cash for a BMW.

Merseyside Police hit back by hiring a twin-engined Squirrel pursuit helicopter fitted with Nite-Sun searchlights, Skyshout loudhailer and infra-red visual aids. Capable of 172 miles per hour, it was more than a match for the fastest getaway driver, its night vision equipment able to track people in darkness even after they had fled from their cars. It brought immediate results. 'They hated it,' says a serving detective who pursued the ram-raiders. In the early hours of 5 January 1989, the helicopter shadowed a stolen, high-powered car in a chase that began in Manchester and carried on along the M62. The car driver was Stephen Lunt. 'We chased him all the way back to Liverpool. He ended up in Toxteth. A police car went up the back of Lunt's car and he nearly lost his foot,' says the officer.

Less than twenty-four hours later, in the dead of night, three masked men drove through an unmanned security gate at Liverpool Airport and pulled onto the tarmac next to the white helicopter with police markings. The three alighted, carrying axes, and hacked at the chopper's side windows. Unable to smash through, they petrol-bombed it. The bottles bounced off, causing little more than scorches to the paintwork. As the helicopter's standby flight team emerged from a nearby cabin to investigate the noise, the men sped off.

If the police were shocked by the gang's audacity, they were less impressed with their efficiency. 'They made several mistakes,' says the detective. 'Instead of trying to smash the windshield to throw in the bombs, they should have just opened the door, because it was unlocked. Then they used diesel instead of petrol and they couldn't get it to light. What they really should have done was ram it with their car. That would have fucked it up. Instead it was only out of action for a few days. We never convicted anyone for it but we had a pretty good idea who it was.'

The nerve of the ram-raiders was breathtaking but the cops were beginning to get results. Over the next few weeks they rounded up many of the main gang members. One was Uchegbu. As he was being held at

Admiral Street police station there was a disturbance outside and a petrol bomb was thrown into the building. Heavily-armed officers thronged the magistrates court when he was brought up. Uchegbu was remanded in custody, charged with burglary, car theft and possession of amphetamines.

At his trial, prosecutor Stuart Clare said there had been a string of offences that bore the same hallmark. 'Similarities include the use of two stolen high-powered cars which are often later found burnt out, burglaries from the same kind of shops, escaping at high speeds in cars with the lights off and heading for the Toxteth area oblivious of the dangers to people unfortunate enough to be on the road at the same time. It is alleged that Uchegbu was at the very centre of this gang. In fact since he has been in custody these kind of offences have virtually ceased. Also, when the police helicopter was instrumental in the catching of one car, within twenty-four hours it had been attacked and keys which fit the stolen car used in that attack were found in Uchegbu's possession.'

Uchegbu and Sonny Boy Osu were jailed for a total of fourteen years. Osu was already on a suspended sentence for conspiring to steal a rare £130,000 left-hand drive Ford RS200, one of a limited edition of only twenty. Their fence, Delroy Showers, had also been caught with Stephen Lunt trying to sell a haul of stolen furs and leathers to an undercover cop. Showers was jailed for five years and Lunt for a year.

In Risley Prison, Uchegbu and Osu were chosen to lecture young car thieves in an American-style pilot scheme to shock youths away from crime. 'The only way these kids will face up to reality is to rub their noses in it. I make them pick up the pots we use as toilets. I show them toothbrushes that have razor blades melted into them and tell them how they'll be used for sex by long-term prisoners,' Uchegbu told reporters. 'The terrified youngsters, usually too shocked to speak, are marched out of the prison as quickly as they came in,' reported the *Daily Post*.

The ram-raiders had made quick profits but the real money was in drugs. It was here that Warren would now make his mark. His name came up again and again in drugs squad inquiries but with little concrete evidence. 'At that time, Warren was probably doing simple ten-pound street wrap deals on the streets of Toxteth,' says a customs investigator. 'He was perceived to be just a dealer. But if you surrender the streets, some of these people grow into monsters.'

5

THE UK CARTEL

Warren entered the premier league of a business

dominated by big players: the Turkish Maffya,

the Moroccan Tangiers Cartel, the Colombian

cartels of Medellin and Cali, the Sicilian Mafia

and the Triads

MICHAEL SHOWERS was about to meet nemesis. The business suits, the politics and the angry outbursts on television were a façade. For all his flowery words and fine mind, Showers was unable to resist the easy money of the drug world. By 1990, the man who had campaigned so loudly to keep smack out of Toxteth was masterminding a plot to flood the streets with heroin.

The first British customs knew of it was when an Afghan named Haji Umar approached their liaison officer in Pakistan and told how he had been offered money to courier twelve kilos of heroin – worth two million pounds on the street – to England. Umar had been told the man who would collect the drugs was 'Michael, a black man, a Moslem, a good man'. Umar was keen to help the authorities and agreed to go through with the deal, working as a participating informant. Operation Rain Man became one of the biggest drugs investigations British police and customs had ever been involved in.

Umar arranged to pick up the heroin from a camp for Afghan refugees. Local *mujahadeen* commanders were paid off to ensure safe passage from the dangerous North West Frontier region. Umar flew to Manchester in November 1990 to hand over the consignment, which was to be sold on by Showers to Mohammed Sabir, a Bradford grocer, and Ahmed Bakhtiar from Leeds. The deal would be consummated at the Excelsior Hotel at Manchester Airport. Customs officers dressed as hotel staff, air crew, waiters, bell boys and cleaners dispersed throughout the building, waiting for the conspirators to conclude their business. Negotiations dragged on for six days while Showers, Sabir and Bakhtiar made arrangements to pay the courier for two bags of heroin and sell it on the streets to finance the rest of the deal.

Conscious of Showers's violent past, the officers were perpetually fearful that he might kill Umar and take the drugs without paying. The tense operation was not without its lighter moments, however. 'In the middle of this, the Australian Rugby League team arrived to play Great Britain and we found ourselves dealing with two coachloads of supporters, all hooligan Australian drunks,' said one officer. 'One of them tried to pick up one of our girls on reception and they kept trying to drag us off to the bar to drink lots of lager.'

On the sixth night a young Asian courier from Bradford crept into the hotel through a fire escape and handed over an instalment of £11,000. He was arrested as he stepped into a corridor and quickly confessed. Showers was apprehended at his home in Childwall. The next night, as the fallen community leader languished in the remand wing at Strangeways Prison, Manchester, his seventy-eight-year-old mother Daisy was knocked down and killed by a stolen car near her Toxteth home. Detectives arriving at the scene in Selborne Street – where the 1981 riots started – found that witnesses simply 'melted into the crowd'. One man who did speak to officers almost died within an hour: his car was deliberately rammed on several occasions by a Rover and when he abandoned it and fled on foot the chasing driver tried to knock him down. Eventually a seventeen-year-old admitted a variety of motoring offences in connection with the death and was put on probation for two years. But the mystery was never cleared up and rumours persisted that the death of Mrs Showers, an active mother of eleven, was some kind of brutal warning to her son.

Michael Showers's trial at Manchester Crown Court lasted five weeks and heard testimony from sixty-six witnesses. He was found guilty and jailed for twenty years. As he was led from the dock, a relative called out to him in Italian, urging him to 'be brave'. Showers followed the Tommy Comerford tradition of thanking the judge.

'It is a strange sort of community liaison officer who is prepared to obtain kilos of high-quality heroin, knowing the damage it would cause on the streets of the city for which he is supposed to be caring,' commented customs officer Tony Coady at the time. 'There is no doubt that a major part of the heroin was destined for distribution by him in Liverpool and his arrest was a major coup for us. He was, at that time, probably the most-significant UK national we have ever arrested in the fight against heroin.'

He was about to be dwarfed by the man who would succeed him. Even as Showers was being taken down to the cells, the vacancy at head of the Black Caucus had been filled.

COCKY was about to leap from the underworld to the overworld: the elite of the global drugs trade. It was a stratosphere of private planes and luxury yachts, of £1,000-a-night hookers and limited edition sports cars and champagne on tap. The kind of world a Toxteth scally could only dream about. He reached it by cutting out all middlemen and buying directly from the sources of supply. In the narco-world of the late 1980s, that meant organised crime at its highest level.

Villainy had finally gone global. International air travel, modern communications and the financial big bang had opened up the world. The new mafia combines had their own ships, aircraft, factories, front companies, hit squads, politicians and judges. They 'owned' governments, bought islands and laundered billions. They even had their own trading floor: Amsterdam, the stock exchange of the European drug market.

In 1985, a Dutch dealer bragged to undercover agents that he was 'the world's largest supplier of hashish'. A year later, a British Member of the European Parliament called Amsterdam 'the cesspit of Europe.' Both comments reflected Holland's role as a central conduit for illegal substances of all kinds. The MEP, Andrew Pierce, sat on a European Community committee which recommended that all countries adopt the same enforcement and sentencing for drug offences. It was a direct attack on Holland's liberal policies.

Though possessing, processing or selling drugs was a criminal offence in the Netherlands, the authorities distinguished between 'soft' and 'hard' drugs, tolerating marijuana and hash on the grounds that they posed little risk to health or public safety and that scarce resources were better used against heroin, cocaine and acid. Possession of up to thirty grams of cannabis, a substantial amount, was allowed. But it was the country's growing importance as a trans-shipment centre that most alarmed its European neighbours. No-one knew how much entered the Netherlands and was then forwarded to the rest of the continent; no official figures were kept. This attitude seemed unconscionably lax to other governments. It was as as if the Dutch did not care.

Tokers and jugheads flocked in particular to Amsterdam, one of Europe's most beautiful cities. They were attracted by its air of relaxed decadence that by the mid-Eighties was sliding into sleaze. In one year the number of canalside coffee shops selling cannabis – and adorned with the tell-tale marijuana leaf – trebled. Many were fashionably decorated in chrome, glass and ferns; the oldest and most famous, the Bulldog, was a former police headquarters. The daily price-fixing for cannabis was announced by pirate radio, while the *Golden Blow Guide* helpfully listed all the drug cafes in the major Dutch towns and cities.

Drug tourists, stag parties and weekend trippers, many of them English, converged on 'the Dam'. Most made for the red light district, where neon-lit, lingerie-clad prostitutes stood like mannequins behind one-way shop windows while queues of gawping men filed past. Organised crime found the city an oasis, perfectly situated to import cocaine by ship from South America and heroin overland on the so-called 'Balkan route' from Turkey. Chemical drugs like LSD, amphetamine and MDMA (Ecstasy) were manufactured in local laboratories that were rarely, if ever, raided. Customs checks were minimal and the security at Amsterdam's Schipol Airport was widely regarded as a joke. And right next door was Belgium, with strict banking secrecy, perfect for placing funny money. One town just over the border consisted of two bars, three houses – and seven banks.

'I have an hour-and-a-half-long presentation to explain why Holland is the main base for international drug criminals,' says Tom Driessen, the boss of a Dutch police team that tackles Colombian drug cartels. 'We have good communications, the biggest and seventh-biggest ports in the world [*Rotterdam and Amsterdam respectively*], a central position in Europe, good infrastructure and a good communication network. And like the British, the Dutch like to trade. This is a country where people are always thinking about doing business and that is also good for organised crime.'

The Dam was a magnet for drug entrepreneurs like Curtis Warren. British investigators believe he gained an all-important *entrée* to this champagne subculture through older Liverpool crooks who had blazed a trail before him. One officer has speculated that the introduction came via a Liverpool mafia stalwart named Stan Carnall. 'Stan was very highly involved with the Dutch criminal gangs. He was a regular through Manchester Airport. He made so many flights he ended up with more air miles than a pilot.'

Eleven years older than Warren, Carnall was a typical 'ODC' – an 'ordinary decent criminal' – with multiple convictions including armed robbery and drugs importation. He was a cool, experienced customer. 'Stan was very lax, very come-day, go-day. Though there was never any evidence of a direct partnership between him and Warren, they spoke quite often. Curtis had a lot of respect for Stan. You could hear it in his voice on the telephone. He always referred to Stan as the Big Fella. In a lot of ways, if Stan said do something then Warren, out of respect, said okay. Warren's attitude was that arguments are bad for business. He didn't want hassle. Also, Stan had been around for a long time and Curtis respected that,' says the officer. Like Carnall, Cocky became a regular through Schipol. In Amsterdam he found that any drug was available, in any quantity, for knockdown prices.

One of the first hints that he might be moving into importation came by chance. Customs picked up a courier entering the country through Dover with a hard-backed Bible hollowed out in the middle. Inside was a packet of heroin. Officers persuaded the courier it was in his best interests to co-operate with them and allowed him to continue his run.

'He travelled to Liverpool under strict customs office control where he made a phone call to Curtis Warren's home,' says a customs officer who worked on the case. 'The phone number was worked out by numbers which had been scrawled onto separate pages of the Bible. Alone they meant nothing but together they made Warren's number. The call was made and a woman picked up the phone. She passed the receiver over to Warren.'

The courier told Warren he was in town and 'had the drugs'.

'Who is this?' replied Warren. 'I have no idea who you are, you must have a wrong number.' The line went dead.

'There was no way to link the drugs to Warren except by the courier's word and that wouldn't stand up in court. To this day we cannot prove that he was involved. We believe there must have been a code word of some kind which triggered his response. He was sharp – it was clear to see even then – but at that point we weren't too concerned because we saw him as just another small-time dealer.'

But Cocky was moving up, fast. 'He was hard to keep track of, his name kept coming up in plenty of different places and in relation to matters of drugs,' says

Detective Chief Inspector Mike Keogh, formerly of the North West Regional Crime Squad. 'He didn't really have a place to call his own, his home was pretty much the bed of whichever woman he could persuade to take him home, and he had quite a few. He never did anything by land telephone line, everything was cellular. And he changed his numbers and phones regularly, every four to six weeks. He had a deal with a perfectly legitimate cellular phone business which would swap his phones whenever he wanted to. He occasionally used cloned phones but that wasn't really his style, he was most likely paying off someone in a legit business to keep him untraceable.'

The major Liverpool distributors operated what were known as 'cartwheel conspiracies', as one drugs squad officer explains:

> The target is in the centre, but is so wealthy he can run the business without ever getting his hands dirty. He changes his mobile phone every other day. He sleeps with a different woman every night. Down one spoke of the wheel is the stash house, where the drugs are warehoused. Down another is the money house, often belonging to a trusted mum or dad. Down a third spoke is the phone house, where runners man a battery of stolen, cloned mobile phones. Down a fourth is the phone dealer. Down a fifth is the man with the Tokarev [*a semi-automatic pistol popular with Liverpool gunmen*]. Down the sixth, seventh and eighth spokes are street dealers.

At some stage, Warren became the importer who supplied all of the bosses, who kept all the wheels spinning. He entered the premier league of a business dominated by big players: the Turkish *Maffya*, the Moroccan Tangiers Cartel, the Colombian cartels of Medellin and Cali, the Sicilian Mafia and the Triads. They were led by impossibly exotic, ruthless men, many from the poorest of backgrounds; men both cruel and generous, disciplined and reckless, smart and stupid. They would spill money like water then kill over a tiny debt; take matters of pride and honour to ridiculous extremes, then betray their best friends. And the richest, most flamboyant and most dangerous of all were the cocaine barons of Colombia.

'Because of our liberal policy on prostitution, the Colombians like to be here,' says Dutch police officer Tom Driessen. 'We have regulated prostitution so it is contained in certain areas. Many of the girls are from South America and so there is a whole scene in these areas with many Spanish and South American bars and restaurants. We are a tolerant, multi-racial society. It has caused problems though; the Americans call us the Miami of Europe. The big criminals in the UK move to Holland to do business with the South Americans.'

One of these would be Curtis Warren. To understand his meteoric rise, it is necessary to take a short detour into the world of the 'snow' kings.

COCAINE comes from the coca plant, grown mainly in the neighbouring South American states of Peru, Bolivia and Colombia. In the 1970s Colombia, already the biggest supplier of marijuana to the United States, became the first of the three to develop the processing facilities to make powdered cocaine hydrochloride. It became the dominant partner of the triumvirate, controlling a classic commodity market with price stability and supply and demand rising steadily.

The market was driven by five men: the three Ochoa brothers – Jorge, Juan and Fabio – and their friends Gonzalez Gacha and Pablo Escobar. They bought coca leaves from poor farmers, transported them over hill tracks by donkey or lorry to jungle labs for processing and turned a Third World cottage industry into a multi-billion-dollar enterprise. By the mid-Eighties their cartel, based in and named after the industrial city of Medellin, was selling cut-price wholesale coke by the tonne. One forest factory discovered in 1984 had seven airstrips, beds for 100 people, mechanics' workshops, a clubhouse for pilots and 11,500 kilos of cocaine, worth an estimated £1.2 billion.

Their chief market was the United States. Mainly for geographical reasons, there tends to be a south-to-north flow for coke in the Americas and an east-to-west flow for heroin from the Middle East to Western Europe. Such was the Colombians' zeal that eventually the US market became saturated and then they, too, looked to Europe. While the United Kingdom had the worst heroin problem on the continent, it was almost virgin territory for the coke barons. And in the drug business, virgins get raped.

The pivotal year was 1985. The Colombians sent a young couple to open up distribution in England. Keith Goldsworthy was a twenty-nine-year-old unemployed chef from Devon. His wife Claudia just happened to be a cousin of Jorge Ochoa, co-leader of the Medellin Cartel. They arrived in London and set to work. At the same time a mysterious criminal called Nikolaus Chrastny, was opening up a parallel London outlet. With thinning hair and thick-framed glasses, Chrastny could have passed for a banker but was a James Bond-style villain, born in Czechoslovakia, a German national and on the run since 1973 for a gems robbery in Munich. Crucially, he had links to some of London's heaviest villains, men who could distribute the product and whose pedigree impressed the Colombians. He also had a line to Escobar and the Ochoas and met them face to face.

'I originally planned on getting between 150 and 200 kilos of cocaine,' Chrastny later told customs officers, 'but they liked the idea of opening a further European market so much that they asked me how much I could take. I ended up with 392 kilos.' He paid for the first thirty-eight and was given the rest on credit. The Colombians were so keen that Fabio Ochoa visited London personally to sort out the deal. Chrastny was soon shifting his huge stash. In one meeting alone at a hotel he paid a South American bagman $2,300,000, while his wife spent half a million pounds on clothes in a month.

Within a year, seizures of coke in the United Kingdom doubled.

Chrastny was eventually arrested in June 1987 at a flat in Harley Street, central London. He was moved to a police cell in West Yorkshire because of fears he might be killed, only to escape by sawing through the bars. He has not been seen since. Only fifty-seven of his 392 kilos were ever recovered. Meanwhile Goldsworthy, who had been flying hundreds of kilos into the US in his private Cessna and then shipping it to Britain, was caught in Miami and jailed for twenty-two years. His wife was charged with laundering millions of pounds but fled with their young daughter six days before her trial at Knightsbridge Crown Court, leaving behind a secluded home in Fulham, west London, bought for cash, and more than £200,000 in bank and building society accounts.

Losing its two main bulk distributors was a blow to the Medellin Cartel. It fell back on individual smugglers, known as 'mules', who carried relatively small amounts through air and sea ports. Law enforcement officers saw a surge in the number of 'stuffers and swallowers' who packed bags of coke into any orifice or ingested it wrapped in cellophane. Many were organised by Jamaican Yardie gangs. While they were not moving large quantities in the way that Chrastny and Goldsworthy had, there were so many of them that the tide became a flood.

In 1988 Richard Lawrence, the then-chief investigation officer for HM Customs and Excise, described cocaine as 'the greatest concern for the future' because of indications that the South Americans were trying to re-establish an infrastructure. Seizures that year reached 362 kilos, exceeding those of heroin for the first time. But the arrogant, violent Medellin men were over-reaching. In August 1989, they assassinated Luis Carlos Galan, a front runner in the forthcoming presidential election. The Colombian state responded with a massive offensive: a civil war between good and evil. Soldiers raided jungle hideouts and hunted down the narco-bosses. US drug enforcement agents weighed in to help, closing off many of the cartel's Caribbean trans-shipment routes. Gonzalez Gacha was killed by police in a shoot-out. Other combine leaders were locked up.

As the Medellin Cartel crumbled, so the Cali Cartel, based further south, took advantage. It was run by Jose Santacruz-Londono and brothers Miguel and Gilberto Orejuela, once close allies of the Medellin men who now carefully distanced themselves from the war with the state. Their master stroke was the mass-marketing of crack, a cheap, highly-addictive crystalline mix of cocaine and baking soda that raged through the urban ghettoes of the United States like a plague. Soon the Cali Cartel controlled an estimated eighty per cent of the world's cocaine. Its leaders – intelligent, sophisticated and ambitious – also turned their attention to Britain. They believed that their greater subtlety and guile would succeed where the macho buccaneers of Medellin had stumbled. What they needed were the contacts to move their powder in bulk and here they had an extraordinary stroke of luck. They found that British criminals were on the verge of forming their very own drugs combine: a UK Cartel.

AT THE HEAD of this network were two heavy-duty crime figures from London and Liverpool: Eddie Richardson and The Banker. Richardson, a rugged scrap metal dealer in his fifties, was one of the few genuine legends of the British underworld. With his brother Charlie he had run the pre-eminent mob in south London in the 1960s. Though the rival Krays grabbed most of the headlines, the Richardsons were considered by many to be the superior outfit. According to their chief enforcer, 'Mad' Frankie Fraser, 'Using racing terms, there would be no race, comparing the Richardsons with the Krays. The Richardsons were miles in front, brain power, everything.'

While the dynamic Charlie was seen as the brains of the outfit, Eddie, a tall, dark-haired ex-boxer, was more feared. In 1966, he was jailed for his part in a murderous affray at a night club. In 1967, both brothers and some of their henchmen were given long jail terms in the notorious 'torture trial', at which it was alleged they had used electrodes and pliers on those who displeased them, though they denied it. Eddie served nine years of a fifteen-year stretch and then quietly resumed his scrap business.

He was the kind of man whose reputation impressed the Colombians. So when, in 1988, he was introduced to a Cali front man, a mutually beneficial relationship was swiftly cemented. 'Richardson brought a kind of stature to the operation,' said senior customs officer Hugh Donagher. 'He was introduced to the South Americans as one of the main criminal *capos* in England, a guy who could provide muscle to protect the London end of things and, at the same time, help to raise money on the strength of his name and reputation. Richardson was never especially bright but people like him can be very useful.' (quoted in Jon Silverman, *Crack of Doom*).

Richardson was already importing Thai cannabis through Gatwick Airport, where he paid baggage handlers to remove cases containing drugs. He now used the same route for cocaine. One successful forty-four kilo importation was worth around £10 million on the street, a fortune in British terms but small change to the Colombians. To bring in what the they considered serious loads, Richardson looked to Southampton docks, where he was confident of getting containers through unchecked. He also, according to customs sources, offered this 'import facility' to a clandestine acquaintance: the Banker.

The Liverpudlian was the most careful of crime lords, a man of innate suspicion and almost Sicilian slyness. He told underlings only what they needed to know and favoured public telephone boxes to reduce the risk of wiretapping. His care had paid off. The police had never been able to penetrate his organisation; indeed, it was believed he had officers on his payroll. What neither he nor Richardson knew was that at the time they were teaming up, they had been under Customs and Excise surveillance for months.

Investigators gleaned that while Richardson was organising a mixed coke and cannabis shipment from South America, the Banker was arranging a massive consignment of hashish from the Far East. Customs officers were dispatched from Britain to follow the supply line. They observed a large shipping container being loaded with massive amounts of cannabis brought down from northern Pakistan. They estimated there was four tonnes of the stuff packed inside the steel box, ready to sail.

Before the hash could leave, in March 1989, Richardson's container arrived at Southampton from Ecuador. It contained a batch of hollowed-out balsa wood; concealed inside was two metric tonnes of cannabis and 154 kilos of cocaine. The coke alone was worth around £40 million, the biggest load targeted at the UK at that time. Some if it was marked 'Calidad', indicating its source was the Cali Cartel. Customs were waiting. They seized the drugs and arrested Richardson and several co-conspirators. The Banker was not one of them; there was no evidence to link him to that load. But the raid caused him a major inconvenience. He immediately suspected that the alliance had been compromised. The Banker never took chances. His four tonnes of cannabis, still sitting in a container, was simply written off and left to rot on Karachi harbour.

Eddie Richardson was jailed for twenty-five years for drug trafficking. The Banker again escaped unscathed. He was tipped off about the operation against him and doubled his defences. It did, however, reveal another interesting arm of his network: he had been trying to open a supply line into Japan. Two Scouse lads had been sent to Tokyo to meet a contact. They were not the brightest of boys. Unable to speak the language or find their way around, they took a taxi from the airport to a city centre hotel, checked in and hit the bar. Officers from the Japanese Narcotics Squad, who had been primed by their British colleagues, watched the pair get stupendously drunk.

'For the next few days they stumbled around the city from bar to bar attempting to find their way around, without success,' says a customs source. 'They would occasionally make calls from street payphones in the hope of making contact with the dealer they had been assigned to meet. But during the whole two weeks they were in Japan they did not once get him on the phone or meet him.'

Eventually, they ran out of cash and nervously made a call back to their master in Liverpool. They claimed they thought they had been rumbled by the authorities and were being followed. They were, but didn't know it. 'They were absolutely terrified of the trouble they would be in when they got back to Liverpool, so they made up this story about being followed. In fact, they were completely inept and were unable to work in the environment they had been sent to.'

Clearly the Banker needed more capable collaborators. One man had come to his attention, a rising young criminal from Granby with a natural authority, ice for blood and an eye for the main chance. They would form the most formidable partnership in British crime.

IN 1991, Curtis Warren's name cropped up in a wide-ranging investigation by the number four Regional Crime Squad, based in the Midlands. It was called Operation Bruise and was sparked by an informant. In August 1990, a car was stopped on the M6 and a man named Graham Titley was arrested in possession of counterfeit notes.

The police offered him a deal: co-operate and we'll put in a good word for you. Titley co-operated. He had a long criminal record, including indecent assault, burglary and handling stolen goods; unsavoury but essentially low-level. Yet when he came up for trial in February 1991, the crime squad's second-in-command wrote a letter to the judge stating that Titley could help to smash 'major criminals throughout the UK and Europe... who are engaged in the large-scale distribution of drugs and counterfeit currency' and 'paramilitary organisations in Northern Ireland who are using the proceeds of drugs sales to fund their terrorist activities'.

Faced with such a letter, the judge was lenient, sentencing Titley to eighteen months. He was released after seven and became an informer. Initially he helped to target a middle-aged man from Stoke-on-Trent who the police believed to be in the 'upper league criminal fraternity'. According to one source close to Operation Bruise, Titley said the man was only a bit-part player. 'The real main man was a guy from Liverpool 8. He wasn't just into currency, he was into drug smuggling. They reckoned he was bringing cannabis over from Spain via Holland, probably on lorries. As a result their inquiry switched to Liverpool. They began investigating the main target and found that one of his associates was called Curtis Warren, who also lived in Liverpool 8 and who wasn't considered more than a low- to mid-ranking street hood.'

Bruise showed how far British law enforcement was lagging behind the traffickers at that time. In an attempt to track suspect vehicles leaving Holland for the UK, the Regional Crime Squad contacted the Dutch police. 'The Dutch had access to a satellite tracking system, which we did not have in those days. They lent it to the RCS, who tried several times to place the tracker on a suspect lorry, both on a ferry and in Liverpool, but it just wasn't possible. So the device sat in a detective's desk drawer for three months, without them realising that the Dutch were charging them twenty-five pounds a day for it. They knew the precise location of the desk but not much else.

'Warren was suspected of organising his own shipments but only in quantities of between twenty-five and fifty kilos of resin at a time, which really didn't put him in the big league. The crime squad came across a telex between Warren and Holland over an importation of tee-shirts and trainers. It stated, "The tee-shirts and trainers are wet, we are returning them." We believe this was a code. Tee-shirts meant cannabis resin and trainers meant herbal cannabis. He was sending them back because they had not arrived in reasonable condition and were unsellable. Cannabis is affected when it gets wet, particularly if it has come in by boat and has been soaked through.'

The Midlands officers naively decided to mount observations in Granby. 'There was one very bullish detective who boasted he could do surveillance anywhere. I told him that it was impossible to work that way in Liverpool 8 but he wouldn't listen. They went up to the Triangle but within two hours they were out of there. They were lucky to escape with their lives.'

By then, the RCS investigation was coming apart at the seams. It emerged that the informant Titley, with the support of undercover detectives, had used a mixture of threats and inducements to pressure people into buying or forging fake American Express travellers cheques. He then tipped off the police and claimed rewards totalling at least £100,000 from Amex. A series of prosecutions – none of them connected to Warren – foundered at court. One case, in which some men from

South Wales had been urged to forge cheques, was described by the judge as 'a scandalous, corrupt incitement which led to the defendants being fitted up to commit crimes none of them would have dreamed of committing otherwise'. At least one officer from the Midlands Regional Crime Squad knew or believed that Titley was acting as an agent provocateur, said the judge. Such conduct is strictly forbidden; Home Office rules say no informant must ever 'counsel, incite or procure the commission of a crime'.

Warren was never charged with any crime in relation to Operation Bruise. Still the intelligence file on him continued to grow, especially when Bruise was absorbed into a far bigger operation involving police and customs officers from all over the country. Police in the north-east had received information from a very well-placed informant that Warren had formed an alliance with a major Colombian drug ring. Customs officers and cops in London, Bristol, Manchester and Leeds were also taking a deep interest.

On 8 June 1991, Warren's friend Andrew John, the tall, handsome karate champion, was shot four times near Granby Street. He was found slumped at the roadside in a pool of blood and died three hours later in hospital. The shooter, a local man, was later jailed for eight years for manslaughter. He claimed 'AJ' had previously attacked him with a baseball bat. If Cocky was aggrieved at the death, he had little time to mourn. He had bigger things to worry about.

THE SUMMIT

What Joey did not know was that the ingots were an ingenious method of moving drugs. Inside each huge lump of lead, impervious to X-rays and so thick that unless you knew where to drill you had little chance of finding anything, would be a steel box containing cocaine...

6

THE COLOMBIAN CONNECTION

When cut and sold on the streets for around £80,000 a kilo, it would yield a profit of at least £70 million

CARACAS, the capital of Venezuela, is the most northerly city in South America. Looking out to the Caribbean and the huge sweep of the Atlantic, it is perfectly located for trade with the east coast of the United States and with Europe. It is a place to work hard and play hard, a modern, go-ahead metropolis of glitzy high-rises, bustling traffic and beautiful women, a city with a sense of purpose. It is also a corruption-riddled hub of worldwide drug distribution and awash with filthy-rich Colombian mobsters.

In 1990, a start-up company called the Conar Corporation rented a small office suite in the centre of town. Its business was import-export in products ranging from sugar to batteries. It was run by two men, Marco Tulio Contreras and Jesus Camillo Ortiz Chacon, with a secretary, Ivonne Cruzatty, recruited from a local employment agency. Miss Cruzatty's brief was to answer the telephone, take notes, type and file letters and generally help out. She spoke good English and was soon translating for her bosses on the phone, especially when the firm diversified into exporting metals. Nothing in the wording of those conversations gave her an inkling that Conar existed for the sole purpose of sending high-grade cocaine around the world.

Conar was a classic front company, its role to provide cover for enormous loads of coke hidden inside 'legitimate' goods or containers. The point man in the Cali Cartel's new assault on the European and US markets would be Mario Halley, a personable, multi-lingual young Colombian. Halley was a natural salesman, well-connected and shrewd beyond his twenty-two years. His potential was spotted early; by young adulthood he had been sent from his native Colombia to Europe, settling in the Netherlands and successfully applying for Dutch citizenship. There he set to work. There was much to do.

The account of how the Colombians and the Liverpool mafia tried – and partially succeeded – in flooding the UK with cocaine is murky and complicated. Much of what follows must be read with one fact in mind: Curtis Warren was ultimately cleared of all charges against him. But to adequately chart the course of events that would lead to the biggest seizure of cocaine in Britain up to that time, it is necessary to piece it together as it has been related by various, sometimes conflicting, sources.

What is not in dispute is that in Amsterdam Mario Halley met a Liverpudlian ex-boxer who was resident in Holland. Halley treated him royally, jetting him to California on Concorde and entertaining him in Venezuela. It was a getting-to-know-you period on both sides. With trust established, Halley was introduced to Curtis Warren and, through him, to a shady figure named Brian Charrington.

Charrington, in his mid-thirties, was an intriguing study. Born and raised on the grim Hemlington estate in Teesside, he served an apprenticeship of petty crime and picked up a raft of convictions for theft, burglary and handling stolen goods. He was suspected of moving into drugs in the mid-Eighties and was soon regarded as a large-scale cannabis smuggler, using as a front a secondhand car showroom, Longlands Garage.

Prematurely bald, Charrington oozed charm and had expensive tastes. He flashed bags of cash, spent weeks every year in Spain, raced offshore powerboats and owned a flying school, two private aeroplanes, a specialist diving vessel, a yacht and a fleet of cars including a Rolls-Royce, a Bentley, a Mercedes and BMWs. Addicted to risk, he was a big-league player dubbed 'Target One' by customs officers. 'I started working on Brian Charrington in 1989,' says one. 'He was a jack of all trades. He was into everything but mainly cannabis. We took out a couple of jobs at Dover but we could never put them on him.'

What that customs investigator did not then know was that the enigmatic Charrington was also a police informant. Since at least 1981 he had been 'talking dirty' to Ian 'Bertie' Weedon, a detective in the Cleveland drugs squad. Much of what he offered concerned the activities of relatively lowly robbers and thieves, some of whom ended up in prison. When Weedon moved up and on to the number two Regional Crime Squad, reaching the rank of detective sergeant, he continued to 'handle' Charrington. Then a complication arose.

While Weedon worked in the RCS's crime wing, its drug wing was targeting Charrington in an operation codenamed Python. An RCS co-ordinator saw the potential conflict of interest and, according to one source, Weedon was directed to cease contact with his informant. He didn't. Instead he lobbied a friend and superior officer, Detective Inspector Harry Knaggs, who was in charge of drugs wing (south) at the RCS, based at Teesside. Knaggs regarded Charrington's information as being 'of high quality'. According to a sworn statement later made by Knaggs, a copy of which has been obtained by the authors, he could not understand why 'someone was not using BC's [*Brian Charrington's*] potential' as a top-echelon informant. He also knew that the operations against Charrington were yielding few results and 'thought it was my duty to use whatever source we could to get information [*about*] international drug trafficking'.

Knaggs took Weedon's side and in July 1990 gained permission to operate Charrington jointly as an informant. He had few illusions about who he was dealing with. 'As at the summer of 1990, BC was considered to be one of the top importers of cannabis into the UK from North Africa via Spain and France,' he wrote. 'As a consequence of this it was believed that he... had developed many contacts in the drugs realm both here and abroad.' Knaggs knew that the best informants rarely come with clean hands. But were Charrington's too dirty?

Charrington was told that a million-pound fund had been set up by the Government to pay top informants and he could expect substantial rewards for 'the right results'. As a participating informant he would effectively be immune from prosecution as long as his own role in any crime was 'a minor one' and he kept his handlers fully informed. If he was caught doing something he had not told his handlers about, he would be 'fair game'. Charrington accepted and was registered as an RCS informant under the apt codename Enigma One. A close associate was registered as Enigma Two.

The relationship between the two Enigmas and the two officers was fraught and at one stage Knaggs and Weedon were again told by their superiors to break off contact with the pair. The Enigmas were alarmed. 'They said that they were talking to some very heavy people, who did not just break arms and legs, they killed people,' recorded Knaggs. 'They had actually been in Holland when a London criminal had been killed and they themselves had had guns held to their heads. They said if things were to come to an end, so be it, but they would like to continue.' When one of their tips bore fruit and led to the arrest and jailing of a cannabis importer, Knaggs and Weedon argued that it was proof of their worth. They believed there was plenty more were that came from, a feeling confirmed in spades by Charrington's next and most sensational tip.

IN MARCH 1991, the Tynemouth lifeboat was called out to rescue three men who had abandoned ship in stormy weather off the north-east coast of England and were adrift in a small inflatable. One of them was Brian Charrington. He and his friends had been sailing out to meet another boat when a heavy storm struck and they were unable to get back to port. The following day, none the worse for his ordeal, he flew to Holland with a friend named Curtis Warren. How the pair first met is not known – it was possibly through mutual acquaintances on the Spanish Costa del Crime – but it seems they struck up a quick rapport. When Charrington returned from Holland, he spoke to DS Weedon, who in turn phoned DI Knaggs:

> [*Weedon*] reported to me that BC… had been over to Rotterdam with a man called Curtis

Warren and... had met a Colombian national called Mario Halley, obviously a close associate of Curtis Warren. DSW [*Weedon*] told me that they had been put up in an expensive hotel, seen large quantities of what appeared to be very good quality cocaine and they had been treated like royalty by Halley, who had huge amounts of money. Talk had been of a huge importation of cocaine into Europe from Colombia or Venezuela within the next five to eight months. At the time they said they already had a suitable vessel which had been purchased and was going over to South America which would have a replacement hold fitted and into which 2,000 kilograms of cocaine would be concealed and then despatched to Europe... Halley had asked BC if he would like to go to Colombia with him to meet the organisers and possibly form part of the crew. Curtis Warren had also been invited.

It should be emphasised that the only source of this information was Charrington and that Warren was later cleared in court of any involvement in a cocaine importation conspiracy. But at the time, the two Teesside detectives felt they had hit the jackpot. If Enigma One was telling the truth, it was the biggest job any copper could expect to pull; the largest narcotics importation into Europe ever. The Colombian cartels were the most potent criminal organisations in the world; here was an informant offering an 'in' at the highest level. On top of that, the story had elements which could be checked out. Flight records showed that Warren had indeed been to Holland with Charrington. And the names of Warren and Halley rang bells; the Cleveland officers were aware that they had cropped up in a high-level operation called

Bruise being conducted by their RCS counterparts in the Midlands. With a growing sense of excitement, Knaggs and his immediate boss drove down to meet officers from the number four Regional Crime Squad in Staffordshire and passed on what they had heard.

Charrington was balancing on a knife edge. 'The guy must have balls of steel,' says one source familiar with the case. 'I think it was an ego thing with him. He thought he could outsmart everybody.' The risks were brought home when he showed DS Weedon an eight-inch bundle of documents. It contained confidential intelligence reports from law enforcement agencies in England, Spain, Holland, Canada and Scandinavia and direct references to Operation Bruise. He claimed Warren had given him the file. If his claims were true, it meant Cocky had a top-level mole. For all his bravado, Charrington was deeply uneasy. When asked if he would help to target Warren specifically, he refused.

Yet that autumn, Charrington did travel to South America with Warren. What happened there is a matter of enduring contention. What is beyond doubt is that somebody put together a deal to bring unprecedented amounts of Colombian cocaine into Britain.

THE ESSENTIALS of any large-scale smuggling enterprise are money, transport, storage and a plausible front. The money for the deal was put up by the Liverpool mafia; in particular, the Banker. Transport and storage at the UK end were arranged by his friend Brian 'Snowy' Jennings, a haulage contractor and wheeler-dealer with fingers in many pies. 'Snowy was a thief but people thought a lot about him,' says one source. 'He was a genuinely nice guy. He was worth a fortune but dressed like an unmade bed.' With the arrangements in hand, all that remained was to find a business that could appear to be making a legitimate importation.

Enter Joseph Kassar. An entrepreneur of Ghanaian birth, he graduated from Manchester Business School before starting a number of small businesses, mainly in textiles. His acumen and ambition brought him a good lifestyle and a white mansion, with lawns sweeping down to a brook, in a middle-class Manchester suburb. Among his longest-standing contacts was a Liverpudlian who supplied him with goods ranging from wool to cocoa beans: Brian Jennings. Late in 1991, Kassar started exporting reconditioned plant and machinery to Ghana, mainly for road construction. But he was in trouble. As the recession bit, he faced business and personal debts of around £375,000 and a £200,000 mortgage.

Kassar put a proposition to a distant cousin, Emmanuel Nana-Asare, known as 'Joey', who lived in south London and imported fruit and vegetables. Kassar said two of his pals, 'Mario and Brian', wanted help importing scrap metal from Venezuela. A profit of up to twenty per cent was promised. Kassar said he was too busy to get involved but wondered if Asare might be interested. It sounded good. Asare set up a firm called Jena Enterprises and was given the number of the Conar Corporation in Caracas. After numerous trans-Atlantic calls and faxes, he arranged to import forty tonnes of aluminium and eighty-five tonnes of lead in ingots. What Joey did not know was that the ingots were an ingenious method of moving drugs. Inside each huge lump of lead, impervious to X-rays and so thick that unless you knew where to drill you had little chance of finding anything, would be a steel box containing cocaine.

In September 1991, nine days before the load was due to leave Venezuela, Curtis Warren and Brian Charrington arrived at Dover in a new Jaguar, telling customs officials they were going to France for a holiday. Both showed British Visitors Passports, valid for one year and useable only in Europe. Both, however, had ten-year passports concealed in their pockets. From France they flew to Malaga, then Madrid, then on to Caracas, booking into the Hilton Hotel. Mario Halley was also in Caracas; Ivonne Cruzatty saw him in the Conar office with two Englishmen.

Prosecutors would later claim – unsuccessfully – that Warren was in South America to oversee the departure of the drugs. Certainly the ingots, with paperwork checked and stamped, left Puerto Cabello, Venezuela's main port, at this time. At the Dominican Republic, the containers were unloaded and placed on board the mv *Caraibe*, which then set sail across the Atlantic to Felixstowe, her final destination being Piraeus in Greece. Halley left for New York, while Warren and Charrington returned to Europe. In Spain they put their ten-year passports into an envelope and posted it to a flat in Amsterdam. Then they reversed their original journey, picked up the Jag in France and drove onto a car ferry, showing their Visitors Passports at Dover 'proving' they had remained in mainland Europe the whole time.

Charrington did not initially tell his police handlers about the trip. When he did, they could scarcely believe their ears. He said he had been introduced to a drug lord of unimaginable wealth, as DS Knaggs later recounted:

> BC said that the man he had met in Colombia was called E [*name withheld*], who owned a large yacht called *The Lady*. E's yacht was anchored at La Guera and then sailed on to the Rochas Islands off Colombia. A number of influential people were aboard the yacht and very beautiful

girls, for example, Miss Colombia. After sailing, E took them by private plane into the Colombian jungle where he visited one of his drug factories – but BC stayed at the plane and he did not see the factory. Talk of E having a personal fortune of 900 million dollars buried in the jungle around the factory site. E gets the US dollars back from the US in imported partitioned water tankers.

Charrington said a Turkish contingent who were major heroin importers had been in Colombia to meet the same people, as had a group of Italians. With the substantial caveat that Enigma One's word must be suspect, this suggested a confluence of the most influential crime groups in the world: a cocaine cartel, the Italian Mafia and the Turkish *babas*. As top-level drugs intelligence goes, this was as good as it gets. He repeated his claim that '2,000 kilograms' of cocaine was heading for Europe but said he had no idea how or when it would arrive. 'BC said he could give us the biggest job there had ever been but that it had to be realised that he had to be heavily involved with these people to gain their trust,' recorded DS Knaggs. 'BC said he wanted a realistic reward and also some protection from smaller agencies that might be involved.'

Trust was in short supply. On October 8, the North East RCS finally disclosed to Customs and Excise that Charrington was an informant. The effect of this news can only be imagined. Not only did protocol dictate that customs should have been told much earlier but also they had been targeting Charrington for months – in co-operation with the RCS – in the still on-going Operation Python. Customs officers were, and still are, deeply critical of the relationship between Charrington and his handlers. They believed Enigma One should have remained Target One.

Events now unfolded at increasing speed. On October 16, Mario Halley flew into Manchester Airport for a whistle-stop meeting with Curtis Warren. Two days later, the *Caraibe* docked at Felixstowe. Kassar told his cousin, Joey, who had no idea what was really going on, that the lead could be stored on an industrial estate near Liverpool's famous Aintree racecourse until they found a buyer. Snowy Jennings paid £2,000 to rent a unit. It was here, allegedly, that the cocaine would be removed from the ingots. Warren spoke repeatedly to Kassar and Halley during this time, using two new mobile phones, while Halley, every inch the international sales executive, was calling Milan, Amsterdam, Piraeus and Caracas. The Colombian already had a Conar Corporation bank account set up in Amsterdam. Now the drugs were on British soil, it was time to pay up.

THE CARACAS POLICE drugs unit first learned about Conar in October 1991. They were too busy to investigate immediately but someone did tip off British customs that a major shipment was due to arrive, probably in a consignment of metal. So when the *Caraibe* arrived at Felixstowe, a rummage team paid particular attention to her cargo. They took photographs of several containers and examined the ingots from the Conar shipment. One was removed and an attempt made to drill into it. The drill bit was too short to penetrate to the hidden box and snapped inside the lead. The searchers gave up; anyway, they were looking for concealments within the container, not the ingots.

It was a disaster. Just inches away from them was a suspected 500 kilos of cocaine – and they missed it.

Apparently the Colombians knew that HM Customs did not possess any drill that went deeper than 25cms, and had adapted their packaging accordingly. The containers at Felixstowe were cleared by customs on October 30 and were sent by rail and lorry to the Aintree lock-up. The *Caraibe* sailed on with another 500 kilos still aboard. 'It went on to Piraeus. From there, they were going to bring the drugs overland to Holland. But the Yugoslavian Civil War broke out and blocked their land route. They stopped that plan and shipped it instead,' says a customs officer.

Jesus Camillo Ortiz now arrived in England and checked into a hotel near Aintree. As Conar's deputy chairman, he knew how to extract the cocaine from the ingots. Each weighed two tonnes and had to be lifted several feet off the floor to allow someone underneath to cut away the lead and reach the steel box inside. While this was allegedly going on, Halley checked into the Park Lane Hilton in London. He bought at least three BMWs for cash, planning to send them abroad. It was good way of moving a lot of money out of the country. He also picked up an English girlfriend and was having a good time. Joseph Kassar too was suddenly flush. He gave his wife a plastic bag with £40,000 in cash stuffed inside. He also ordered new plant to be shipped out to Ghana and drew up a list of vehicles he intended to buy for his West African business.

As for Curtis Warren, all anyone could prove was that he had travelled and met with certain people and made certain phone calls. The only task remaining was to dispose of the empty lead ingots. Snowy Jennings paid his (innocent) son-in-law to dispose of the scrap metal and it was buried under tonnes of rubble. A week later it was dug up and sold, ending up at a yard in Newcastle-upon-Tyne where it was melted down. The deal's financiers could now celebrate. They had paid £14,000 a kilo for almost-pure cocaine. When cut and sold on the streets for around £80,000 a kilo, it would yield a profit of at least £70 million.

It seems that the authorities first knew of the importation in early November, when Enigma One told DS Weedon that 500 kilos had come in and the job 'had gone off perfectly right under the noses of customs, who did not have a clue'. Charrington claimed he had only learned the details of the shipment after its delivery and so could not have warned the police in advance. His involvement was to be in laundering the proceeds for Halley. On one occasion he produced a sack with £900,000 in it to prove his point. He was changing the sterling into dollars, using bureaux de change in London. He also said the Colombians were pumping five tonnes a month into the USA and Europe, using the same method and the same shipping line.

Enigma One was playing a very dangerous game. Knaggs noted, 'The Colombians think nothing of killing any official of any nationality, with life being to them extremely cheap. BC said it was urgent we get on with it and if we were not interested in the job to tell him now so that he could get out, as anyone even suspected of informing would be murdered. BC said only a handful of people resident in the UK knew of Halley's activities and if it became obvious that the leak came from England, then the Colombians would eliminate them all.'

Inexplicably, it seems that little effort was ever made to recover the drugs. 'Not then, nor at any subsequent time, did the customs or, for that matter, any senior police officers, ask for myself or DSW to pursue an investigation into the 500 kilogram importation that we had been told about by BC,' recorded DI Knaggs. 'Had they done so at this time, we could have had a positive result. Everyone's eyes were on the next job'.

ALMOST IMMEDIATELY after the dispersal of the first shipment, a second was set in train using the same method. Thirty-two cylindrical ingots, each four feet high, would leave for Liverpool on the freighter mv *Advisor*. They would contain another monster load of cocaine: 900 kilos, worth £150 million on the street. The Cali Cartel was going for broke. (Fourteen tonnes of cocaine would be seized in Britain and Europe in 1991, up from virtually nothing six years earlier).

Customs were persuaded at last to meet Charrington and establish what to do with him. The meeting was arranged at a hotel in the seaside resort of Scarborough. Present were Knaggs, Weedon, Charrington and an experienced customs investigator. It did not go well. Drink was consumed and there was 'an element of confrontation and argument,' according to Knaggs. Charrington made a crack about Weedon and Knaggs being on the take. It was intended as a joke but fell flat. The customs officer questioned Weedon's integrity and Knaggs got the distinct impression he 'thought DS Weedon and myself were bent'. However customs did eventually agree to pay Charrington a reward – the figure of £500,000 was bandied around – if he helped them identify the source of the shipment. He agreed and gave them the name of the shipping company. He also revealed the drugs would again be in ingots.

That December the Venezuelan police raided the Conar Corporation and closed its offices. Nevertheless, the shipment continued, setting sail a few days later. This time it was being monitored by customs and the police. Charrington told them the plan was for the ingots to be unloaded at Felixstowe and then taken by road to Liverpool.

They arrived on 12 January 1992. This time Kassar rented a warehouse in Derbyshire to store the ingots. Charrington continued, with official sanction, to launder money so his cover would not be blown; at one stage he even asked a customs officer if he could get him a better exchange rate, as the bureaux de change were 'pissing him off'.

Before the authorities could move on the gang, there was yet another development, this time in Holland. On Saturday, January 18, Brigadier Simon van Rijn of the Dutch police led a team of officers on a raid at a warehouse and an adjoining property. They arrested three men including Jesus Camillo Ortiz. 'He was actually wearing goggles and gloves and holding a drill to an ingot when he was arrested,' said one of the Dutch officers. In the warehouse were thirty-five lead ingots and a variety of metal-cutting tools. Each ingot held thirty-seven packets of cocaine. A total of 845 kilos was recovered.

According to DI Knaggs, the Colombians now contacted the 'men in the UK to warn them that the consignment at Felixstowe would have to be sacrificed'. The innocent Joey Nana-Asare received a telephone call from a Liverpudlian called 'John'.

'Don't touch the consignment,' John ordered. 'All my friends have been picked up in Holland. We'll find a better way of bringing it in.'

Asare was mystified. Why would anyone be arrested over a pile of metal? 'This was the start of my nightmare,' he later recalled. 'I told him, I am doing genuine business. But he just hung up.'

Minutes later, John rang back. He was curt.

'I told you. Forget about the consignment.'

'What do you mean?'

Again the phone went dead. Shocked and intimidated, Joey found the number of a solicitor in the *Yellow Pages*. Within twenty-four hours he was talking to customs. Meanwhile Curtis Warren was spotted in Smithdown Road, Liverpool – yards from where he had previously robbed a post office – using a public telephone box to dial Kassar's home in Accra. Later that day Kassar rang Asare from Ghana. The police were listening in. Asare complained about the call from the mysterious John.

JK   *He said what?*

JNA   *He said, "Forget the consignment. All my friends have been picked up in Holland. We sent the consignment through Greece. The forklift driver fucked up. Now all my friends have been picked up so don't go to Felixstowe. Don't touch anything." He starts giving me orders. In fact, I was bloody annoyed.*

JK   *Joey, listen. All you have to say to him is, "Talk to Joe."*

JNA   *That is exactly what I said: "Have you spoken to Joe?" He says he does not know how to get into contact with you, so I said, "Give me a number, I can talk to you [Kassar] and then we can get to the bottom of this." Then the guy says, 'Look, I've run out of money,' and that's it.*

Kassar ignored the advice to 'forget the consignment.' He told Asare he would come over to England and instructed him to find a new warehouse for lead. He also warned him to 'stay off the phone.' It was too late. Operation Singer was up and running.

That Wednesday, the lead and its hidden cargo arrived at a warehouse near Stoke-on-Trent. At night, it received a secret visit from a ten-strong police-customs team. One of them was customs officer Peter Hollier.

> The bottom of the first ingot was cut open and revealed a tight casket in the bottom with a lipped entrance. I prised open the lips and inside were twenty-eight packages of cocaine. We opened another two ingots that night and they took some work because we were not exactly sure how to get into them. It was very strenuous. It took us almost three hours to get into the first ingot but we had to stop during daylight and only returned again when it was dark. There were twenty-eight or twenty-nine packages in each ingot.

Officers removed 905 kilos of cocaine with a purity of between eighty and ninety per cent, the biggest single haul seized in the UK up to that time. Then they re-sealed the ingots and put the warehouse under observation.

At around the same time, Warren flew to Amsterdam and met Halley. He returned three days later and drove a Rover Sterling to Cheshire to meet Kassar, who had flown in from Ghana to sort things out. The ingots – having secretly been emptied – were moved again, first to an industrial estate on Merseyside and then to a storage depot in Runcorn. Staff were told that someone would be 'picking up one of the ingots and taking it away for testing'. A middle-aged man from Liverpool turned up in a car followed by a friend driving a flat bed truck. The ingot was loaded onto the truck. After a circuitous route it was transferred to a lorry and driven to Huskisson Dock on the Liverpool seafront, where it was unceremoniously dumped. It was to lie on the quayside for three weeks, untouched, before being collected and returned to Runcorn.

The Liverpool gang, said Charrington, now knew there was no coke in the ingots. They were expecting 'a pull' [*an arrest*] but believed there was little hard evidence against them. In March, Charrington travelled to Fuengirola in southern Spain to meet Halley and find out what was going on. Weedon and Knaggs went as well, shadowing him. Halley never showed up; the Cali Cartel's European sales manager had been arrested in Holland, supervising yet another 800-kilo shipment. He was charged with conspiracy to import cocaine. Warren was now under massive surveillance and believed a spotter plane was following him. But Joe Kassar, perhaps because of his dire financial position, was determined to push ahead. He booked into a Cheshire hotel with his Swedish mistress and moved all thirty-one (empty) ingots back to yet another warehouse in Stoke. With arrests imminent, Charrington decided he would be better off in Spain for a few days.

JUST AFTER 10PM on Sunday, March 29, customs officers and police burst into Joe Kassar's room in the Kilton Inn, near Knutsford. He was in the bathroom. As he saw the officers, he tried to throw away a piece of paper with a Vodafone number on it. They had little trouble arresting the mild-mannered Kassar but Warren was considered a different proposition. He had convictions for violence against police officers, albeit when he was a teenager. He was located at a girlfriend's house in Liverpool. A contingent of officers from the

Midlands Regional Crime Squad, which had been working on Warren since Operation Bruise, travelled up to join the bust. They booked into the Adelphi Hotel in central Liverpool posing as the 'West Midlands County Council', saying they were something to do with the inquiry to the Hillsborough football disaster.

'We were warned he had a rottweiler dog and that he was built like Mike Tyson,' says a customs officer. 'We had an armed police team but unfortunately it was nine in the morning, with kids going to school and the binmen coming round. It wasn't ideal. I was sent round the back of the house and I thought, if he comes running out I'm going to have to hit him with the bin because it's the only way I'm going to stop him.

'Anyway we smashed our way in and he didn't try to leg it. But he was giving us a right mouthful. All kinds of abuse. Then this police inspector came in and gave him a mouthful right back. I had a quick look around, then wrote down what he was saying – which wasn't very nice – and asked him if he wanted to sign my notebook as a statement of what had happened. He was sitting on the settee and his exact reply was, "How can I sign your notebook with my hands cuffed behind my back, you cunt?" The cops had slapped the cuffs on him and I hadn't realised. As for the rottweiler, fortunately it was quite old and very docile.'

Warren had £1,000 in cash, a Bearcat scanning device for intercepting police frequencies, and an envelope with a British Visitor's Passport inside. Beside his bed was a mobile phone – bearing the same number on the scrap of paper Kassar had tried to hide.

'Curtis was taken to the central detention centre. He saw one of the Midlands officers and said, "Oh! You're with the West Midlands County Council. You were staying in the Adelphi, weren't you?" The cops got a real fucking fright. Curtis knew everything that went on in Liverpool.'

Around a dozen other men were arrested. Most remained silent, though one or two who had been involved in a minor way in moving or storing the ingots did answer questions. They said they were acting entirely innocently and knew nothing of any drugs. All were charged with conspiring to import cocaine.

7

FIASCO

Warren's release from custody had made him a hero in the eyes of some of the Toxteth community. He was the living embodiment of the buck ethos.
He was coming to believe he was untouchable.

THE TRIAL of the Operation Singer defendants promised to be long and complex. Ten men faced charges of conspiring to smuggle 'Class A' prohibited drugs. They included Curtis Warren, Brian Jennings, Joe Kassar and a number of alleged bit-part players involved in moving or storing the lead ingots for both shipments. A vast amount of cocaine had been recovered. There was an inside witness, Joey Nana-Asare, and a secret informant, Brian Charrington. Credit card transactions and flight manifests revealed a trail of suspicious journeys and apparently incriminating meetings, backed up by a mass of surveillance material. British officers had even visited Venezuela to gather more evidence. The prosecution felt it had an iron-clad case to put before a jury. But in a hall of mirrors, nothing is as it seems.

Rot set in early and the cause was Brian Charrington. In April 1992, a month after the arrests, a reward of £100,000 had apparently been approved by both police and customs, payable to Enigma One. It is believed to be the second-largest award of its kind up to that time. The application to the Central Drugs Fund was made by DI Harry Knaggs, who wrote, 'The informant supplied the identity of the shipping company... the approximate date of arrival at Felixstowe, the identities of those involved and – most importantly – the method of concealment. The information supplied was essential to the success of the operation.'

The money was never paid. It was blocked by senior customs officers, who were deeply unhappy about Charrington's role and suspicious of his motives. According to one customs investigator, 'Informants are in it for three reasons: money, an insurance policy or to knock out the opposition. Sometimes all three go together. Anything anyone else tells you is bollocks.' Charrington, they believed, had gone for the treble. While he could not be touched for the second shipment because of his 'participating informant' role, customs believed he had benefitted royally from the 'first run'. They were also sure he had been involved in side deals of drugs he had told no-one about. It would be unconscionable, they felt, to give him immunity. They decided to arrest and charge him, thrashing out the details at a top-level meeting with Cleveland Police.

Even if they were right and Charrington was up to his brass neck in it, it is unclear how customs ever expected to secure his conviction. Not only was there the formidable complication of his informant status but also no drugs had ever been recovered from the first run. How could it be proven that any cocaine had been imported at all?

Yet on June 26, as his private plane landed at Teesside Airport from Spain, Enigma One was arrested. He was stunned. Officers also raided his Nunthorpe home and noticed a bulge in the ceiling. They found a bag containing £1.79 million in his loft, along with £1.4 million in Swiss francs. 'We took the money to be counted at the Bank of England and were told the notes were new and had been out for just ten days. Most of the notes were also contaminated with cocaine because they had been through so many dealers' hands,' says a customs source who has no regrets about the bust.

Weedon and Knaggs were incensed. 'A tragic error of judgement,' recorded Knaggs. They appealed to their superiors for the charges to be dropped, with no success. So instead they put their careers on the line and went for broke. Weedon approached Tim Devlin, the then-Tory MP for Stockton South and parliamentary private secretary to the Attorney-General, Sir Nicholas Lyell. According to Devlin:

> Weedon said I was one of the Government's law officers and I could sort it out. I told him it was improper and probably a breach of police discipline that he'd come to see me at all. Weedon replied that his boss, Knaggs, had been to see his senior officers and told to sit tight. He was bloody frightened and said the Colombians were coming over here with guns. So I told him, 'Leave it to me and I'll try to sort it out.'

Quoted in David Rose
In The Name of the Law

Devlin lobbied Keith Hellawell, then Cleveland Chief Constable (and now the national 'drugs czar') and Sir John Cope, the Paymaster General and responsible for HM Customs and Excise. Devlin also 'pulled strings' with the prison authorities to have Charrington moved back to a Teesside jail after he was beaten up in Strangeways Prison in Manchester; met Charrington's wife, a walking jewellery store who said she wanted all their confiscated money back and safe passage from the country; and even visited Charrington in jail, where he moaned that the authorities had welshed on their side of the deal.

Finally, on 19 December 1992, the Attorney-General chaired a remarkable meeting to discuss the case. Present were Charrington's barrister, Gilbert Gray QC, senior members of the customs legal department, and a second ministerial law officer, Sir Derek Spencer, the Solicitor-General. Mr Gray wanted the charges dropped. *Observer* journalist David Rose, who gives the customs version of the case in his book *In The Name of the Law,* wrote:

> That a lobbying campaign can have led to a meeting between the two senior government law officers and defence counsel in order to discuss whether a pending criminal trial should take place or not was an event unprecedented in British criminal history. It represented an ultimate blurring between the political and the judicial arms of the State. One expects such things to happen in the more corrupt jurisdictions of the Third World, but not in Great Britain.

Charrington's barrister presented statements from Knaggs and Weedon attesting to his worth as an informant and indicating they would testify in his defence if he was tried. Knaggs's asserted that Charrington was 'the best source of intelligence there has ever been into the major cocaine families operating from Colombia and Venezuela' and said his information 'would most probably have resulted in stopping cocaine entering Europe'. The Customs Board of Management was stymied.

In January 1993, Charrington appeared before a stipendiary magistrate in Manchester. A customs prosecutor stood up, said they had reviewed the evidence and could not support the charges. Enigma One walked free, returned briefly to his home in Nunthorpe, then slipped out of the country. The matter might never have been made public had not a Darlington-based freelance reporter, John Merry, got hold of a story about a rift between customs and the RCS over the case. Tim Devlin phoned Merry at home and asked him not to pursue the story. Merry taped their conversation and sold it to the *News of the World*, which gleefully gave it full exposure.

The trial of the remaining defendants had been set down from Manchester Crown Court. It was dramatically shifted, however, when a defendant on a separate serious drugs charge was sprung from a prison van by an armed gang and escaped, raising fears about security. [*The man was Mancunian Stephen Mee, who would later work with Warren – see Chapter 12*] The new venue was Newcastle-upon-Tyne. Armed police would patrol the court precincts and Joey Nana-Asare would be kept under close guard. Warren was transferred to Frankland Prison, Durham, nearer to the court. One other defendant apart from Charrington would not be there. The likeable Snowy Jennings died while on remand in Strangeways. He took many secrets to his grave.

In April 1993, the trial began at Newcastle Crown Court before Mr Justice May. It was to last forty-three days, hear from 179 witnesses and cost an estimated £40 million. Warren faced two charges of importing cocaine between 1 January 1991 and 30 March 1992. He was represented by the eminent Queen's Counsel Michael Beresford-West, an Oxford-educated opera lover who had spent his National Service with the Intelligence Corps in the Middle East before being called to the bar. He had a tough job ahead. Even though Charrington had now vanished abroad and would never testify, the case against Cocky appeared watertight: the surveillance, the phone records, the circuitous route to Venezuela, the meetings with Halley, Kassar and others, the cocaine itself, the arrests of Ortiz and Halley in Holland.

His position worsened when Cleveland Police immediately applied for a public interest immunity (PII) order covering its dealings with Charrington. PII certificates – which forbid the disclosure of specified information – may be granted by a judge if the identity of a police informant could be compromised or if national security issues are at stake. The system has been widely criticised; it allows the prosecution to speak to a judge and seek a gagging order without the defence being present. Defence lawyers are not allowed to view the contents of the certificates and argue that they may be used to hide crucial evidence. Ultimately the decision rests with the trial judge. Despite defence pleading, Mr Justice May supported the application. The case began.

One of the first Crown witnesses was Robinson Aruinzones, a senior criminal investigator with the Caracas drugs unit. He described how cocaine was moved from South America across the world using

Venezuela as a bridging post. 'The investigation into Conar began in October or November 1991 after a confidential call to us. But because we had another job, involving a fourteen-tonne shipment to Texas, we did not start our inquiries immediately. The Conar case involved people who were sophisticated international businessmen. They exported cocaine to New York, Holland and Greece.'

As a string of prosecuting witnesses took the court through the labyrinthine details, Cocky watched and learned. Every day spent listening from the dock, every laborious hour spent reading depositions in his cell in Frankland Prison, was another lesson in law enforcement. Old lags would say, *Don't serve time, let the time serve you.* Warren also knew who his friends were. One man turned up every day to give moral support from the public gallery. Phillip Glennon was a wealthy, middle-aged businessman with a conviction for armed robbery back in the early Seventies. He would later be described in a separate court case as a 'wealthy crook who made his money through drugs' and 'a major drugs baron'. He has never been convicted of any drugs offence.

Warren's spirits rose as holes began to appear in the prosecution case. It was revealed that Joey Nana-Asare had been paid by customs for his help – around £20,000 plus around £19,000 for expenses – though a customs officer denied defence suggestions that the money was to ensure his attendance at court. The real bombshell, however, was a ruling by the judge concerning the absent Mario Halley. The court had heard how he went to Liverpool with Warren when the first load of drugs were being removed there; how he met Charrington, Warren and others when the cocaine was being sold and distributed; and how he spent the next few days buying top-of-the-range cars for export in Park Lane showrooms, paying with bundles of cash. Yet this, said Mr Justice May, was not enough.

'Whereas it might be possible to suspect and perhaps infer that Halley was concerned with drugs generally... there is, in my judgement, no possible evidential basis for inferring that Halley was concerned with the particular importations which are the subject of this case,' he said. Any evidence of Warren's contact with Halley could, under the Police and Criminal Evidence Act, adversely affect the fairness of the trial, added the judge. And with that, he ruled it inadmissible. It was body blow from which the prosecution never recovered.

'The judge said, so what if he went to Colombia? What did he do there? There was very little left at the end of the day,' recalls Keith Dyson, a Manchester solicitor who represented Kassar at the trial and currently acts for Warren. Yet Halley was at that moment languishing in a Dutch jail, awaiting trial for his role in the importation of 955 kilos of coke, again in ingots. The judge also excluded evidence relating to Warren's trip to Venezuela

At the end of the prosecution case, before a single defence witness had been summoned, Mr Justice May ruled there was insufficient evidence to sustain a conviction against Warren. He instructed the jury to acquit. Cocky rose and left the dock. What followed has since passed into criminal folklore. According to reports in several newspapers, Warren left the modern courthouse and walked into the street. He then stopped, turned and went back. He took the lift up to the third floor, where a small huddle of shell-shocked customs officers were gathered, and strode up to them. 'I'm off to spend my £87 million from the first shipment and you can't fucking touch me,' he said.

Keith Dyson, Warren's solicitor, denies the incident took place. 'The £87 million story is apocryphal. It never happened.' True or not, it came to symbolise Warren's self-confidence and sense of invulnerability.

Another legend has grown up around the Cocky Watchman's return to Granby. According to law enforcement sources, he cruised the streets in an open-topped Lexus as scores of friends and well-wishers came out to greet him. His release from custody had made him a hero in the eyes of some of the Toxteth community. He was the living embodiment of the buck ethos. He was coming to believe he was untouchable, something he would later brag about in a phone call to a close friend, Tony Bray:

CW *Hey, I come out smelling of fucking roses all the time, don't I?*

TB *You're a lucky sod, you. You've got the luck of the devil with you, haven't you?*

CW *Do you reckon?*

TB *Fucking telling you. You always come out smiling.*

Next, Warren and a girlfriend went for a two-week holiday abroad. On his return, he was stopped by an unusually large group of customs officers.

'Welcome back Mr Warren, is it nice to be back out?' one of them asked sarcastically.

'Yes, thanks to British justice,' replied Warren.

To their chagrin, Warren and his girlfriend were taken away and searched. Nothing was found but the girlfriend was furious.

'Why did you have to answer back,' she demanded.

'It just came out,' said Warren.

THE TRIAL of the others continued. Further cracks opened in the prosecution case. Defence barristers contended that there was no evidence the first shipment of ingots contained cocaine. The men who had moved the ingots around or disposed of them said they were acting entirely innocently. Joe Kassar refuted out-of-hand that he had been involved in narcotics, saying indignantly, 'I should be a multi-millionaire if I was concerned with the first shipment. All I had was a very brief dealing with the lead.' His counsel scorned the evidence of Nana-Asare. 'It is a false supposition to assume that if Asare is innocent then my client must be guilty. Mr Asare's evidence was dishonest and HM Customs and Excise have assumed my client's guilt from the outset and then proceeded on inadequate evidence to attempt to prove it.'

Other defence barristers pitched into the star witness. One claimed he 'ran to customs and proclaimed his innocence, transferring himself from a prime suspect to a paid witness. Was he buying himself a place in the witness box rather than the dock? You would not buy a used car off this man... not in a month of Sundays... Joe Asare is plainly an untruthful man who was playing for high stakes and at the appropriate moment jumped ship.' Some of the customs evidence – including documentation with the wrong time on it – was described as a 'disgrace'.

On Thursday, July 8, Mr Justice May began his summing-up:

> The prosecution has to prove separately for each count and separately for each defendant that the cocaine was imported. For the second importation, the cocaine was intercepted and recovered and its antecedent entry into this

country in the lead ingots via Felixstowe has been established and not challenged. For the first importation, no cocaine was recovered. If you are not sure that there was cocaine concealed in the lead ingots of the first consignment, then you will acquit all the defendants on count one.

The judge referred again to his earlier decision to discount any evidence relating to Mario Halley. He went on:

There is virtually no direct evidence in this case that any defendant knew the ingots contained or had contained cocaine. There is no direct evidence that the first consignment contained cocaine. The direct evidence from which the prosecution seeks to satisfy you that cocaine was imported in the lead ingots of the first consignment includes the following: first, the source of the ingots, the Conar Corporation in Venezuela; secondly, the fact that the cocaine was imported in exactly similar manner and circumstances to the second importation. You [*the jury*] should consider... the possibility that the first consignment might have been a genuine importation of lead and contained no cocaine, or might have been a dummy run without cocaine but with concealed compartments to test whether the lead would pass through customs without trouble or suspicion as a prelude to the second importation. If you are not sure it is an inference which you do draw, then you should acquit all defendants on count one.

After two days of deliberations, the jury found Joseph Kassar guilty as charged. They could not agree verdicts for two other defendants involved in the movement of one of the ingots. The men would later be cleared at a re-trial. The rest were acquitted and walked free immediately. Kassar, aged forty-two, chancer and fall-guy, copped the lot. 'One and a half tonnes of cocaine means utter degradation, both physical and moral, and perhaps death to thousands of people,' the judge told him. He was sent to jail for twenty-four years, one of the longest sentences ever imposed for a drugs offence in the UK. It was scant consolation for the officers of Operation Singer.

THE FALL-OUT and recriminations from that trial linger on. A year after it ended, the police launched an investigation into the conduct of certain Cleveland officers involved in the case. Operation Mantis was conducted by an outside force, Thames Valley. The inquiry took four years and produced a report running to forty-eight volumes. A separate internal inquiry, Operation Teak, was conducted by the Cleveland force and overseen by the Police Complaints Authority. In June 1997, Detective Sergeant Ian Weedon was suspended from duty. His phone calls had been tapped and his house raided. Yet the strongest recommendation to emerge from either inquiry was that Ian Weedon be 'admonished'; at the time of writing, this had not been done, though Weedon had been suspended for four years.

Weedon and Knaggs, who retired from Cleveland Police in 1993 and now works in the Middle East, insist they did nothing wrong. They point out that as late as February 1995, Weedon was being instructed to liaise with Charrington with the full knowledge of senior officers, with information being passed to the National Criminal Intelligence Service. The outrageous Charrington even tried – unsuccessfully – to sue the police from a Spanish bolthole for the reward money he had never been paid.

At least he was free. Mario Halley, the brash young Colombian who had helped pump cocaine into Europe, was by this time in a Dutch jail serving an eight-year sentence. The prosecutor had asked for sixteen years, but a psychologist told the court that Halley was childish and slow in his mental development, and did not deserve a long sentence, despite the seriousness of his crime. He also said that detention would have a damaging psychological effect on the Cali Cartel salesman.

Meanwhile the stockpile of cocaine from first shipment was pouring onto Britain's streets. Police nationwide recorded a twenty-eight per cent rise in coke seizures in 1992. In Greater Manchester, always a ready market for narcotics, cocaine-related arrests rose by almost sixty per cent. The drug landscape had been changed irrevocably. The genie was out of the bottle.

8

'MAD, INNIT?'

'Drug dealing is a thousand times

more addictive than drug taking.'

Anonymous dealer in

Coked Up, Channel 4 TV

PAUL ACDA and Colin Gurton faced each other across the desk in Acda's windowless Manchester office. It was a functional room, grey, plain and modern. Open files lay between them on a plastic desktop with a single computer terminal and phone. A lone pot plant stood forlornly to one side. There was a framed photograph of Acda, then an army officer, meeting the Princess Royal and another of his family. The only other splashes of colour came from the bright shields and pendants dotted on the walls, gifts from foreign customs and police forces, symbols of duty and pride. Today they seemed to reflect a kind of reproach.

The mood was sombre. Acda, a bespectacled bear of a man with a passing resemblance to the foot-in-the-door TV reporter Roger Cook, seemed distracted. As the Assistant Chief Investigator for HM Customs in the north of England, he had been closely involved in the Full Bloom/Singer investigation and had always been deeply sceptical of Charrington's role. He was used to the highs and lows of what politicians called the 'war on drugs'. Today was a low. Gurton, forty-four, a senior investigating officer (SIO) once described in a *Readers' Digest* feature as 'methodical and cagey with a dry sense of humour', looked even slimmer and paler than usual; his face was as wan as the office walls. Conversation was muted. There was not much to say.

After months of work, what had they got? One conviction, a bunch of acquittals, a court case that had cost millions. Cops and customs at each others throats. Charrington untouchable, Warren free. There were no two ways about it: Operation Singer had been a total fucking disaster. Even worse, Warren had spent hours reading the evidence, listening in court and learning every detail of how the operation had been planned and executed. Newcastle Crown Court had been the best classroom any professional drug smuggler could want.

Acda broke the silence. 'Well, we really showed our hand there, didn't we? Warren's seen our Crown jewels and now he knows exactly how we operate.'

Gurton agreed. 'He couldn't have had a more perfect learning experience.'

They both fell silent again. Losing two main targets like Charrington and Warren was the bitterest of pills to swallow. Now what?

'At least we know Warren's not going to change,' said Acda, forcing some enthusiasm. 'At some time or other we're going to have to go and have another look at him. I know there's no point in doing it now but he'll be back. We'll let the dust settle and see where he's going.'

More pressing was the question of how to rebuild relationships with the police. Customs had been appalled at the police handling of Charrington but it was hardly an exceptional incident. Distrust, even enmity, between the two organisations was of long standing. Under the pressure of fighting the drugs explosion it had broken out into barely-concealed warfare. It was customs officers who had first uncovered corruption in Scotland Yard's central drugs squad in the early 1970s and had used their ensuing moral superiority to advantage in lobbying for pole position in the fight against drugs. 'Customs investigators, aided by a superb intelligence network and a reputation for honesty, dominated the field for much of the 1970s and early 1980s,' reported the *Daily Telegraph*. It was a situation that irked the police.

By 1983 the drug problem was so serious that the Home Office urged chief constables to take a more active role. Turf wars escalated. While customs were tasked with stopping importation, which often meant arresting suspects at ports and airports, detectives preferred to follow contraband to its end destination to take out everyone involved. A lack of dialogue led on more than one occasion to customs officers unwittingly arresting undercover officers or couriers planted by the police. Both sides squabbled over the kudos on big busts and often claimed credit for the same seizures. One solution proposed by the police was for a new, elite anti-drugs force; naturally they would take the lead role. That went down like a grit sandwich with customs. Individual customs officers took to referring to the police as 'the Oscar Bravo', a mickey-taking reference to a police radio call sign. The police reciprocated; certain high-ranking officers were apt to dismiss customs as 'baccy guards' who should stick to hassling cigarette and booze smugglers and leave crimefighting to the professionals.

All of this was going through Acda's mind. Hell, they'd even had different codenames for the investigation into Warren. The police had called it Operation Singer while customs insisted on Operation Full Bloom. It was pathetic.

'We can't have another operation like that with such a lack of consultation,' he said. 'If our separate offices and the regional crime squads can't co-operate like grown-ups then we might as well forget it and all go home.' They would never trap Warren without pooling manpower, resources and, in particular, intelligence.

Colin Gurton sat lost in thought. Though he looks like a tax inspector and speaks in the classless monotone of estuary English, behind the metal-rimmed glasses is the hint of an implacable nature. Without even trying, he impresses as the last person you would want on your tail. And maybe he had an idea.

CURTIS WARREN had also been doing plenty of thinking. He knew he had walked too close to the edge, been too self-assured, too... cocky. Yet he had no intention of cashing in while he was ahead. He was just getting started. For the first time in an aimless life of unemployment, petty crime, borstal and prison, he had found his vocation. His tactile mind, unrivalled street smarts and intimidating demeanour were a formidable combination. He also had tact, a rare quality in the underworld. With the zeal of the late convert, he threw all of his energies into his new career. The prize was worth it.

He would have to make changes if he was to continue unscathed. The most important was his adoption of a 'cell' structure. Terrorist armies often used cells of three or four people to carry out missions. Each person in the group is allotted a task – intelligence, logistics, transport, security – and all are isolated from other, similar cells. If one cell falls it cannot implicate anyone else. Warren may have learned the tactic from Mario Halley; the Cali Cartel were masters of insulated cells, employing an army of surrogates responsible for every detail of the trafficking business, from car rental, to pager and phone purchase, to the storage of cocaine in safe houses, to the keeping of inventory and accounts. Wherever the idea came from, Warren needed no second bidding. 'I think he figured it out himself. He had an exceptional mind when you consider his poor educational background,' says a customs officer.

Cells suited Warren's ability to compartmentalise, to keep many different things in his head without mixing them up. 'His cell structure was really good, just like the IRA's,' says a current chief superintendent who pursued him. 'Two strangers might be standing next to each other in a bar and start chatting just by chance. They could both be working for Warren, both be in the same line of business, yet neither had a clue about the other one. That's how he worked it.' He was also utterly unsentimental; if he felt a cell was compromised he would lop it off and never deal with any of its members again. 'If someone screwed up, he would cut them out of everything. Immediately, they became nobodies. They either went off somewhere never to be heard of again or would go right to the back of the pile as low-level street dealers, but they were never trusted again.'

Cocky also needed a plausible cover for his activities, a job to explain at least some of his income. An obvious one was club and pub security. Until the late Eighties, those of the 650 licensed premises in Liverpool city centre that employed doormen did so independently, advertising for staff as needed. Then came the rave scene.

Illegal but popular warehouse parties opened the door for opportunists to control both access and the distribution of Ecstasy and amphetamines. As rave moved mainstream, the door gangs became 'legitimate', setting up security companies and aggressively expanding by assimilating or driving out the old bow-tie-and-monkey-suit bouncers. Some of the new firms were honest and law-abiding; many were not. As they vied for lucrative city centre doors, rivalries were often settled by 'straighteners' – bareknuckle fights. By the early Nineties, one group was predominant.

An established guarding security company, it moved into Liverpool city centre and began taking over the provision of door security at numerous entertainment venues. This organisation was a registered company which, until its expansion, was known as a provider of security in the local construction and retail sectors, but had not previously come to the attention of the police.

The swift displacement of existing door security firms was engineered by making cash payments to key incumbent door supervisors to secure their services. Physical intimidation and violence was meted out to those who refused. Any licensees who refused to accept their services were threatened with disturbances on their premises.

Information was received which indicated that the company's door supervisors either sold drugs in the premises they regulated or otherwise vetted and took a cut from – 'taxed' – other dealers operating within 'their' premises. The philosophy of this approach is given in the expression 'control the doors, control the floors'.

Sheridan Morris
Clubs, Drugs and Doormen,
Police Research Group

Whether or not Warren was friendly with this particular firm, he certainly exercised great influence over the employment of doormen through his numerous contacts and the respect he commanded. Calling yourself a 'security consultant' was useful for tax returns. Several years later, Stephen Vaughan, a Liverpool boxing promoter and property developer, told the Sunday Times he had employed 'Warren's security company' for his fight promotions and 'paid him about twenty-eight or thirty cheques for about £300 each'. What the company was called and what Warren's role was is something of a mystery. Surveillance officers who tailed Cocky say he certainly had little hands-on involvement in any such enterprise. He may, however, have been the power behind the throne at more than one firm.

The immediate post-Singer period also saw Warren cement his relationship with the Liverpool mafia. He had done the right thing – kept his mouth shut – and was accepted as a stand-up guy by the crime hierarchy. And no-one could gainsay his ability to make money; it was unrivalled. His talents were even tipping the balance in his most crucial relationship, with the Banker. 'It became clear that Warren was taking over the initiative from his mentor,' says one officer. 'Curtis had made the big time through his connection with the old man and had been taken under the wing of the organisation. Now he became its front man.'

As such, he would never have to dip his hands in powder. He despised drugs anyway. Once he had arranged the deal, it was nothing to do with him. Pushing the stuff to users was someone else's problem. 'The Top Man brings in the gear, which is quickly broken up and sold on to the Ten Kilo Men, who then sell it on to the One Kilo Men. They then usually distribute it to their network of dealers who sell it on the streets. Warren was by now the biggest of all the Top Men. He would never be associated with the direct selling of the product, and the bigger he got, the more divorced he was geting from the street scene,' explains Paul Acda.

The Ten Kilo men were generally local gang bosses. Often based on family ties, they would control distribution in their patch, be it inner-city areas like Anfield or suburbs like Maghull. Merseyside had up to ten well-established crime families, hermetic cliques with a prickly territorial pride. Some were rivals, mainly over door contracts or petty squabbles, and there was occasional bloodshed. Warren dealt with them all. 'He became the conduit through which all the other drug traffickers and dealers passed,' says another source. 'Everything had Warren's hand in it somewhere. He was the top rung and you had to be tasty to deal with him, a good dealer in your own right. He didn't mix with time-wasters.'

Warren had a pet expression which peppered his conversations, a response to the vagaries and strangeness of life: 'Mad, innit?' It was a phrase he would find himself using more and more.

IN THE WEEKS after the Singer-Full Bloom trial, Customs and Excise found plenty of things to keep them busy. Their Manchester HQ in a modern block beside the River Irwell was the centre for all customs investigation in the north-west. A delicate sting operation was in the offing which involved setting up a bogus company and resulted in the conviction of two Colombians for a plot to smuggle 250 kilos of cocaine through Manchester Airport. There had been other developments. The redoubtable Delroy Showers had been picked up by police in Scandinavia, where he had been masterminding a multi-million pounds drugs racket from Holland involving heroin, cocaine, cannabis and amphetamines. Information was passed from the fledgling National Criminal Intelligence Service to foreign authorities and Showers was arrested in Denmark while trying to sort out a deal that had been bungled by his underlings. He was jailed for eight years.

But Curtis Warren remained an itch for both customs and the police. It was decided to keep tabs on him and certain other key suspects. A joint team of four officers was set up. 'We started by looking at Merseyside crime as a whole, with two police and two customs officers doing basic intelligence. We wanted to find out who Curtis's people knew, what mobile phones they had, who they were living with and where, their movements, just to get an idea of what they were doing,' says Colin Gurton. The team was based in Salford, thirty miles from its target area, for security.

One of the first things they learned was that Warren was living with Stephanie Glennon. An attractive blonde, she was a care assistant at a private Liverpool nursing home and the daughter of Phillip Glennon, the Liverpool businessman who had watched the Singer trial from the public gallery. Warren and Stephanie lived in a luxury waterfront flat in newly gentrified Wapping Dock, close to the famous Liver Building and – in an irony not lost on Warren – overlooking the Customs and Excise Museum. Entry was by intercom. Stephanie converted one room to house her considerable wardrobe; it was crammed with the latest designs by Gucci and Versace. Her boyfriend was always on the move: knocking around Dingle in a Peugeot, cruising through Toxteth in a Jaguar, popping up on the Wirral in a Lexus. He had a wide circle of friends and acquaintances and a mobile phone constantly glued to his ear. He lived well but not ostentatiously. But what was he up to?

IN AUGUST 1993, a highly confidential memo landed on Paul Acda's desk. Written by one of his senior men, it re-capped Broadway, the operation several years earlier which had uncovered the partnership between the Banker and Londoner Eddie Richardson. Though that had resulted in the seizure of thirty kilos of Liverpool mafia heroin, its prime target had escaped untouched. The memo urged a fresh investigation of the Banker and his associates, to be called Operation Crayfish:

> [*The Banker*] was the motivator and originator behind the [*Operation Broadway*] seizures... In the end there was insufficient evidence to prosecute [*him*] and he continued to take an active role in drug smuggling on Merseyside. He had a significant role in the background to Operation Full Bloom/Singer, where a successful first run of 500 kilos of cocaine was followed by two runs and the seizure of 1,000 kilos of cocaine in lead ingots. He still has under his control around 200 kilos of cocaine from the first run.
>
> He and [*a relative*] went to London to meet two Turks known to import heroin. There is an informant on him – the first time anyone has done so – who says he is paranoid about revealing his

activities. He tends to fragment information to a number of associates.

There is information that he will restart his activities after the end of the Full Bloom/Singer trial. He has assets both here and abroad worth around £50 million. He owns pubs, a health club and a night club. He runs them successfully and seems to have a very good lifestyle.

He is well-versed in surveillance techniques in law enforcement agencies and will only use public telephone boxes. Some of his meetings are at his club or at business premises. He has many contacts with law enforcement agencies on Merseyside. His own bank tipped him off about our inquiries relating to [*Operation*] Broadway.

The estimate of the Banker's assets at £50 million made him possibly the wealthiest criminal in British history. The memo recommended a joint venture between customs and the Regional Crime Squad, housed with maximum security away from any customs or police bases. 'When it is up and running the initial resources should be expanded to more than the existing four officers,' said the memo. It was a start, something for the team to get their teeth into after the disappointment of Newcastle. There was no mention of Warren. But within a matter of weeks, he had moved centre stage.

When Curtis Warren swanned up in his Honda Legend at Burtonwood service station in November 1993 [*see Chapter 1*], it was as though someone had tripped a switch. His proximity to a such a huge load of heroin – the Turkish driver, Hidayet Sucu, was later jailed for sixteen years at Snaresbrook Crown Court – was enough to put him centre stage for the fledgling Operation Crayfish team. He may have had nothing to do with it the drugs; he may have just been out for a ride. But from that moment on he would inherit Brian Charrington's old mantle. Curtis Warren was Target One.

9

FRAGGLE ROCK

Criminal life is a succession of deals.

The average modern wiseguy has four or

five deals in the air at any one time.

Robert Lacey, *Little Man*

FOUR MEN hatched the working plan for Operation Crayfish at a secret meeting at the offices of the North West Regional Crime Squad, tucked away in a modern block near the Manchester United football ground. Present were Paul Acda, Colin Gurton, RCS boss David Thornton and his junior Tom McAllister. They agreed to target the major Merseyside-based drugs importers, with Curtis Warren at the top. They would devote unprecedented time and manpower. The two agencies would work as one. Hatchets would be buried. Failure was unthinkable. Crayfish would be the biggest joint operation ever undertaken by British law enforcement.

Concentrating so many resources on one city, when crime in the whole region had been rising remorselessly, was a bold step. But Liverpool's pre-eminence in the drugs trade made it an irresistible target and only the most intensive investigation could hope to succeed. The most pressing need was good-quality intelligence. They had four officers already working on this but needed to boost their strength. The collating of data on major criminals was now in the hands of the new National Criminal Intelligence Service but it was having teething troubles. In its 1993–4 report, NCIS noted that 'the number of intelligence officers working out of the North-West office remains unrealistically low to achieve the aim of providing excellence in local criminal intelligence.' It had been forced to recruit extra staff to tackle the backlog of reports awaiting input on its database.

There had also been tensions among the original joint intelligence team. Two of them did not see eye-to-eye and, when it became plain that their working relationship would be fractious at best, they were replaced. Another clash came over a customs stipulation that they would not work with any Liverpool police officers. 'We didn't trust them,' admits a customs source. 'We were getting a lot of intelligence about officers with criminal contacts.' While the sentiment was exaggerated – no-one was seriously suggesting that most Merseyside cops were bent – paranoia had become the norm.

The RCS – now renamed the National Crime Squad and which tackles major criminals with officers taken on secondment from local forces – dug its heels in. Either Merseyside officers were on the team or the job was off. Customs backed down. But their suspicions of police officers outside their immediate team remained. 'We trusted only one, in the Force Intelligence Bureau, and no one else. We occasionally took the odd very senior officer into confidence but that was it,' says the source.

Next came the choice of who should be in on the hunt. Within the RCS, the natural choice was the Dedicated Drugs Unit based at Bebington on the Wirral. They had been set up to target top-end drug crime and had a good informal relationship with customs. They were also accustomed to working apart from their colleagues. They had their own offices, vehicles and support staff, rarely mixed with other units and were outside the 'canteen culture', taking lunch at their desks or on the road.

Secrecy was vital. To house the team without raising suspicions, a military building was chosen well outside the city but close to the M6 and the M62. It was a sparse, no-frills set-up. Someone christened it Fraggle Rock, the name of a children's television programme about a fictional Cornish lighthouse inhabited by a bearded Scottish keeper and his dog; beneath them is an underworld of strange creatures which they can often hear but never see. 'Being a military establishment, it gave us good cover and was perfectly located for motorways and transport networks,' says one of the team. 'It already had an armed presence because it was a Ministry of Defence site, so there would not be any added suspicion and it also meant we had a ready-made secure compound for our vehicles.'

A protocol was drawn up as the joint team moved from intelligence gathering into operational work. It was a written policy log which could be adapted as the need arose. It was to be a binding agreement and meant that all work was shared. Policy areas were a matter for Acda and Geoff Nicholls, the co-ordinator of the RCS, a vastly-experienced detective from Manchester. Operational decisions rested with Gurton and senior detective Mike Keogh.

'Customs would take on the international trafficking side and the police would deal with internal trafficking matters,' says Acda. 'It was a very flexible team which shrunk and expanded when necessary depending on operational needs. We did not want to replicate what happened with Singer and have all these spats. Everyone could win this way. The police might make an arrest but we'd get just as much pleasure out of it because we were in this thing together. No-one sat there on their own and said, "What's mine is mine and I am not going to share it".'

Initially a police sergeant and five officers set up at Fraggle with around fifteen customs personnel. The core of this group would be on Crayfish full-time, with more bodies pulled in as necessary. A police computer system called CLUE was installed and every sliver of information went on it. Covert surveillance – watching from buildings, vans or bushes – was almost impossible in inner-city Liverpool. Warrants were granted for electronic bugging devices and for intercepts to be placed on telephones used by Warren and other targets.

The first strike came almost immediately. The Crayfish team intercepted a call to a Liverpool phone box in which the collection of seven kilos of heroin was discussed. On 30 April 1994, police raided the Wavertree home of thirty-six-year-old Leroy Thomas and found parcels of heroin under a bed and in the garage. The value was estimated at £414,000. Thomas was later jailed for six years. 'It was significant at the time but later busts would make it look puny,' says Acda.

While Cocky and his men were wary of bugging devices, they knew that British law does not allow telephone intercepts as evidence in criminal courts. Tapping lines is governed by the Interception of Communications Act. Permission must come from the most senior officers; in police forces, often only a chief constable. They must be satisfied that the crime is serious, that normal methods of investigation have been tried and failed or would be likely to fail, and that the use of the equipment would be likely to lead to an arrest and conviction. All applications must go the Home Secretary to receive final authority in the form of a warrant. Authorisations last for one month, after which a fresh application must be made.

The *Alice in Wonderland* part of the Act relates to court proceedings. No evidence may be admitted or no question be asked in cross-examination which would lead to the suggestion that officers had tapped phones. It is an offence even to discuss evidence of phone taps in open court. Still, phone bugging would provide crucial information to the Crayfish team. A special British Telecom department tapped the lines and recorded the calls. Police and customs sent 'readers' to transcribe the tapes. Often it was difficult to decipher what the callers were saying; sometimes they spoke in code and almost always they kept their conversations vague. This could lead to surreal moments when even the subjects could not understand each other, as when Warren and his friend Tony Bray talked at cross purposes.

TB   *How about, er, the other fucking caper, the
      first little oppo?*
CW   *What?*
TB   *How about the first little op?*
CW   *Isn't it?*
TB   *You know which one I'm on about don't
      you?*
CW   *Oh aye, yeah.*
TB   *Fucking mad that.*
CW   *Well I hit the nail on the head, didn't I?*

TB	*I thought, fucking hell. I said, "Are you sure?" He said, "Oh, that's it, just tell him that, know exactly what I'm on about," he said.*
CW	*Oh dear.*
TB	*I went, oh dear me.*
CW	*Mad, innit?*
TB	*They don't want any of that though.*
CW	*Who?*

The Crayfish team also placed electronic bugs in houses, cars and meeting places. The extent of their infiltration has never been revealed but some of the team were masters of the black arts. It became common to tag target vehicles with transmitters which would allow them to be tailed from up to two miles away. Two officers in a car with a lap-top computer could follow from a safe distance. The difficulty was putting the tags on the vehicles; sometimes it resulted in officers being mistaken for car thieves and being set upon in the small hours by insomniac dog walkers.

The most valuable of all sources were informants and it was here that the team struck gold. Early on in their investigations, they 'turned' an insider who was able to provide valuable information on Warren's operation. The informant, whose identity is still a secret, agreed to work with them partly because he was scared of the people with whom he was mixing. It was the first direct 'in' on Cocky's operation.

Warren had his own network of look-outs and spies, according to a Crayfish investigator. 'There is a cul-de-sac in the Dingle [*an area just south of Toxteth*] where several of Warren's associates lived and we used to see him down there a lot. It was one place you could never get any surveillance done. Every time you drove down there, all the curtains would be twitching. There was also an old factory that had been converted into luxury flats on the outskirts of the city. A few of the top white guys lived there. They could talk to each other over their garden fences and you couldn't eavesdrop without very sophisticated equipment. They gave one person a house at the entrance to the plot. He was known as the Gatekeeper and his job was to check who was going in and out, in case they were cops.'

The watchers began to learn a lot about Warren. For all his contact with the Liverpool mafia, he never forsook his Granby crew. 'His mates saw him as a bit of a gravy train, a street scally who, all of a sudden, found the trappings of wealth. He went from nothing to having everything he wanted. The Lexus and Range Rover came along. But he also looked after the troops.'

One of his hang-outs was Park Road, a Toxteth street lined with pubs. 'He felt safe there. He would leave his Legend parked with the keys in the ignition and the window open and no-one would go near it. He would not use violence for the sake of it but he was prepared to have the frighteners put on somebody even over a relatively small debt. It was all about reputation. At one time there was a series of rip-offs in Liverpool where people were following others to drug deals and stealing their money. On one occasion it was Curtis Warren's money. It was returned post-haste.' He had people around him who could enforce, men like Johnny Phillips. 'But they never commanded the respect that Warren did. With Warren it was latent, an undercurrent. You never had to test the mettle.'

Of all the Crayfish targets, Warren was the hardest to keep tabs on. 'He would make decisions that would drop us right in it. We'd be cursing him but afterwards we had to admire his sharpness.' He kept a close watch on perceived traitors. When warned that one acquaintance was jealous of him and was acting as 'a double agent,' Warren replied, 'I've got the dossier on him, don't worry about that.'

Gradually the number of people working out of Fraggle Rock increased. Soon there were nearly thirty loosely attached to the secret HQ, often working around the clock. 'Drug dealers don't exactly keep office hours. There tends to be very little activity before lunchtime, a bit in the afternoon and then a whole lot at night and into the early hours of the morning. We had to change our lifestyles. There was no other way to do the job and we were all committed. If you weren't, you were out.'

IF OPERATION CRAYFISH had a motto, it would be 'Target the Transport'. 'The name of this game is transport,' says Mark, the surveillance officer who spotted Warren at Burtonwood service station. 'If you can sort that out you can not only bring your own stuff in but also bring orders in for others and take a commission for it.' Buying drugs is easy, selling them not much harder. Moving them in large quantities across national borders is the difficult part.

Mons Travel was a small agency nestling in a parade of shops in West Kirkby, at the mouth the River Dee. It was owned by sixty-five-year-old Trevor Haskayne, who put up posters in local pubs offering cut-price weekend trips to Amsterdam. His coaches would leave Liverpool late on a Friday night and return forty-eight hours later, giving travellers time to sample the attractions of the bars, coffee shops and the red light zone. Unbeknown to the passengers, the coaches would also be carrying hidden bags of Ecstasy and speed.

Haskayne hired John Moore to mind the drugs on a coach trip set for 4 December 1994. The bus left on time but Moore had been on a bender the previous night and woke with a crushing hangover to find he had missed it. In a flap, he drove to Manchester Airport and bought a return flight to Schipol for more than £400. When the coach returned the next day, Moore was on it.

At Dover, the passengers disembarked with their luggage for a customs check. The holdalls containing Ecstasy were deliberately left in the hold and in the racks above the seats. It did not take long to find them. A search team boarded the vehicle and unzipped the bags, revealing a mountain of pills, around 950,000, with a street value of at least six million pounds. Haskayne would later receive a thumping eighteen years in prison for his part in the shipment; his lackey Moore got six years. The Crayfish team took pleasure in the knowledge that they had fouled up a run that would have flooded the British market for weeks.

'It was at about this point that we realised that we didn't need to go for Curtis himself, we just needed to go for the most vulnerable aspect of his operation: the transport network,' says a Crayfish officer. 'Curtis never touched his stuff, we knew that from the outset, but the people he was supplying would have to physically shift it and they used a variety of methods. If we could crack these, we could really get in and create a big problem for the Top Man. It would also make him nervous of his own people because he would suspect informers, and a nervous man is a vulnerable one.'

Warren never betrayed any nerves but he was trusting fewer and fewer people. He was convinced no-one took his advice and would later complain about it in a phone call to confidante Tony Bray.

CW   *They don't listen, do they? You know what*
       people are like, they are stupid.

TB   *Fucking hell. You tell em, don't you Cock,*
       and they still want to do it their own way.

CW   *Innit.*

TB   *It's like pissing against the wind, isn't it*
       son?

Warren sighed. 'No wonder Jesus had a hard time, everyone questioning him.'

THE FILIP from successful busts was soon tempered by fresh discord. Customs and Excise had different work and pay patterns to the police. The customs staff received flexible allowances of up to £11,000 on top of their salaries for working or being on call beyond their normal hours. The police, in contrast, were paid hourly overtime which, given the inhuman hours the Crayfish team were having to work, mounted up spectacularly and put severe strain on their budgets.

'Customs could go out and work thirty hours straight, kip for two hours and then work another twenty-four and this would be covered in their allowance,' says a Crayfish policeman. 'We would have to go home when the overtime got too great, because the force couldn't afford to pay us. Consequently there was a feeling that customs were doing all the work.'

The team came up with two solutions. Firstly, they put more effort into intelligence and less into surveillance. 'Everyone realised that we couldn't keep going out and doing long, long watches. So instead of sitting watching a car park for two days waiting for a truck full of drugs to arrive, we would seek to pinpoint times and locations more precisely.' Secondly, many of the police officers effectively chose to work for nothing. 'The police guys got fed up with the arrangements and decided they couldn't leave observations before the job was done,' says Colin Gurton. 'They began to say they would take the time off in lieu rather than get paid, so they could stay on the job longer. Whether they ever took that time off is moot. It was utterly selfless of them.'

Often police working practices proved the most effective, as Gurton acknowledges. 'They have an observation log in which every movement on a job is written down. That recorded everything and meant we could later input all that information on our databases. It was a better structure than customs officers' notebooks. Also police have operational orders written down at the start of the day and submit paper work at the end of the day to say what action they have taken. Customs are more flexible; they are given a job and it's up to them how they build up the case. We decided the police method was better because again we could track exactly what everyone was doing over time on the database.

'Having a mix was excellent because we could call on the resources needed. If we needed a firearms team or a helicopter, we could call in Merseyside Police. We had the resources of the Regional Crime Squad at our disposal and customs teams all over the country. It meant we could operate everywhere without having to inform local forces. Customs officers would give orders to police officers and vice versa depending on who was running the particular job. If drugs were running live, a customs investigating officer had to be there on the ground. If the job involved firearms, it was under a police superintendent.'

Acda and McAllister had also decided to take legal advice at every step of the investigation. They weren't about to go through the fiasco of Singer/Full Bloom again. Together they went to see one of the country's leading prosecution barristers, David Turner QC. He had immense experience in prosecuting Customs and Excise cases and was invaluable for advice about evidential matters leading to arrests. 'We first tried to take out the limbs of Warren's operation but it soon became clear this wouldn't be enough to secure his downfall. Every time we would take off a leg or an arm, we could go to our counsel and say, "Is this enough to get the big guy?" If it wasn't then we'd go back and go for another limb,' says Acda. Turner became a key part of the team, although outside the investigation.

Such was the furtive nature of their work that Crayfish officers could not be seen directly to take part in busts or give evidence in court; that could have exposed their operation before they were ready to take down the bosses. 'We had to disguise our involvement. When we gave jobs to the traffic police it was ideal because they could claim the arrest without knowing too much about what they might be dealing with. We didn't let them know it was Crayfish work. We couldn't be seen to be appearing in court as that would also have tipped them off about our operation. Cheshire Motorway Police suddenly became the best drugs squad in the country. All they had to do was find a reason to stop that vehicle. They could always come up with something.'

One such stop was another coach run, this time handled by a Cheshire operator called Clive Morris. A listening device was placed in one of his vehicles and it was stopped returning from Belgium in May 1995. A rummage crew found a secret compartment accessed from beneath a rear seat and leading under the vehicle's toilet compartment. It contained fourteen kilos of heroin, worth up to two million pounds, and 408 Ecstasy tablets.

Three men, including Morris, later received a total of twenty-eight years in jail.

Mixed runs, known as 'groupage' loads, were typical of Warren. 'He was a placer; he'd place people into whatever drug they wanted,' says Acda. 'If you wanted a tonne of cocaine, he'd put you into a tonne of cocaine, if you wanted fifty kilos of cannabis, he'd put you into that. You received it, sold it and paid him. If you were to lose the shipment anywhere, Curtis still got paid. Always. He would also cut off anyone who got caught and never deal with them again.'

The busts seemed to have little impact on Warren's business. 'He could afford to lose one run in three and still make plenty. And there's no doubt he was getting a hell of a lot through,' says a Crayfish officer. Both the sophistication of his concealments and his salesmanship were becoming legendary. One coach believed to have drugs stashed on board was secretly searched while on a ferry. The rummage crew found nothing and were forced to let it go. They later learned it had contained 100 kilos of heroin, which were sold within forty-eight hours.

The occasional miss was a fact of life. Customs manage to seize only an estimated ten per cent of drugs entering the United Kingdom. The police seize one per cent. Eighty-nine per cent gets through. Once the drugs had gone, there was only one other way to catch the dealers. Trace the money.

ONCE A WEEK, every week, Peter McGuinness left his home in the Liverpool suburb of Dovecot and took a cab to Lime Street station, a sports bag clutched in his right hand. The forty-one-year-old father of grown-up children would board the train to London, taking a standard-class seat and stashing his holdall on the overhead rack. A burly minder joined him. They would chat for a while then sit back, open their newspapers and relax. The journey was dull, the trains often delayed, but at least it was lucrative. Inside the bag was £250,000 of someone else's cash.

McGuinness was the bagman for the Liverpool mafia. Having served a jail term for drug-running, he became instead a money-runner, collecting the underworld's illicit gains – crumpled fivers, tenners and twenties, often contaminated with security dye or traces of cocaine, speed or heroin – and taking it to be laundered.

Money laundering is the moving and processing of ill-gotten money to make it appear legitimately earned. According to a 1998 United Nations report on the 'World Drug Problem', it has three stages:

> **Placement**. The initial entry of funds into the financial system serves the purpose of relieving the holder of large amounts of actual cash and positioning these funds in the financial system for the next stage. Placement is the most vulnerable stage of the process, as the chance of discovery of the illicit origin of the money is greatest at the beginning.

> **Layering**. The next stage, describes a series of transactions designed to conceal the money's origin. At this level money is often sent from one country to another and then broken up into a variety of investments, which are moved frequently to avoid detection.

> **Integration**. In this stage, the funds have been fully assimilated into the legal economy where they can be used for any purpose.

McGuinness's trips to London always ended at the same place: a small bureau de change at 22 Notting Hill Gate, west London. The shop was owned by Ussama 'Sammy' El-Kurd, an enterprising Jerusalem-born Palestinian who started in business with a small tobacconists before dabbling in car hire and video rental. Trade did not go well. Every day, Sammy looked out wistfully at the thousands of tourists wandering past from the Tube station to visit the shops and stalls of Portobello Road market. Some would stop in and ask where they could change their dollars or yen into sterling. Sammy saw an opportunity. In a corner of the shop he installed a booth with a window and an employee to change cash for tourists. Outside he hung a small sign displaying his daily rates of exchange. And at some stage, he became Europe's most prolific money laundering outlet.

The biggest UK denomination note is fifty pounds. Other currencies, however, have much higher denomination bills. In Holland the 5,000-guilder note, worth approximately £1,400, is not unusual. Consequently, a bag of sterling can be changed for a slim wad of foreign cash that fits into a jacket pocket and can easily be taken abroad for banking or spending.

El-Kurd would change all the sterling anyone wanted and ask no questions. Word soon spread. 'He was doing so much business, he simply did not have enough high denomination notes in the shop at all times, so he was forced to go to high street banks and other bureaux de change shops to exchange his cash for what he needed,' said Senior Investigating Officer Dave Thompson. Often,

El-Kurd would hit the phone in the shop's basement, frantically trying to locate more foreign notes. He would dispatch his staff to collect the money but they were not allowed to travel by taxi; he made them go by bus or Underground to save money.

Once changed, the cash was often taken by couriers to the Netherlands or Belgium, from where it was wired to bank accounts in Switzerland or Dubai. Some of the money was used to buy more drugs, which were then imported into Britain to start the whole cycle again. By mid-1994, El-Kurd was changing cash for criminals across the country. He was careful not to betray his growing wealth, living in a modest semi-detached house in Greenford, Middlesex, with his second wife and their three children. But his conduct was so blatant that the authorities were soon onto him. 'If you change £100,000 at a bank till, someone is going to get suspicious,' said Thompson.

In September 1994, surveillance was mounted on his shop. 'It was incredibly important for intelligence. We were able to follow the spokes radiating out from the shop to cities all over Britain. One of the most productive lines was to Liverpool. Almost every day couriers from there would show up with bags crammed full with cash and leave with their pockets lined with foreign notes.'

On one occasion, one of El-Kurd's employees changed more than £100,000 at a Thomas Cook branch in the West End. Once he had left, customs officers raced inside. They wrote a Customs and Excise receipt for the sterling and took possession of the lot. It was tested at a laboratory and proved to be covered in cocaine, cannabis and heroin from the hands of users and dealers.

Peter McGuinness upped his visits from once to twice a week. His bag often contained Scottish, Irish and Manx notes, indicating it was the proceeds of drug dealing across the British Isles. He appeared to be organising other Liverpool couriers, some of whom used National Express coaches, shoving bags of money on the luggage shelf or under seats. 'The couriers' activities were really quite astonishing,' recalls a member of the surveillance team. 'Our guys followed one into a pub where he started working. He put the bag on the floor behind the bar and did a full shift. Then he picked up the bag, with about a quarter of a million pounds in it, and went home. He took the train the next morning.'

McGuinness was once observed on a platform at Lime Street. He put his bag on the ground and wandered off to a payphone. 'Our obs team were astonished, they didn't know what was happening. Was it some kind of hand-over? It turned out the guy made a call, then returned to his bag and boarded the London-bound train, second class. It just shows how blasé these people were about carrying huge sums of cash.'

Having purchased foreign notes, McGuinness would usually hand over the small bundles to the couriers who would take them abroad. One member of the gang was later described as the airline KLM's best customer, having made 143 trips to Holland, often going every day. Sometimes he didn't leave Schipol Airport, simply handing over his cash to another in the chain of couriers and returning to Heathrow on the next flight.

ON CHRISTMAS DAY 1994, Delroy Showers was exercising in the yard at Horsens State Prison, 150 miles west of Copenhagen. The regime there was gentle: inmates had colour televisions, personal computers and direct-dial telephones in their cells. Showers, an escape risk, was usually watched while he was jogging but as it was Christmas he was given a little leeway. No-one spotted the rope slung over the four-metre high perimeter fence. By the time the alarm was raised, Showers was gone.

'Without a doubt he will be back among his underworld friends,' said Detective Inspector Noel White, urging people in Liverpool to watch out for him. 'He must not be approached. He has a history of violence. He also has an intricate network of friends.'

Three weeks later, that network was partly exposed to the public for the first time in a full-page *Sunday Times* feature headlined 'Men Who Run Crime UK.' The newspaper intoned, 'A dozen British crime families have formed a national mafia-style alliance and seized control of the country's drug trade, worth more than £3 billion a year.' It named gang leaders in London, Liverpool, Glasgow and Newcastle.

Some of it was exaggerated and some of it was old but it was the first time that any newspaper had touched on the Liverpool mafia and its malign influence. It pointed out that Liverpool was a 'key staging post' for drugs to Scotland and north-east England, briefly reprised Eddie Richardson's demise and revealed:

Part of the Richardson cocaine consignment was to have been sold in Merseyside. Intelligence sources have revealed that it was bound for Brian "Snowy" Jennings, who was one of the richest men in Liverpool but drove a secondhand car and lived in a council house. Jennings's partner was Tommy Comerford... recently released from prison after being jailed for fourteen years for importing heroin. The financier behind the pair has never been charged with drug smuggling. He uses Athens as a meeting point for his heroin contacts from Pakistan, has £57m in a bank account on the Isle of Man and recently placed £235,000 in cash into an Irish bank. His client list includes the Showers family, who were responsible for supplying heroin and cannabis to Merseyside for a decade.

There was no mention of Curtis Warren, which was a relief to the Crayfish team. The last thing they wanted was for him to be spooked before they could close the net. Their policy was one of stealth. They were still a long way from getting the 'big guy' but there were plenty of arms and legs to be going on with. On 30 April 1995, the police busted William Fitzgerald, an associate of Warren's whose name had first cropped up in the ill-fated Operation Bruise. He was found in a flat with thirty kilos of cannabis resin in a bag. He denied all knowledge of the drugs but would be jailed for two years. It was another Crayfish success.

The next day, David Ungi was shot dead and Cocky's carefully spun web began to unravel.

'If you want trouble, go to Liverpool.

What's going on there is frightening.'

Member of the Cheetham Hill Gang

Manchester, May 1995

THE Gang War of 1995–6 had no single cause. Liverpool's underworld had been volatile for several years, with conflict over territories and between security firms wanting to control club doors. Guns, seeping into the city, added to the tension. Up-and-comers with fresh drug loot in their pockets could be spotted out and about in town most nights, cruising in their Golf GTis and Shoguns, flashing gold and flexing muscle. 'Town' was buzzing and so were they.

If there was a watershed, it can be isolated to Christmas Day evening, 1994, at The State nightclub, a popular dance-round-your-handbag venue featured in the hit film *A Letter to Brezhnev*. Two young men were thrown out for causing trouble. 'We'll be back,' they threatened. The doormen had heard it all before but this time it was no bluff: Darren Delahunty returned with a pistol and fired seven times at the bouncers as they crushed into the doorway for cover. Two were hit in the legs, buttocks and back. The attack was recorded on a security camera and within weeks a DJ had dubbed garage music over the footage and was re-playing it on a screen as part of his show: Delahunty crouching against the recoil of his pistol, the short burst of flame in grainy black and white, the doormen in a heap. Delahunty was later jailed for fifteen years but a line had been crossed.

The following month, Merseyside Police raided houses and night clubs and arrested seventeen people after a year-long probe into drug-dealing, extortion, arson, kidnapping, witness intimidation and protection racketeering by door security agencies. Operation Aladdin was aimed at the men behind the door wars. It was a necessary measure but, by taking out some of the key players, its immediate effect was to destabilise the status quo. Suddenly it was open season on the doors; petrol on the embers.

Several simmering conflicts exploded almost simultaneously. By far the worst – and the only one which would resonate outside the city – was between some of Curtis Warren's predominantly black or mixed-race Granby crew and white criminals from the neighbouring Dingle. The man in the middle was Warren's former partner in extorting prostitutes: Johnny Phillips.

A well-connected underworld source:

> It goes back to an incident involving a black bouncer in Liverpool. This guy is massive; he's built like two Mike Tysons. He was working in a club when some members of a very tough white family came in and started throwing their weight about. One thing led

to another and this bouncer knocked one of them out.

They swore they'd get revenge but they bided their time. About a year later, the bouncer was getting out of a parked car with another guy, the boss of a door security firm. Two men appeared with guns and started firing at them. They ran off and got away. The door boss suspected the white family was behind it. He and some of his associates travelled immediately to Manchester where they knew people who could supply them with guns. A full-scale war situation developed.

Johnny Phillips worked for Curtis Warren and was also friendly with the door boss. Phillips wasn't in the door business himself but would sometimes dictate to clubs which doormen they could employ. A pretty powerful man. He stepped in as a mediator, to try to calm the situation down and resolve it. But the mediation broke down. Because Phillips had put his reputation on the line it became personal with him.

Always powerful, Phillips was now a man mountain – a 'steroid-pumping giant' in the words of one detective – who had taken to jogging around leafy Sefton Park wearing body armour under his tracksuit. He had moved out of Toxteth to the slightly smarter Aigburth a mile away and was reputed to be Warren's lieutenant in south Liverpool, running protection rackets and keeping drug dealers in line. He was much avoided and widely feared.

The first shots in the war were fired in February 1995. Twenty-four-year-old Colin Fitzgibbon was walking to his home in the Kensington area of the city when he was blasted in the back with a shotgun. Fitzgibbon was a member of a large extended family from the Toxteth-

Dingle area. Those suspected of the shooting were members of what the police labelled the Black Caucus. Three men were charged with attempted murder, including Mark 'Sonny Boy' Osu. (Osu would spend thirteen months in custody before the charges against him were dropped.)

But the spark that lit the conflagration came at Cheers, a dismal, flat-roofed, concrete block on Aigburth Road that had been converted from a Conservative Club to a themed wine bar. According to the *Guardian*, 'A local black businessman and some associates tried to take it over and the white regulars tried to drive them out.' The 'businessman' was Johnny Phillips; the 'white regulars' included brothers and cousins of Fitzgibbon. One of them, David Ungi, found himself barred.

Ungi, thirty-five, was a married father of three boys, and a former amateur boxer and secondhand car dealer. As a senior family member, he took it upon himself to resolve the dispute in the accepted manner: a one-on-one 'straightener'. Phillips accepted the challenge and the fight was arranged. On March 20, the two men squared up. Ungi won.

Under the rules of the straightener, that should have ended the matter. But Phillips, always a loose cannon, was not prepared to accept defeat. A rumour spread that his opponent had fought in skin-tight leather gloves and had concealed a knuckleduster under one of them. The following day, as David Ungi drove up outside his home, a man stepped from a parked car and shot at him. He survived. The gunman was never caught but the rumour-mill said it was Phillips. Alarmed at signs that the 'south side' was splitting into two warring camps, the police launched secret operations against both sides. But before either operation could get off the ground, events took a fatal turn.

Shortly before 5.30 PM on May 1, David Ungi slowed his red Volkswagen Passat at a Toxteth road junction. Either by coincidence or deliberately, a black Volkswagen Golf GTi blocked his path. Inside were two young black men. Ungi exchanged words with one of them. The man's response was to pull a gun and crack off several shots. Ungi fell to the ground, fatally wounded. The killers sped away. Their victim was taken to the Royal Liverpool University Hospital but was dead upon arrival.

The personal columns of the *Liverpool Echo* filled up with dozens of poignant death notices in a manner not seen since the Hillsborough football disaster. 'Davey was an innocent man gunned down in the street by gangs for no reason whatsoever,' said his distraught widow, Jean. 'This has nothing to do with crime in the city. My husband was a quiet man, very generous, he was always there if you needed him and to stop trouble if needed. He loved his family very much.' A huge white floral tribute was placed at the death scene against a low garden wall, its blooms spelling out the word 'BROTHER'.

Ronnie Ungi, thirty-two, appealed for witnesses to come forward and name the gunmen. 'The sooner they are caught, the sooner we can bury our brother,' he said, standing at the shrine of flowers where his brother fell. 'All he had was a straight fight in a pub and this is how they retaliated.' He denied his brother was involved in crime. 'I don't know where these rumours have come from. If you check my brother's background you will see that he has no criminal record, he has never been in trouble with the police. It has got nothing to do with racketeering or drugs and that's it.'

The next day someone poured petrol through the door of Cheers and struck a match. Two days after that, six houses were sprayed with bullets in Halewood, a few miles south of Toxteth. The war had begun. Phillips, who knew he would be a prime suspect for the murder, went voluntarily to a police station to deny any role in the killing. His alibi was good. A few days later, he flew to Jamaica for a holiday. Three other men, including Ricardo Rowe, were questioned about the killing but were released without charge

On May 9, two white men burst into Vic's Gym in the Kensington area of the city. Amid the weights and training machines, they singled out Rowe and shot him in the hand. On May 15, a man was wounded in Netherley and another in Dovecot. Over the following weekend five people were injured in two shootings, including the boss of powerful door security firm who was not connected to the Toxteth feud. Once again, the city was making headlines for the wrong reasons:

SHOOTINGS BLAMED ON RIVAL BLACK AND WHITE GANGS
The Times

GANGSTERS PUT LIVERPOOL TOP OF GUN LEAGUE
The Observer

TOXTETH LIVES IN FEAR
Daily Telegraph

RACE TENSIONS FLARE IN DRUG DEALERS' CROSSFIRE
The Guardian

While some of the stories characterised the violence as black versus white, one of the most informed reports came in the *Observer* on May 28:

> For the police and community leaders the last
> four weeks have been a nightmare as two, perhaps
> three, turf wars have erupted. One involves gangs

which control security at the city's lucrative pubs and nightclubs. The others centre on less lucrative issues of pride and territory. The picture is confused because the same men involved in the bouncers' war are brought into disputes between local criminals, blurring the line between gang activity and other disputes. According to police investigating the shootings, these are men who 'live by their own code' and settle their own problems, often with an organised brawl. Councillors, press and law-enforcement agencies admit that the identity of the warring families and groups and their leaders is the city's biggest 'open secret'.

Chief Constable James Sharples called a meeting of his top officers. Through his mind were running thoughts of the public order predicament faced by his predecessor Ken Oxford. Now guns were involved. He outlined his strategy: to put round-the-clock armed patrols on the streets. His staff were behind him. The open use of weapons by gangsters could not be tolerated. 'My officers will fight fire with fire,' pledged Sharples.

That night he ordered the force's armed response vehicles (ARVs) into action; armoured Volvo 850 estates capable of up to 150 miles per hour. Inside each was a team of officers dressed in paramilitary black, with army-style helmets, bullet-stopping vests, Heckler and Koch MP5 sub-machine guns (adapted to single-shot mode) strapped across their chests and Smith and Wesson .38 calibre revolvers in hip holsters. They had orders to stop and search suspects at gunpoint. Checkpoints were set up at key locations.

In the weeks that followed, some individuals were searched up to half a dozen times in a day. The strategy, unique in mainland Britain, had its critics. Solicitors complained that their clients were being targeted and harassed. Some undoubtedly were. The left-of-centre *Guardian* was scathing: 'Liverpool, it seems, has succumbed to its unequalled talent for self-dramatisation. In response to a succession of petty firearm attacks, almost exclusively involving gangland figures and causing minimal harm to the innocent, they have wheeled out a force worthy of a role in Terminator 3.' Easy words for a London-based leader writer to pen.

'The situation was very tense,' recalls a firearms team member. 'There was no time to relax during that whole summer. Every patrol required the utmost concentration. Every time we stopped a car, we had to treat it as a hostile situation. One officer would cover with the firearm while another did the checking. I lost count of the times we forced people out of cars to lie flat on the ground while we searched them. It must have been frightening for many of them but we knew who we were looking for. We'd seen photos of the main players and we knew their haunts. I was actually quite surprised by the amount of respect we commanded from the community. There was a real sense that we were there to help, more than any time I've ever known on the force.'

On one occasion, the officer stopped two main men in the Granby gang. 'The two guys were driving around Dingle in a car. We'd seen them circle a small circuit of roads twice. They might have been scouting a location or scoping us so we decided to give them a tug. On their third pass we pulled out in front of them and went into our defensive-stop procedure: one officer ordering them out of the car, others at the rear using doors and the bonnet of the vehicle for cover.

'Even though we'd done many stops before, you just don't know if someone's going to pull a weapon and take a pop at you. You can never read minds. They were slow in reacting and that made us twitchy. They came out after a few moments and got on their knees. Then we had them on the ground and did the vehicle search and checked them out. We found nothing but didn't exactly get co-operation from the suspects. By this time there were people coming out of houses wondering what the commotion was. I had to go onto crowd control duty. There was a woman screaming at us to leave the men alone. But I remember an old black guy telling her to shut up and to let us get on with our job.'

Five weeks after his brother's death, the police stopped thirty-year-old Colin Ungi in a car. He said he was going to buy a cake. He was dressed for the trip in body armour and had a loaded, Russian-made Tokarev pistol, one of the more fashionable handguns in Liverpool at the time. Ungi, who had a previous conviction for manslaughter, claimed he was afraid for his life and needed the gun for self-defence. He was arrested and charged with possessing a firearm. He and his brother Brian, twenty-two, would also be charged with the attempted murder of Ricardo Rowe at Vic's Gym.

On the evening of Colin Ungi's first appearance in court, there was a major disturbance in Toxteth. Streets were sealed off by the police as youths in balaclavas set cars alight and hurled stones in Park Road. 'People have taken to the streets to vent their anger and frustration,' said Ronnie Ungi. 'My brother should have been released on police bail. The atmosphere in Toxteth now is like a powder keg, the tension is so great.' The brothers were eventually cleared of attempted murder after the prosecution declined to offer any evidence but Colin was jailed for a year for the gun offence.

An inquest shed little light on David Ungi's death. 'People fear reprisals for helping police with our

Curtis 'Cocky' Warren

Curtis Warren: 'He was big, not tall but burly and big-necked, with close-cropped hair and a soft-spoken Scouse accent. He smiled, but not with his eyes…'

i

Tommy Comerford and his wife *Photo © Liverpool Echo*

The buccaneering Tommy Comerford, drug dealer par excellence, enjoying a cruise on the QEII with his wife. He was one of the pioneers of large-scale drug importation to the United Kingdom.

Above

The response Merseyside Police met when trying to mount anti-drug surveillance in the tougher parts of Toxteth.

Below

Michael and Delroy Showers, the formidable brothers considered by police to be Warren's predecessors.

Michael Showers

Delroy Showers

Mario Halley *Aged 22, the Cali Cartel's precocious 'European Sales Manager', who plotted to flood the Continent with cocaine.*

Operation Singer
Lead ingots containing cocaine. Warren would be acquitted of involvement with the drugs.

Mario Halley

Operation Singer

Charrington (centre) with Warren (rig

Operation Singer

Above *Warren, (right) and Brian Charrington (centre) with another man at Heathrow Airport. Unbeknown to Warren, the charismatic Charrington was leaking information to the police.*

iv

The Coach House   *Photo © Liverpool Echo*

Above *Warren's executive home: The Coach House at Meols on the Wirral, with flagged patio, Koi carp in the filtered pond, and a sophisticated alarm system.*

Above *The Turkish lorry containing 178 kilos of heroin, seized in November 1993. Warren's presence in the vicinity of the load sparked Operation Crayfish.*

Operation Mix

Above *Dutch officers drilling into lead ingots to recover 400 kilos of cocaine.* **Right** *What the Dutch officers saw when they opened the container from Colombia at the climax of Operation Mix.*

Operation Mix

Right *The British drug gang smashed by Dutch police in October 1996, in order of importance, with Warren top of the tree.*

Curtis Warren

Stephen Whitehead

Stephen Mee

Ray Nolan

John Farrell

William Fitzgerald

Right *Scouse bagman Peter McGuinness and bureau de change boss Ussama El-Kurd, who laundered the Liverpool mafia's criminal loot.*

Peter McGuinness

Ussama El-Kurd

Tony Bray *Photo © Liverpool Echo*

Stan Carnall

Tony Bray *Warren's friend and confidant, jailed in connection with the corrupting of Elmore Davies.*

Stan Carnall *Currently serving ten years for heroin dealing and a mentor to Warren and others.*

Phillip Glennon Snr *Father of Warren's girlfriend, Stephanie. Glennon walked free from charges of conspiring to pervert the course of justice.*

Elmore Davies *Showing off a haul of guns shortly before he was arrested for corruption.*

Phillip Glennon Snr

DCI Elmore 'Elly' Davies *Photo © Liverpool Echo*

inquiries,' Detective Chief Inspector Alan Buckley told the hearing. He said that illegal handguns, many smuggled from former Eastern Bloc countries, were now readily available to the city's criminals.

'Is it true that you can even hire a gun by the day?' inquired coroner Roy Barter.

'That is what our intelligence suggests,' replied Buckley.

Recording a verdict of unlawful killing, Mr Barter made a strong appeal for people to assist the police in the investigation. It fell on frightened ears.

The police had some successes. In a raid at a service station on the M6 they seized eight pistols and 399 rounds of ammunition destined for the city. A reconstruction of David Ungi's murder was broadcast on the BBC *Crimewatch* programme. And Johnny Phillips was arrested at Manchester Airport returning from his holiday and charged with attempting to murder Ungi the day after their straightener.

Still the shootings went on. On June 4, bullets were fired at a house in Princes Avenue, Toxteth. On June 8, twenty-two-year-old Lee Parry was shot nearby. Three days later, Edward Shaw from Moses Street, Toxteth, was stopped in Aigburth in a car with two sub-machine guns, one fitted with a silencer, and two self-loading pistols. It was later claimed in court that he told police he had been forced to mind the guns by 'the Ungis'. Shaw categorically denied it and claimed it was the police who suggested the name. He was later jailed for five years for possessing guns and ammunition with intent to enable another to endanger life. On June 19, Stephen Anderson was shot in Moses Street, the city's fourteenth shooting since David Ungi's death. Anderson lingered for five months before dying.

Police also took the rare step of naming two men they wanted to trace in connection with the Ungi murder – Barry 'Bunji' O'Rourke and Darren Jackson. Neither had been seen since the shooting. It was widely rumoured that they had left Britain and were living in Jamaica. On July 28, shortly after O'Rourke's name was released by the police, his home was sprayed with bullets.

The tension was palpable in the streets of Granby and Dingle. Front doors were deadbolted at sundown. Curtains winced at the sound of a car. The pubs of Park Road were deserted. Brooding men sat in their living rooms in bulletproof vests, guns to hand, constantly chattering into mobile phones.

CURTIS WARREN was one of many people hauled into the police station for questioning at this time. He was extremely cool; one officer tasked with watching his reaction to questions said Warren betrayed no tension or emotions at all. Yet he should have been worried. South Liverpool gossip had it – though the police discount it – that Cocky had ordered David Ungi's murder. Some of the White Clan were convinced he was behind it. The police had a theory that the two men wanted for questioning, Jackson and O'Rourke, had been spirited away to the West Indies with Warren's assistance. Once there, so the story went, they had demanded money to start a new life. Instead, Warren had them killed. Tony Bray related the police version of events to Warren in a phone call.

TB   *Tell you what, you know, the shite they think up is unbelievable. The special people [possibly a reference to Special Branch] have got the plod in Jamaica looking for the bodies of the other two.*

CW   *Yeah?*

TB   *This what they've got down: you give the order to do the other fella [David Ungi], they done the business for you and then you got them out to Jamaica, right?*

CW   *Yeah.*

TB   *They wanted more money to keep their mouths shut. You have got connections with gangsters there, so you got them slotted. Fucking mad, isn't it?*

CW   *Yeah.*

TB   *They've got you down as fucking putting the hit out but you got them slotted because they [wanted] some more money to keep quiet. Fuck, so now they're all looking for these fucking two bodies in Jamaica.*

CW   *Mad, aren't they?*

At the time of writing, Jackson and O'Rourke are still missing. There is no evidence that either is dead. One urban myth has it that they were spotted by a Merseyside detective who was watching a video of a Chris Eubank world title boxing contest; there were O'Rourke and Jackson at ringside at the fight in Newcastle, sitting next to Johnny Phillips. The story has never been verified.

In truth, the Gang War was the last thing Warren wanted. With the ARVs on the streets, the constant harassment and the climate of fear, the movements of dealers and their runners were severely curtailed. It was bad for business and forced him to take sides when he did not want to. Cocky had friends among the White Clan and had even been caught on surveillance photographs in the company of one of their leaders, apparently holding a meeting to defuse the situation.

He had nothing to gain from a petty squabble over a pub.

'We believe that Curtis tried to step in as a mediator and settle the feud,' says Colin Gurton. 'Even though he appeared untouchable and wasn't scared of anyone in Liverpool, he might just have been concerned that some nutter might pop up over his hedge and blow him away for the heck of it. He wanted the gun battles to stop as much as anyone. The drug trade had pretty much come to a standstill in Liverpool. The police crackdown was causing him too much heat and he wanted an end to it.'

Though not afraid of any gangster, he was less certain of the police. 'He was convinced that the Merseyside firearms teams would shoot him on sight if they spotted him,' says a senior officer formerly in the drug unit. 'He was certain of it. Jim Sharples's decision was that if the gangsters were going to use guns, then he'd show them real firepower. It had a very significant effect and Warren thought they would use it as an excuse to take him out.'

His sixth sense was on full alert. On one occasion he was in a cafe with Tony Bray when his radar turned on a young man sitting at a nearby table. Warren confronted him and accused him of being an undercover police officer. Ashen-faced, the man fled. Bray later confirmed through a police contact that Warren had been right; the plain clothes constable had been sent to observe Cocky from outside the cafe but against instructions had gone in and ordered a cuppa. Bray recounted to Warren what his contact had said.

TB *He admitted that was* [an undercover officer] *in the cafe.*

CW *Did he? What did he say?*

TB *He was told… just to observe. Not to be*

> *sitting in there. He got a bollocking cos he*
> *could have got killed.*

CW   *What did he say when I got on him?*

TB   *He fucking shit himself…*

CW   *What did he say about it?*

TB   *He said he thought you were going to duff*
       him up. But if you would have done,
       nothing could have happened anyway.

CW   *What did he say about me getting right on*
       him, though?

TB   *Oh, he said, "Fucking hell. He got right on*
       that, didn't he? He's fucking eagle-eyed."

CW   *Ha!*

TB   *The fella was just told to sit outside and*
       watch us go in, not fucking slurp tea next to
       us.

CW   *Innit. What did I say to that bizzy that*
       day?

TB   *I can't remember. You said, "Hello officer,*
       you fucking…" Something mad, wasn't it?
       He fucking jumped up and legged it out,
       didn't he?

CW   *Yeah.*

TB   *His head must have gone though. He got a*
       right rollicking when he got back.

CW   *Did he? What did [his boss] say?*

TB   *"You fucking dickhead, you could have got*
       killed," he said. "I told you to sit outside
       and watch. That's all I told you to do. Not
       go in thinking you was a fucking hero."

CW   *Ha!*

To avoid such close encounters, Warren was
spending more time outside the city. While still using
the flat at Wapping Dock, he bought a £350,000 home,

the Coach House, on Meols Drive, Hoylake, facing the entrance to the Royal Liverpool Golf Club. It was every inch the executive property, the epitome of white middle-class living: flagged patio, an extensive garden with sprinkler system, Koi carp in the filtered pond, a sophisticated alarm system to deter burglars, spacious rooms laid with tasteful rugs, a discreet Peugeot in the garage.

Cocky was also thinking of upgrading his transport. One day he arrived at the heliport at Squires Gate, Blackpool, in his black Lexus and enquired about helicopter flying lessons. 'He came up four or five times so his face became quite recognisable to us,' recalls one of the instructors, who asked not to be named. 'He was big, not tall but burly and big-necked, with close-cropped hair and a soft-spoken Scouse accent. He smiled, but not with his eyes. He had pockets full of cash, always paid with cash, crisp new notes. He was affable and had a habit of putting his arm around you, which was quite intimidating. He came to us for a trial flight, with several other people, all of them a bit bigger than him but it was obvious he was in charge.

'We were going to take him up in the little Robinson R22 two-seater but when we were walking over to it on the tarmac he spotted a bigger helicopter and said he wanted to go up in that one, a Bell 206 Jetranger. Then he saw the even bigger twin-engined Jetranger – nice and shiny, blue-coloured – and decided that was the best one and that he'd rather go up in that. So he packed all his friends into it and off we went, down over Liverpool and the Wirral. He was asking all kinds of questions about the helicopters, what they could do, if they could be landed on a yacht at sea. I told him that a twin-engined helicopter like the one we were in cost about £1.1million and he didn't seem to flinch much at that.'

Warren once flew for an hour and a half, paying £750 from a wad of cash in his pocket. 'I let him take the controls sometimes, but he never really settled at them, he wasn't a natural. If you are dedicated, you can do your pilot's licence in about six months but he didn't really get a feel for the helicopter.' On one trip, they flew over Barrow-in-Furness on the tip of Cumbria, a town noted for the production of Trident nuclear submarines. Warren pointed out Barrow Football Club. 'I own that,' he claimed. [*The question of whether or not Warren did have a stake in Barrow AFC is, at the time of writing, the subject of a Dutch asset-seizure application*].

Flying high, Warren should have been at his zenith. But the Gang War was a constant sore. British newspaper stories about the shootings were apparently faxed to Cali bosses in Colombia. They were concerned that it might jeopardise their lucrative long-term relationship with the Liverpool mafia. 'Warren was told to sort it out,' says a detective. Yet for all his power and influence, there was little he could do. It had become a blood feud and there was no restraining some of the participants. 'We have crossed a threshold and there is no going back.' said Jim Sharples. 'The informal pressures that used to exist – the rules that said don't use a gun – have gone. It began as a fashion to carry firearms. Now it is a fashion to use them. We cannot just put the genie back in the bottle.'

IN SEPTEMBER, Johnny Phillips was arrested after his Honda Legend was chased through north Manchester and Lancashire. He was charged with causing actual bodily harm to one police officer, assaulting another, damaging two police vehicles and driving dangerously, and was released on bail. The following month, charges that he attempted to murder David Ungi were thrown out at Liverpool Magistrates Court when the only witness failed to show up. There was said to be a £50,000 contract on Phillips's life.

On October 1, the home of Ronnie Ungi was riddled with bullets. A few days later, Johnny Phillips's house in Aigburth and his £30,000 BMW 328i convertible were sprayed with automatic fire. He vacated the house with his wife Maria and young daughter Chelsee and moved to a flat in Toxteth, closer to his allies. In November, Brian Fitzgibbbon, described by the *Liverpool Echo* as 'the man who led one of Merseyside's most notorious drug gangs', was arrested. Fitzgibbon had been duped into buying a machine to make Ecstasy pills from undercover officers. He handed over tablets in part exchange for the machine. Police also found guns, ammo and amphetamines in a raid. Fitzgibbon admitted conspiring to supply drugs and was jailed for fourteen years. Other members of his gang were also jailed.

On November 20, his cousin David Ungi was laid to rest. A cortege of thirty-one limousines followed the hearse to Our Lady of Mount Carmel Church in Toxteth, where Ungi had been baptised, made his first communion and been married. Cars double-parked along the street and more than 150 mourners made their way into the church while an estimated 1,000 people gathered outside. There was a flatbed lorry covered in flowers and a floral tribute from his sons that stood five feet high and contained his photograph on a dove. The *Liverpool Echo's* In Memoriam section stretched to five pages of tributes. Mr Ungi's mother Vera composed her own memorial notice, turning her son's name into an acronym, which started: 'D for Distinguished, A for Admirable...' and carried on to 'I for Incomparable'. It had been a tragic year. There had been forty-two shootings in Liverpool, causing death or injury to twenty-nine people.

Among the bullets, Operation Crayfish continued unabated. In August 1995, a Jaguar driver was stopped by Cheshire Motorway Police on the M62. He was carrying 5,000 Ecstasy tabs. In October, a lorry was 'knocked' at a service station near Newbury, Berkshire, having arrived from Spain via France. It was carrying 250 kilos of cannabis concealed in a lorryload of onions to disguise the smell. Warren was believed to have a big interest in the load and had been observed setting it up at a meeting in Skelmersdale, Lancashire. A father and son from Skelmersdale were later jailed for seven and four years respectively. Customs also picked up a lorry driver at Portsmouth with 200 kilos of cannabis in a consignment of shoes.

Yet Cocky was not unduly concerned. He was making a fortune. Having abandoned his flying lessons at Blackpool, he turned up at Barton Aerodrome on the edge of Manchester and said he was interested in buying a helicopter. 'We put the deal together for him,' recalls one of the staff. 'He was actually a really nice guy, cracked a lot of jokes. He looked rather a frightening character but we had no problems with him at all. He was stocky, imposing. Always casual, dressed in tracksuit bottoms and the like.

'He got some way towards getting his pilot's licence but there are six written exams to take and a lot of reading to do and he really wouldn't take to the reading and the paperwork at all. All the same, he was very keen to buy a helicopter, so we set up a deal to buy a little Enstrum. It's what we use for training, and costs about £70,000. But he went to Holland, said he had some business to attend to there. We ordered the helicopter on his behalf but before the deal could be completed, he disappeared.

We tried to trace him but couldn't. It rather left us in the lurch but we decided to buy the helicopter for ourselves. That was the last we saw of him.'

Curtis Warren had vanished.

THE WORLD WIDE WEB

'Liverpool is the number one

UK centre of excellence for drug smuggling'

a Senior Investigator

HM Customs and Excise

AT the time of Curtis Warren's disappearance, the Liverpool mafia were the most prolific drug importers Britain had ever seen. While by no means having a monopoly – the main London dealers were far too powerful to allow that – they had contacts all over the globe, tentacles reaching everywhere. No narcotic was too addictive, no substance too vile for them to sell. Though the Cocky Watchman became the most high-profile of their number – in some ways the figurehead – he was by no means alone.

Typical of the city's drug elite were two white criminals – John Haase and Paul Bennett – who operated independently of Warren to forge the so-called 'Turkish Connection'. By the early Nineties, Turks controlled the supply of Middle Eastern morphine base to Europe and were causing serious concern among British police and customs officers. Their gangs were clannish and difficult to infiltrate but Merseyside Police struck lucky. Bennett, a married man, had ditched a girlfriend when she started using heroin. Perhaps as an act of revenge, she told a detective constable that he was importing the drug. Surveillance revealed that Turkish *babas* [godfathers] were regularly travelling to Liverpool to meet Bennett and his accomplice Haase, an ex-member of a notorious armed robbery gang known as the Transit Mob. Huge amounts of cash were handed over in plastic bags and taken back to Turkey to buy more drugs. When customs officers moved in to arrest the defendants, they seized eighty-seven kilos of brown heroin.

On remand in prison, Haase and Bennett asked to see customs officers. They were facing long jail terms and were desperate. They offered a deal: information about a container of weapons on board a ship at Liverpool docks in return for a sympathetic word in the judge's ear at their trial. They said the container door was protected with bags of Semtex plastic explosive. Bomb disposal experts blew the door off and found fifty weapons, including Kalshnikovs and Armalite rifles, and more heroin. Haase and Bennett provided further addresses where firearms and heroin were found and suggested they had exposed an arms network supplying the IRA.

At Liverpool Crown Court in 1995, the pair admitted conspiracy to supply heroin. They were both jailed for eighteen years and each had £840,000 confiscated. Their chief lieutenant received fourteen years and five Turks were jailed for between four and twenty years. 'It is rare that the courts deal with somebody so high up the ladder,' the judge told them. Yet barely a year later, Haase and Bennett were free. In what the Home Office called a 'unique' deal, the sentence for both had been secretly reduced to five years in return for their help. When newspapers uncovered the story, despite considerable Government efforts to suppress it, there was an outcry. Some suspected that Haase and Bennett had perpetrated an elaborate confidence trick and that the consignment of guns was actually their own.

Warren, who prided himself on his information network, was kept abreast of the Turkish Connection by his pal Tony Bray, who reported what newspapers were saying about 'the two loons', Haase and Bennett. Unbeknown to Warren, his phone was being tapped by a foreign police force.

TB   *A big thing in the* [Liverpool] Echo *about them other two.*

CW   *What is it saying?*

TB   *Fucking showed all the guns they give over and all that. But the police are saying we knew it was their own guns, they are saying they are not supergrasses and all that. Their customs fella said, "Look, the only way you get that time off a sentence is when you give us good information, which they done, we don't deny they done that."*

CW   *Yeah?*

TB   *"We helped them, they helped us... they fucked off," it said. They are supposed to be living in Mexico somewhere.*

CW   *Fucking Mexico!*

TB   *Dear me.*

CW   *Mad aren't they?*

TB   *Bet you they are sick that come out, son.*

CW   *Well, they won't be happy.*

In fact they were not in Mexico but back on the streets of Liverpool. A few weeks later, Bray told Warren about a report in the *Echo*'s morning sister paper, the *Daily Post*.

> TB   *There was a big thing in the Post today...*
> *said they were working for MI5.*
>
> CW   *Yeah?*
>
> TB   *The Home Secretary has admitted they were*
> *working for MI5... they were to grass people*
> *up on big, big arms deals coming into the*
> *country and loads of gear and all that, and*
> *they have done a good job, he said. But*
> *now, because their cover's blown, they are*
> *no good to anyone, so they have had to let*
> *them go.*

Whether or not they ever did provide any information on others is a moot point. What is not is the amount of money that was washing into the Liverpool economy from the drug trade. The city had undergone a renaissance since the nadir of the Militant years, exemplified by the restoration of the Albert Dock, but it did not seem enough to explain a sudden boom in bars and cafes.

> One of Liverpool's greatest mysteries is where
> the money comes from. Strangers are struck by
> the run-down feel of a once-great port that has
> fallen on hard times. Yet, amid boarded-up
> shops, there are pockets of wealth: a designer-
> clothes shop, a flashy night club... Expensive cars
> cruise the streets, and a remarkable proportion
> of the kids flaunt mobile phones. They cannot

all be the dependants of Premier League
footballers.

Independent on Sunday

Nowhere was more attractive for drug dealers than the
club scene. Where there were clubs, there was Ecstasy –
or, to give it its chemical acronym, MDMA. It was one
drug that no-one could monopolise; it was easy to
smuggle and was increasingly being made within the UK
at secret laboratories tucked away in countryside, Wales
being one favoured location. With their contacts in
Holland, where most labs still were, Liverpool smugglers
were bringing in as much as anyone.

An illustration of the profits at the lowest level of
this dealing chain came with a raid on Liverpool's most
famous dance club. Cream opened in Wolstenholme
Square in the city centre in 1992, the brainchild of two
enterprising friends, and quickly became the country's
most talked-about 'superclub', rivalled only by London's
Ministry of Sound. Coachloads of revellers from as far
as Newcastle-upon-Tyne, Hull and Nottingham would
arrive every weekend to dance through the night. Cream
was a well-run venue but the management found it
difficult to keep out the Ecstasy dealers. After a number
of arrests at the club in 1994, a new security firm was
appointed to run the door.

But the problems returned. The new door team
comprised tough local men headed by a well-known
martial artist. By early 1995, the police received reports
that large-scale Ecstacy distribution had resumed at
Cream and that some of the door staff were implicated.
According to the evidence given later in court, dealers
were given designated pitches within the club, protected
by bouncers. Each of five pushers sold around 200 tablets
a night at £10 each, a daily turnover of £10,000. An

undercover operation culminated in a massive raid in February 1966 and the arrest of twenty-three people. The boss of the door firm denied any involvement and was eventually cleared of all charges after three crown court trials. Another man was jailed for seven and a half years for conspiracy to supply Ecstasy. [*Cream's management were in no way implicated and now heavily vet their security staff*].

THE CRAYFISH team had not been involved in the Cream job but they were closely concerned in another case involving a famous club. In its heyday, the Haçienda was synonymous with the dance scene. No other venue more successfully adopted the hypnotic, hedonistic vibe of rave than this street-corner Manchester warehouse with its cutting edge DJs and northern ambience. From its so-called Summer of Love in 1988, it led the way, its gloomy modern-industrial interior nightly transformed by a throbbing, chemically-fuelled orgy of threshing young limbs and staring eyes.

The club survived through police raids, threats to revoke its licence, temporary closure, the butchering of its doormen by a Salford gang and the death of a sixteen-year-old girl who had taken an E tab. By the mid-Nineties it was struggling financially but was still a magnet for gangs dealing drugs. It was inevitable that the Liverpool mafia's product would end up there.

A week before Christmas 1995, the Crayfish team had booked a festive office party at an Italian restaurant. They were looking forward to getting smashed and letting the hair down. 'In the end, half the team had to go out and do a job,' says one of them. 'So only a couple of car loads of us ended up going for the meal. We had a good night. It finished late and we were looking forward to getting home to out beds. Most of us had been sleeping on the floors and sofas at Fraggle on and off.'

It was after midnight when the group began to leave. The mobile phone of a female customs officer rang. It was her boss. He told her to pass the word that she and the others would have to be out at six o'clock that morning on a watch.

'But it's Christmas,' she pleaded.

There was a pause at the other end of the line. 'Christmas has been cancelled,' said the voice.

The job they had been called out on was the culmination of Operation Tuxedo, which had involved months of surveillance work on a drug cell run by two residents of the rave capital Ibiza: Liverpool-born businessman Gordon Wilson and his lieutenant Vernon Rees. They had been shipping in drugs for months and employed a collector called David Gould, a man mountain from the West Derby area of Liverpool, to tour pubs taking money from dealers. Gould regularly met Wilson to hand over the cash in a superstore car park in Knotty Ash. On one occasion he was observed at Euston Station handing over banknotes taken from his shoe. He even bought a currency-counting machine. Wilson was making so much money that he sent off his Rolex watch to have extra jewels encrusted.

The call that interrupted the Crayfish party was to tell them that busts were imminent. The next day a Manchester University student, Daniel Hayward, was stopped on the M62 by Cheshire Motorway Police. Step out of the car please, your rear light appears to be defective, he was told. Stashed in his vehicle were 2,000 tabs of MDMA. He admitted he was taking them to sell in Manchester's clubs, primarily the Haçienda.

Hayward's cache was just part of a giant load that had originated in Holland and been driven through the

Channel Tunnel on an articulated lorry. It was tailed to Burtonwood service station on the M62 – the place where Warren had been spotted two years earlier – and was 'knocked' as the driver prepared to transfer some bags to a white van driven by Vernon Rees. Rees tried to drive off but crashed into a customs car. The service station was sealed off and 120,000 MDMA tablets, 108 kilos of amphetamine and sixty kilos of cannabis resin were found in the lorry. It was aimed at the Christmas and New Year market, when speed and E were much in demand.

'The immediate upshot of Operation Tuxedo was that armed robberies on Merseyside increased by eighty per cent in the following January and February; mainly robberies of betting shops and post offices,' says Paul Acda. 'Clearly people had been relying on money from those drugs.'

Wilson was picked up at Manchester Airport, preparing to catch a flight to Ibiza. Gould was arrested at home; later he co-operated with the investigation and was said to be in danger of his life (in January 2000, shots were fired at his house in Liverpool). Wilson later received a whopping eighteen years in prison, Rees twelve and Gould seven for conspiracy to import controlled substances. Hayward got five years for possession with intent to supply. The long terms reflected a trend towards higher sentences for large-scale drug importation. The Crayfish team suspected that Warren was behind the supply. Cocky was reported to have told a friend that he had lost 'a big one' and wanted to recoup his losses as soon as possible.

Manchester was also home to the biggest street market for hard drugs in the country. The Alexandra Park estate in Moss Side is a low-rise enclave of alleyways and walk-throughs, hostile to outsiders and hard to police. It was here that two gangs had engaged in a destructive feud that surpassed even the Liverpool Gang War in ferocity and left several young men dead. By the Christmas of 1995, an uneasy truce prevailed.

The east side of the estate was controlled by the Dodington Gang, probably the most trigger-happy crew of street thugs ever seen in Britain. When not engaged in gunplay with their rivals or each other, they ran a drugs market in a cul-de-sac in the heart of their territory, specialising in heroin, cocaine and crack. Mothers and young children had to walk through it to reach a nearby primary school, nursery and playground.

Inevitably, the source of their cocaine was Liverpool. It was cooked in a crack factory at a house in Manchester by a Granby man, Verdaine Griffin, guarded by a Dodington goon with a machine pistol. The rocks – known locally as 'stone' – were then supplied to up to thirty dealers, several of them children. Some sat astride mountain bikes, others worked on foot. Junkies came from all over the county to score: in one six-day period, 219 transactions were recorded by police. The dealers, in full-face balaclavas and bulletproof vests, worked seven days a week. Most carried mobile phones. The market was raking in more than £20,000 a week, or over one million pounds a year, when it was smashed by Greater Manchester Police. Griffin received a long jail term.

The Crayfish team also kept up the pressure. Two men were arrested after seven holdalls of cannabis were being handed over in a meeting at a Liverpool pub. Both were later jailed for seven years. Unconnected raids on two pubs in Kirkdale yielded a Luger automatic, a starting pistol, a small amount of cannabis and Ecstasy and £7,000 in cash. On the same day, thirty-five-year-old Jeremiah Miller was caught with a kilo of cannabis in an M-reg Suzuki. Miller was much more than just a hash courier. His connections would reveal a new dimension to the Liverpool drug empire.

THE PROVISIONAL IRA takes a dim view of drug dealers. Despite persistent newspaper reports that Provo leaders sell narcotics to finance their military campaign, the truth is that – with a few rogue exceptions – they strongly oppose the trade. Part of their stance as defenders of their community is an intolerance of anti-social behaviour. Dealers are often threatened, sometimes injured, occasionally killed. Punishment attacks have continued throughout the current ceasefire. 'Ireland's not like England, where the criminals have only got the police or other criminals to worry about. There's a third force here,' a Republican source told the authors.

When heroin first impacted on the Irish Republic in the early Eighties, a community group, Concerned Parents Against Drugs (CPAD), was formed in Dublin to oust the dealers. They organised protest marches on the homes of criminals. 'Faced with the people power of the CPAD, the pushers could no longer threaten or intimidate with impunity. Some of the CPAD's organisers were members of Sinn Fein and there was speculation that the IRA had also infiltrated the organisation,' wrote journalist Paul Williams in his best-selling book *The General*.

Ten years later, the Republic was facing an even more concerted assault. The flow of drugs had become unstoppable and again community bodies emerged to effect their own policing. Some came together under the banner of the Coalition of Communities Against Drugs (COCAD). 'In many ways the anti-drugs campaign mirrored the Concerned Parents movement of the 1980s, only this time there was more effort devoted to increasing treatment facilities,' reported the *Irish Times*. 'There has also been a darker side to the way people affected by the drugs trade have responded. There have been up to 40 beatings, a number of evictions and one killing... Members of the IRA have been blamed for some of the most serious incidents, including an attack which left one youth with a severed ear. There is no doubt that without the threat of violence, many dealers who have left their homes in the inner city would not have done so.'

Some of the pushers were bundled off for 'interrogation'. They quickly crumbled. 'They think they're big tough gangsters but when you get them in, they all talk,' one of the interrogators told the authors. 'They don't have the bollix to keep quiet.'

So it was that a chubby, bespectacled crook called Tony Long found himself in a house in a run-down area of Dublin, answering questions. Long, described by a COCAD activist as 'a notorious scumbag', hails from the bleak Ballyfermot district, a sprawling, scruffy council estate that supplies many of Dublin's worst criminals. Apparently Long was at the meeting of his own volition, though he knew the possible consequences of non-co-operation. Whatever his motives, he talked. He related a story of how a gang of Liverpool villains had infiltrated the already-buoyant Dublin heroin market to such an extent that they had become the biggest suppliers to the city. The gang had all of the appearances of a cell structure.

Long had been jailed for seven years in England after he was caught in a taxi cab with a box of guns and ammunition. He ended up in HMP Risley near Warrington. 'I fell in with some people in the system over there. Some pretty serious people. They were long-term prison fellows, they had lots of connections, they could get anything. I was asked about the heroin scene in Dublin. A proposition was put to me,' he told COCAD.

The gang, led by a man nicknamed The Scouser, told Long they would spring him from jail and get him home to Dublin if he would then go to work for them, selling their drugs.

> I agreed. My attitude was, I had done the time and you just come in at the tail end of it and rocket to wealth. Rags to riches stuff. If you're six months in Risley without a conviction in the jail, you qualify for what's known as outdoor activities. I went on three walks: out on the moors, down this other fucking place in north Yorkshire and to some fucking lake place. There was no way I could do a runner from there because when you're going out in the minibus to go to them places they don't tell you where you're going in advance and you can't hang around outside Risley to follow the bus 'cos the bus will just turn back. The fourth time I was brought to the baths in Warrington. It was an old Victorian baths but they had built a new pool in the same building. The public were using that one, the prisoners were using the old one.

Long was instructed to walk through the baths with a red towel under his arm so that the getaway driver would recognise him. Long was wearing two sets of clothes, one on top of the other, a false pair of spectacles and a wig. At an opportune moment, he slipped away from the guards and out of the building, running towards a car waiting with the engine running. One of the guards saw him and gave chase but Long and the driver sped off and made for a flat in Liverpool. Two days later Long took the Sealink ferry to Dublin and started work. He was joined by the above-mentioned Jeremiah Miller, free on licence from a fifteen-year sentence for conspiracy to commit armed robbery. They also had a 'transport manager' a small, quiet man who limped as a result of a road accident and was known in the Irish underworld as Gimpy.

'I'd drive a lorry to Cherbourg and head for Amsterdam, 'Gimpy later told *Ireland on Sunday*. 'I'd meet these Turkish crews near Schipol Airport and get, say, twenty to thirty kilos of heroin and a couple of weapons. We'd load the gear into a lorry and I'd drive it back to Dublin. The Liverpool lads didn't want it going through Merseyside. They wanted their names kept out of it. There was too much pressure on [*them*] from the crime squads over there.'

The drugs were stockpiled at houses in Dublin, according to a COCAD member. 'It was farmed out to different individuals and stored. When someone wanted a kilo or half a kilo they went to Long and he had it delivered. They were doing around twenty- five kilos a week. That is a huge proportion of the Dublin consumption.'

Once the week's money had been collected, it was given to Gimpy. 'I would collect parcels of money from [*a named individual*] and bring it to my house. We often cleared £250,000, well maybe £500,000, every three months. As we were selling a kilo for £36,000 to the Ballyfermot crowd and each one would take three kilos per week, we earned a hell of a lot of money.' To launder the cash, Gimpy used a family from a remote part of rural Ireland. They would drive into Dublin, collect the cash then disperse throughout the country to change the punts into sterling in amounts of between £1,500 and

£2,000 at banks and other outlets. The relatively small sums would escape suspicion.

'I'd get £1,000 in wages each week but make more depending on the currency exchange rates,' said Gimpy. 'Sometimes lads would come over from Liverpool to help out. They had English accents which made them all the more plausible.' Once the cash had been changed, it was handed over to The Scouser.

Jeremiah Miller was arrested in Liverpool as part of Operation Crayfish, bringing his role temporarily to a halt. But he was freed on bail and resumed his activities. In May 1996, Miller was told that one of his heroin batches had been cut so many times that the 'gear was no good' and the Dubliners had rejected it. He was sent back with a new supply. Garda officers stopped him in a taxi and found three packs of heroin hidden in his clothes and a fourth in a holdall. It was the biggest seizure in Dublin up to that time, worth about £500,000. Miller was kept apart from other inmates in Mountjoy prison after threats on his life and was later jailed for ten years after pleading guilty at Dublin Criminal Court. The judge directed that he be deported in 1999 on condition that he serve the balance of his sentence in England.

The Liverpool cell was also targeted by another force. 'Republicans were coming under strong pressure to move against heroin traffickers. Hence, when word got out that a couple of heavyweight Liverpudlians were throwing their weight around, the Provos soon developed a keen interest in them... and in those with whom they were associating,' reported the newspaper *Ireland on Sunday*. Some of them were hauled in for a grilling, as there was a strong suspicion that they were supplying Loyalist paramilitaries.

Tony Long had had enough. He dropped out of the drug business, though not out of crime. He was later convicted of bribing a garda officer. He was described in court as an 'unemployed man of affluence' who had not worked since 1986 but had substantial finances and owned land in County Meath. He paid a £45,000 fine rather than go to jail. Strangely, there were no immediate efforts to extradite him to the UK, even though he was still on the run.

'I know I done wrong,' he told COCAD. 'I was under pressure. I'm over eighteen, I know the fucking score. They did get me home. I didn't think they'd have fucking pressed me. I honoured what I got into. I was never told to stop. I stopped on me own free will and there's nobody in England or Ireland that can say I'd be getting in contact or connection with anybody or drugs in the last year and a half. I just want to set the record straight and hope that it's all fucking behind me.'

He did have an enduring respect for the Liverpool mafia: 'Them Scousers, they're just out of reach.'

TONY LONG sold weapons as well as drugs. Where those guns went is an enduring puzzle. It seems that few of them showed up in the Dublin underworld. A Republican source who spoke to the present authors had his own opinion. 'One of the connections was an Ulster Volunteer Force commander from the Fermanagh-Tyrone border. He had links to Dublin criminal gangs. It could well be that the guns were going to Loyalist paramilitary groups.'

Would this explain an intriguing conversation recorded on the afternoon of 22 July 1996, between Curtis Warren and a close friend? [NB: not Tony Bray]

'Now tell me this,' said the friend. 'Do you know your man, you were saying, erm, from the block [Bloc?] country, the…'

'Yeah, yeah, yeah.'

'Right. Well a fella asked me could I get SU-23s. Er, they're shells.'

'Yeah.'

'The heavy one, they want a, they want a, it's for the country, they want quite an amount.'

'I'll speak to them,' said Warren. 'He's on holiday at the moment, my mate here.'

This oblique exchange raises several questions. Firstly, what are SU-23 shells? There seem to be two possible answers. Sukhoi is a renowned Soviet manufacturer of military aircraft and many of its products have the prefix Su: the Su-27, the Su-35, and so on. However, there is no Su-23 listed in any military catalogue and the company itself, based in Moscow, is non-committal in the face of queries. It is unlikely in any case that Warren's friend was after aircraft components.

A more plausible – and equally disturbing – explanation is that the man wanted shells for a ZSU-23-4. According to the authoritative *Jane's Land-Based Air Defence 1999-2000*, this is a Russian-made, self-propelled, anti-aircraft gun system armed with four water-cooled 23mm cannon, which have a cyclic rate of fire of up to 1,000 rounds per minute per barrel. 'The onboard control system consists of roof-mounted Gun Dish search/tracking radar, sighting system, computer, line of sight and line of elevation stabilisation system,' says *Jane's*. Mounted on a tracked vehicle, it can bring down a jet at a distance of a mile-and-a-half. An earlier line, the ZSU-23-2, is a cruder system towed on wheels on a triangular platform; various models were built by the Russians, Bulgarians, Chinese, Egyptians, Iranians and Poles.

Secondly, who are the people from 'the country' and why would they want shells for this weapon? Could they be Irish terrorist groups? On the Nationalist side, the Irish National Liberation Army is known to have links with several of Ireland's most powerful drug lords, some of whom reside in Holland. Another alternative is that the guns were going to Loyalists. In one conversation with Tony Bray, Warren discussed a tip-off that some of their associates' houses were being bugged. Warren was confident he knew which branch of law enforcement was behind it: 'Told you for many years now. R-U-C. Telling you, not talking crap.' The RUC is, of course, the Royal Ulster Constabulary, the police force of Northern Ireland. Why would Warren be concerned about the RUC? Why would the RUC be interested in Warren? Certainly he has never been charged with gun-running or any offence linked to terrorism.

Warren also referred in phone calls to Special Branch and 'the Special people', the secretive arm of the police that provides information about extremists and terrorists to the Security Service, MI5. He seemed to take it for granted that they were investigating him. Yet not one of the many customs and police personnel that the authors have interviewed for this book has admitted Special Branch involvement; indeed several have denied it outright.

One source did admit that MI5 made a pitch to join Operation Crayfish. Military Intelligence Five, as it was originally known, is charged with protecting the UK from foreign espionage, subversion and terrorism. But in 1995 – with the IRA on ceasefire – then-Prime Minister John Major was pressing for MI5 to assist in the war against drug gangs. In his October speech to the Tory Party conference, he pointedly said that a young person was more likely to be 'killed by a drug dealer than by an enemy missile'. It was interpreted as tacit consent for MI5 to move discreetly against drugs and serious crime.

'A guy from the funny farm [*MI5*] went up to see the Crayfish top brass ,' says a source. 'He said, "What can we do for you? We can do anything you want." There had been a hiatus in the IRA situation at the time. But would they have deserted Crayfish if it blew up again? The bosses listened to what he had to say and then said, "No."'

The offer had been tempting. MI5 operatives are the acknowledged masters of long-distance surveillance, specialists at breaking and entering, bugging and the theft of documents. They have a huge budget and unrivalled gadgetry. Their methods, however, are not conducive to successful criminal prosecutions. 'There has always been a deep-rooted suspicion of MI5,' says a Crayfish officer. 'Detective work and dealing with criminals has nothing in common with James Bond stuff. They may be very thorough in their particular field but they are completely unaccountable. If we let them start riding roughshod over the way we work, we could never secure a conviction against the kind of people we target. MI5 has very little idea of how to gather evidence and gain convictions.'

The caution was well-placed. On Friday, 9 February 1996, the IRA's ceasefire came to a spectacular and bloody end when the Canary Wharf bomb exploded in London Docklands, killing two and caused many millions of pounds of damage. MI5 was criticised for not forewarning the collapse of the ceasefire. Suddenly it was back into counter-terrorism in a big way. Anti-drug and crime work slid down the priority list.

IT IS A LONG WAY from the bleak streets of Ballyfermot to the broad sands of Bondi beach. Perhaps there is no better illustration of the Liverpool mafia's global reach than the story of how it supplied Australia's biggest city – 10,000 miles away – with Ecstasy and amphetamines, the fuel of the rave generation. Gary and Andrew Murphy were two brothers who abandoned life in West Derby on the Wirral for the considerable attractions of Sydney, where they worked as casual bricklayers and labourers. They were well-acquainted with the dance scene and soon noticed the hefty prices Aussies paid for their gear. An 'E' selling for between £10–12 in Liverpool or London could fetch £25–40 in Sydney. Amphetamine at £10 a gram in the UK could bring in £35–45. If they could buy at British wholesale prices and smuggle the stuff over, it would be like shooting fish in a barrel.

It is thought that the brothers first used couriers to smuggle small amounts. Then in 1995, with the help of relatives and friends, they set up two front companies, Watermark Developments Ltd, based in Birkenhead, and Crest International, in Essex, ostensibly to export footwear. They arranged for shoes to be bought, boxed and shipped to Australia. Inside the heels were false compartments containing drugs.

In Sydney, the brothers and their runners made regular cash deposits for transfer back to England. The sums were almost always around £4,500. According to the Australian Transaction Reports Act, banks and finance houses must report cash transactions in excess of 10,000 Australian dollars; these amounts were just under that threshold. The Murphys varied the amounts, the names of the senders, collectors and the places of collection. In England their money was shuffled around domestic bank accounts, a client account handled by a firm of solicitors and cash transfers to a post office and travel agencies.

With substantial liquid capital, Watermark Developments began to acquire properties and employed an accountant to keep track of its assets. The Murphys rented a flat with views of Sydney Harbour Bridge and the Opera House. Andrew had three aliases with false documents and would use them to put his drug money through banks and travel agencies all over Australia. On his return to the UK, he would then go into the financial institutions and collect cash. The Murphys were making so much, so quickly, it was clear they would need more people to graft for them. Some made cash transfers. Others were required to pack the drugs into the shoes back at home.

In September 1995, a young Merseysider was arrested by the Australian Federal Police in possession of two kilos of fake Ecstasy tablets. He bolted and escaped along Bondi beach in his underpants, and is known to have returned to England using a false passport. In December 1995, a courier from Birkenhead was arrested by Australian customs officer at Sydney Airport who found 30,000 tabs of MDMA in a false bottom in his suitcase. He was later jailed for six years but was never connected to the Murphys. They had, however, become Crayfish targets. Officers suspected that their source of supply was Curtis Warren. But the Cocky Watchman was still missing. Where was he?

THE FALL

*Warren lost his rag and was screaming
all kinds of abuse at this man.
But Warren was making the call from his home,
on his mobile, breaking his most strict rule…*

12 GOING DUTCH

'Now he could flood the country if he wanted, or starve the streets of merchandise, forcing prices higher. He could single-handedly affect the supply and price of coke on the streets of Britain.'

A senior Crayfish officer

CURTIS WARREN stood framed in a first-floor window of his rented villa, looking out. His brown eyes scanned the surrounding fields through powerful binoculars, lingering on every bush. Beyond the garden, separated from the main road by a hedge and small dyke, lay miles of tulip beds and flat, featureless farmland. The rear and sides of the house and the gravel drive leading to a double garage were sheltered by high trees. It was a quiet, secluded residence. Only birdsong and the occasional distant train disturbed the peace.

Satisfied no-one was outside, Warren replaced the field glasses on a specially-erected stand by the window, returned to a sofa and reached for his cellphone. The silence was accentuated by the size and bareness of the house. Though its red-brick and red-tile exterior – with the nameplate 'Bakara' – would not have looked out of place in the Cheshire stockbroker belt, its sixteen rooms had little by way of furnishings or decoration. There was a large colour TV and video in one room, a personal computer in another and not much else.

Warren's 'little moonlight flit' had taken him to the Netherlands, the ideal base to oversee his worldwide web. After weeks of searching, officers traced him early in 1996 to Sassenheim, a small, anonymous town halfway between Amsterdam and The Hague. Number 53 Hoofstradt had recently changed hands for 1.2m guilders (£330,000). It was handily placed for both road and rail, the living was easy, and Warren was unknown to the local police. He felt more secure in Holland. He was sure the British police had lost his scent and he was happy to be away from the hassle of the Gang War. Above all, he had developed an irrational fear that the Merseyside Police wanted to kill him. 'It was that, more than any fear of gang rivals, that led him to leave. He wasn't scared of any of the villains in the city but the high-profile police activity was really cramping his movements,' says one officer.

Sassenheim had another attraction. It was within easy reach of Amsterdam, the sex capital of Europe. 'The lifestyle suited him. He was, to put it crudely, like a pig in shit,' says a Crayfish officer. 'He thought he was out of reach and anonymous and he had sex on tap. A typical night was work, out for a nice meal, a visit to a brothel, home, telly and bed. For someone from his background, it was probably the dream come true.'

Sex had always been an obsession of Warren's. Along with cars, gossip and drug deals, it was his main topic of conversation. With Stephanie back home in England, Cocky indulged in casual encounters with no emotional ties. Sometimes he entertained several hookers at a time but they were never allowed to interfere with his work. 'Women are for the night,' he advised his men. Sometimes he would phone Merseyside mates like Tony Bray from high-class massage parlours to gloat.

CW   *All right in here.*

TB   *Is it?*

CW   *Little bluey* [blue movie], *watching it.*

TB   *Oh dear, that's what you want, isn't it?*

CW   *Proper. Can you hear the bath going, the jacuzzi?*

TB   *Oh yeah, I can hear it. That's what you want, isn't it?*

CW   *Silly not to. Just going to get blew off.*

TB   *Best way mate, isn't it?*

'He was talking about buying a new car for when he came home and fancied a bright red 8-series BMW. He got one of his people to go down to a BMW dealership and make inquiries on price and delivery times. There was talk of a cash down payment. From this we took it that he was coming home to collect it and get back to business again on his home turf,' recalls a Crayfish officer. Despite the obvious benefits, the Crayfish team assumed Warren would soon return to England. 'We continued our interest in him but Crayfish was wider than one man. We lost all intelligence on him but even though he was in Holland, we anticipated he would continue to import drugs into this country,' says DCI Mike Keogh.

Continued seizures seemed to bear out Keogh's assessment. In January 1996, the Dutch took out a consignment of Pakistani heroin concealed in lamps. The following month, a large cannabis haul was found hidden in a secret compartment welded to the exhaust system of a DAF lorry owned by a Runcorn haulage firm. Seven men were later convicted. The load was believed to be linked to Warren. On April 1, HM Customs and Excise formed the National Investigation Service 'in response to the increasing threats to the United Kingdom from serious crime'. It merged the 1,600 officers of the various regions or investigation units into one national entity under a Chief Investigation Officer, Dick Kellaway.

In Liverpool, there had been a spate of shootings over the New Year period. In March 1996 someone tried to kill Johnny Phillips as he pulled up outside his flat on his thirty-fifth birthday with his daughter Chelsee. A gunman opened fire as they were getting out of their red BMW. 'Chelsee was in his arms when the firing started. After the first shot John threw her into the car and closed the door,' recounted his wife Maria. He took four bullets in the chest and stomach. The shooter was believed to have been an imported Irish hitman. Phillips underwent emergency surgery and was put under armed guard in hospital. He recovered remarkably quickly owing to his tremendous strength and fitness. It was said that his blood had been so thickened by steroid abuse that it saved him from bleeding to death.

The attack presaged another bloodbath. A ferocious Black Caucus associate had a fight with some of the White Clan in Childwall. A gun attack followed in a pub in Old Swan. On April 18, a Granby hit team set out on a mission. In one day, they shot a teenager four times at his home in Old Swan, wounded a man in the legs in Bootle and then headed to a street of newly-built detached houses in West Derby to take care of one of the top White Clan soldiers. He and a Caucus leader had clashed weeks earlier in the foyer of Liverpool City Magistrates Court; the Caucus man had pulled out a gun and pushed it to his rival's temple, saying, 'That's how fucking easy it would be.' Now he was coming to complete the job.

The triggermen crashed through the front door of a house and ran upstairs where they encountered a man on the landing, his frightened girlfriend behind him in the bedroom. They forced the pair to lie on the floor, then briefly discussed whether they had the right man. 'Shoot him anyway,' said one fiercely and they did: three times in his left leg, three times in the right and once in the right arm. It was a case of mistaken identity. Their victim, left twitching on a carpet of blood, was a twenty-four-year-old police constable, Stephen Hardy. He survived. The prime suspect was the most active shooter in the city. Ironically, as a teenager he had wanted to be a policeman.

On May 16, twenty-seven-year-old Mark Osu, repeatedly named by police as a main player in the Black Caucus, was arrested after a car chase. He was charged with making threats to kill and possession of a sawn-off shotgun but the case collapsed when witnesses failed to turn up. Afterwards, Osu gave an interview to the Liverpool *Daily Post*:

> I think that it is highly likely that I will be shot dead. But I can only die once. Whatever the police think of me is not the point. I am a human being with a contract killing on my life. The police have got a job to serve the public and all I say is that the police do their job without bias. Why should I pack my bags and run? I am strong

enough mentally and physically to cope with whatever happens. I had a girl who I was in love with and we had to split up because of the pressure. She was told that her throat would be cut because of me. How can a man say that to a woman? I just hope the black community now realises it can get justice. They see this as a race war. They see us as standard bearers who have repelled this attack and are still standing. But I know that there are contract killers out there somewhere who will come and try and take my life.

Warren was well out of it. Like most of the city's major criminals, he frowned on the conflict. The last thing he needed was to worry about where the next bullet was coming from. Anyway, some things on Merseyside were more important. That year there was a particularly vital football match that many of 'the boys' wanted to see. A private plane was chartered and tickets dished out. 'If you had a ground-to-air missile you could have solved the drug problem in Merseyside with one shot. Just about every major villain in the city was on that plane,' says a Crayfish source. Cocky, still in Holland, would almost certainly have approved.

A NATIONAL Criminal Intelligence Service memo shows that by 14 May 1996, the British authorities were aware that Warren was renting the Sassenheim villa with a friend called 'Tony Farrell'. They had no idea who Farrell was but knew he had travelled to Colombia several times, probably as a link man between Warren and the cartels. It suggested that the cocaine pipeline broken in Operation Singer had been re-built.

It was also becoming apparent that Warren had no immediate plans to return home and so it was decided to inform the Dutch of his presence. The approach was made by the British drug liaison officer – a link man with foreign law enforcement agencies – in The Hague. Next, a delegation flew to Holland to try to persuade the Dutch to look at his activities. At first they were reluctant; they dealt regularly with the top echelon of world crime and one more rough-arse Scouser was a low priority. 'What persuaded them to make him a target was intelligence which showed he had clear links to South America and the cartels there,' says Paul Acda. He and RCS co-ordinator Geoff Nicholls were put in touch with the elite Prisma team, a special police task force set up to investigate South American organised crime.

Its boss was Tom Driessen, a tall, rangy man with thinning hair and a phlegmatic manner. 'We have lots of contact with our British colleagues. For cocaine gangs, don't look to South America, look to our country. They use Holland as their base. Maybe that's one reason Warren moved here. The British came to us and explained how important he was. They thought that part of his criminal organisation was being moved to Holland and asked if we could help. We thought he might be in contact with one of our targets. They didn't know the name of the man, they only knew he was dealing with South America.'

The British officers allegedly had intelligence that Warren was dealing with a Colombian called 'Mr L'. Driessen had a clear suspicion who he was. 'When Tom heard what we had to say he nearly fell off his chair,' laughs one of the Crayfish delegation. 'The people we couldn't identify, well, the Dutch could. They were Prisma targets. It gave us the connection all the way through to South America.'

Driessen believed Mr L to be Luis 'Lucho' Botero, a middle-aged man from the Cali area. 'He's a powerful man. A few years ago the Police National Colombia arrested guys like Escobar and Ochoa, the first generation of Colombian drug barons. After that came a new group and Lucho was one of them. We think he's one of the ten most important Colombian drug men, and the most important guy for western Europe. Warren's relationship to Mr L was enough to give it a priority for us.'

According to Dutch sources, Botero was one of an emerging cabal from the North Valle del Cauca region, near Cali. He spent six years in prison for drug trafficking before moving to the Netherlands, where he lived with a beautiful woman from the Dutch Antilles. It is thought he operated freely for years, bringing in hundreds of kilos of cocaine in 1991 and 1992. In 1995, governments in the Andean region of South America took unprecedented steps against the cocaine trade. Just as the Medellin clan had risen and fallen, so seven of the eight top Cali leaders were caught. Men such as Botero swiftly filled the vacuum. In March 1996, Prisma officers interviewed a snack bar owner from Amsterdam who said he was under threat of death for owing a vast sum to South American gangsters. He had been responsible for smuggling cocaine into Holland, often hidden in the hulls of boats. Botero, he said, was a 'leading figure in the criminal organisation'.

Commander Driessen felt that Warren could lead him to Botero. He agreed to take up the case and on May 25 launched Operation Mix. Over the next few days, officers checked out the Sassenheim villa and other addresses and a public prosecutor applied for permission for the police to tap a number of phones used by Cocky and his associates. 'Warren was driving around Holland a lot. It's a small country. We couldn't put much surveillance on them because we thought he would see it easily. We also didn't try to put anyone into his organisation because it was too hard. To get in you would need an introduction from one of his people and it was never going to be possible. So we had to analyse the telephone conversations to see what they were up to,' says Driessen.

Warren did not yet know it, but moving to Holland would be his greatest error. Telephone taps, inadmissible as evidence in British courts, were admissible in Holland. Now every word spoken into his portie could be used against him. 'He didn't realise,' says Surveillance Mark. 'It was just ignorance. But it was the most important break we could have got.' However, under Dutch law the target of any phone intercepts must be informed after six months and then has the right to receive copies of all of the tapes. It meant they had half a year to get Warren. There was no time to waste; Operation Mix began as spring turned to summer. The first call was intercepted on Tuesday, May 28, 1996.

COCKY'S CONVERSATIONS proved almost indecipherable to the Dutch. His Scouse accent and use of nicknames was bad enough but his backslang utterly defeated the translators. The old playground code had come in useful. 'To us, backslang was amazing,' says Tom Driessen. 'They learned it in jail or on the streets but it was very clever. They also used false names or swapped names around and never give full details of locations. They'd say, "See you at the place we met that last time, you know, by the thing." We had to figure it all out.'

The Dutch were frequently bemused. When do 'lads' become 'men', they asked? One Prisma officer phoned the Crayfish team to ask where the 'Café Buyus' was.

They consulted every phone directory but could find no trace of it. It was only later that they realised Warren had said 'the café by us'. Two Regional Crime Squad detectives, DS Steve Kyle and DC Pamela Norbury, and three anonymous customs officers known as Tom, Jerry and John, were sent to Holland to help. Several of them were conversant with backslang. They received an explanation of Holland's legal process and were told not to divulge anything to their British superiors without first informing the Dutch via the DLO at the embassy, Cameron Walker.

A secure room was set aside for the listeners and an independent voice-recognition expert was consulted. 'My instructions were to listen to historical conversations and sometimes conversations in real time from various people and to type a summary in English,' said DS Kyle. 'Afterwards, my transcripts were translated into Dutch by a Dutch interpreter.' Nothing was to leave the translating room, not even scraps of paper. Kyle was to make nine trips to Holland between June 3 and July 18. He and the others listened on headphones to five or six separate mobile phones. More than 14,000 calls would be taped over the next six months and the piles of typed transcripts became known as the 'Dutch Product'.

Patterns of behaviour emerged. Warren, a late riser, made few calls in the mornings. From midday his phone traffic would hot up. He had a small corps of 'joeys' or gofers who would run him around while he made dozens of calls, sewing up deals or picking up the latest gossip. The phones were busiest during the early evening and calls continued late into the night. He travelled widely, particularly to Belgium, France and Turkey. On at least one occasion he visited Sofia, the Bulgarian capital and a favoured meeting place for East European drug clans. He arrived in a Jaguar with a bodyguard. Jags were uncommon in post-communist Bulgaria and the pair were stopped by police. Their car was taken apart but nothing was found. 'You are free to go,' said the police. Warren and his minder walked to the vehicle compound to find their expensive motor in bits, and no means of re-assembling it.

Gradually the listeners deciphered Warren's slang. A 'squirt' was a gun. Money was 'goulash' or 'tank'. A bag of cash was a 'bag of sand'. A helicopter was a 'petrol budgie' and an aeroplane a 'paraffin budgie'. Various euphemisms were used for drugs, 'lemon' being the most popular. An investigation was an 'invessy', a police inspector an 'inspessy'. Everyone had a nickname. 'Thingy' was used all the time, for everything. Much of his conversation was mundane, although the tittle-tattle he exchanged with friends did serve to keep him in touch with events back home.

One of his closest friends was Tony Bray, a rugged, happy-go-lucky sometime-doorman in Birkenhead, across the River Mersey from Liverpool. They had met through the night club scene and shared the same sense of humour. Both loved gossip and chasing girls. Bray hung out on the fringes of the underworld and occasionally got into deep water. He had once travelled to the Home Counties with a psychopathic acquaintance to rip off a drug dealer. They sold the man a block of wax for £20,000. When the dealer realised he was about to be conned, and protested, Bray's companion pulled out a gun and – to his horror – shot the man dead. Bray was innocent of the killing but served a jail term after admitting a lesser charge; his travelling companion is still (at the time of writing) on the run.

Bray spoke to Warren on the phone almost every day and would often visit him in Holland. He acted as one of Cocky's men on the ground in Liverpool, sorting out problems and reporting information. Women were an endless source of debate. Warren was forever asking friends for updates on various women he knew and Bray would give him saucy descriptions of mutual acquaintances.

TB   *Fucking little ankle chain, like a dead small denim skirt on, she's dead brown and a little white top showing all her nipples. I'm telling you, she's proper her, mate.*

CW   *Is she ready for me?*

TB   *She's ready. Oh, she was asking when you were coming home and all that.*

CW   *You liar.*

TB   *Proper that mate. I swear to God, Cock. All her hair's down, little white top on, no bra, dead tight top, like a vest showing her nips off and everything.*

CW   *Would you have her?*

TB   *Fucking hell... I tell you what Cock, she is proper, proper fucking gorgeous.*

CW   *You know I can have her any time, don't you? You know what's happening when she's goosing* [her boyfriend], *don't you? She's seeing me.*

TB   *Seeing your head on his shoulders?*

CW   *It's a fact.*

When it came to business, his contacts had strict instructions never to call from home or from cellular phones. Warren would change the subject if he felt a conversation was becoming too revealing; many of his chats would contain several minutes of apparent aimless banter with one small nugget dropped into the middle. As they gradually deciphered the jumbled code, the listeners in their room in The Hague began to learn more and more about Cocky. What they discovered was frequently astounding. One particular importation was an awesome demonstration of his influence.

CANNABIS is the most popular illegal drug and Morocco its biggest cultivator. It explains why so many British crooks are based in Spain, just a fast speedboat ride away from the African coast. By the 1990s, Moroccan resin accounted for seventy per cent of the European market. The cannabis, or 'kif', would be grown by small farmers in the northern Rif region before being cut, processed and sent across the Mediterranean in myriad ways: in motor vehicles, on ferries, by fishing vessels, yachts and light aircraft.

The northern Moroccan men who controlled the cultivation and export were known as the Tangiers cartel. Many came from poor villages, climbing to power with the help of political protection. They included Abdelaziz El Yakhloufi, who had multiple bank accounts, companies and property in Morocco, Gibraltar, Spain and Canada, owned a yacht and fifteen cars and claimed a personal friendship with Fidel Castro in Cuba; Mohammed Derkaoui, owner of half a dozen palaces and fishing vessels; Mohammed 'the Genius' Belmokhtar, of Casablanca, who specialized in transport and warehousing; and, above all, H'midou Dib – The Wolf – a former fisherman who had shipped hundreds of tonnes of hash to Europe from the late 1960s and owned his own port. Dib's accomplices included top government and police officials. He was once labelled in court 'the godfather of all Moroccan traffickers'.

In December 1995, under increasing pressure from France and Spain, King Hassan II launched a brutal crackdown on the hash trade. 'The Moroccans dealt with it in their own way,' says a senior British customs investigator. 'They called it intensive interrogation. It would be known in the West as torture. It was medieval but it brought results. They targeted the entrepreneurs, the farmers, the shippers and the middlemen. They burned fields of cannabis. For three months no one could get a single kilo out of Morocco. It was as if the cannabis business had closed down overnight.' More than 300 suspects were prosecuted. 'Four months were enough to jail and incapacitate all drug barons,' said Morocco's parliamentary investigative committee on narcotics.

Yet incredibly, at a time when barely a joint moved out of the country, Curtis Warren managed to extricate over 400 kilos of resin. It was the smuggling equivalent of the Great Escape and again bore the hallmarks of his cell structure. There was an organiser, a front company, an overseas fixer, a regular driver and several odd-job men. The front company was Sight and Sound, a London-based firm set up ostensibly to lease TV, electrical and sound systems to film crews working in Spain. Its boss was south Londoner John Model who, using a false identity, sent trucks back and forth to the Costa del Sol with equipment. Each time, they returned with large amounts of Moroccan cannabis, concealed by an ingenious method.

Model, however, could not keep his mouth shut, especially after a few drinks. Undercover officers regularly followed him into pubs near his London home and heard him talking about smuggling, concealments and large sums of money. For the surveillance team it was rewarding but gruelling work. 'You would go to work on Monday and might not come home again until a week on Wednesday. You had no idea how long you would be away. We regularly did thirty-six hours without a break and I once did six weeks without a day off,' says one.

GOING DUTCH

In the summer of 1996, several of Model's gang flew to Malaga to organise collection of the shipment Warren had smuggled out of Morocco. It was driven back in a lorry carrying video screens. A joint police-customs team found the lorry in a warehouse and arrested five men, including Model. But after a thorough trawl, they came up empty-handed. 'We searched the whole of the lock-up and the truck with the TV sets in but could see nothing,' says a police officer. 'We thought we'd missed the load, that they'd managed to offload it without us seeing or something had gone wrong with out intelligence. Then one of the customs boys took a look at the TVs.'

Four banks of television screens made up a large 'video wall' of the kind used in pubs and clubs. 'They look strange to me,' said the customs officer, and started ripping one open. 'We shouted for him to stop because he might be damaging a legitimate load but he pulled away the back and front to reveal the drugs inside. They had constructed a special box to hold the drugs which would allow the TV set to be used and not be damaged. They had also replaced the glass screen with one of perspex. It was a very clever concealment.' Model was later jailed for six years for smuggling 436 kilos of cannabis. The main organiser, fellow Londoner Theothoules Ioannu, received eight years. The eventual place of distribution was to have been Liverpool.

As a postscript, the tough action in Morocco was not accompanied by any financial incentive for farmers to change their crops. Record rainfalls in 1996 meant that despite the crackdown, by the end of the year the amount of land being used to grow cannabis had actually increased by ten per cent.

ONE OF the biggest puzzles for the Dutch and the British was the identity of Tony Farrell, Warren's hard-looking sometime-housemate. Then they found out. His real name was Stephen Mee and his criminal record made even Warren's look tame. Born in 1958 in Manchester, he was both violent and an incorrigible thief and by his late teens had picked up a string of convictions. In the 1980s he appeared before courts in Manchester, Oldham, Bolton and Bury for offences ranging from burglary and handling stolen goods to theft and obtaining property by deception. In 1984 he was jailed for six months for his part in a stolen car ring and. On his release he picked up further convictions for handling stolen property and twice absconded from bail.

In 1988, he turned up in Holland, where he was jailed for nine months for grievous assault. Somewhere along the way, he had learned to fly a plane and made some heavy contacts. In 1992, Mee was the lynchpin of a scheme to bring cannabis and Colombian cocaine into Manchester, probably for conversion to crack. The drugs were held on the Dutch Caribbean island of Curaçao for distribution by couriers, preferably couples with children who travelled as tourists. The operation was infiltrated by undercover agents and Mee was caught.

In April 1993, he was on his way to Manchester Crown Court in a prison van for sentencing when it was hijacked by a gang on the M62. Mee was freed and disappeared. The court sentenced him to twenty-two years in his absence. By coincidence, it was that escape which had caused Warren's trial on the Operation Singer charges to be moved from Newcastle to Manchester [see Chapter 7]. Now Mee had turned up at last. He was known to have flown to Venezuela and piloted at least two private flights to Colombia in 1996. On at least one occasion he was secretly videoed by Dutch police and was plainly acting as Warren's intermediary.

As a bulk buyer, Cocky could barter for huge discounts. He might pay £2,000 a kilo for heroin from the godfathers of the Turkish *Maffya*, or £3,000 a kilo for cocaine direct from South America. Criminal gangs prepared to buy from him in Amsterdam and arrange their own transport to the UK would pay £17–19,000 a kilo. If they wanted Warren to ship, they paid £25,000. The bent hauliers or coach operators he used received around £1,500 a kilo for powder or £500 for cannabis resin for taking the loads. Once cut, mixed and sold to addicts and users, the drugs would realise around £80,000 a kilo.

'Curtis had become one of the most dangerous people in the business in Europe because he had direct contacts with the Cali Cartel and the Turks,' says a senior Crayfish officer. 'Only six or seven people in Europe have these kind of links. Curtis was one of only two in northern Europe, consequently he leapt in the eyes of everyone trying to fight drugs. Now he could bring in hundreds of kilos of cocaine directly from Colombia on his own terms and flood the country if he wanted, or store it elsewhere in Europe and starve the streets of merchandise, forcing prices higher. He could single-handedly affect the supply and price of coke on the streets of Britain.'

DESPITE the now multi-national operation to trap him, Curtis Warren did not exist as far as the British public was concerned. His name had barely been mentioned in either the national or local media since the Singer trial because he had kept such a low profile. But journalists were beginning to take an interest. In June 1996, the fearless Irish newspaper reporter Veronica Guerin was shot dead while sitting in her car at traffic lights outside Dublin. Guerin had been investigating organised crime and had infuriated a ruthless drug boss with her tenacity. In the wake of her death, a group of British and Irish newspapers vowed to continue her work in exposing drug barons.

One of those who took that pledge seriously was John Sweeney, chief reporter of the *Observer*. 'I first came across Liverpool's equivalent of Al Capone while on the trail of the Irish heroin barons who ordered the murder of... Veronica Guerin,' he would later write. 'He was a heroin baron and the main cocaine wholesaler for northern Europe, a man more feared than named... That year in Liverpool I started asking questions about Warren. One cop, as tough as they come, said: "Listen. I go against Republican terrorists. And I would not go against people like Cocky unless I had the full support of the job [*the police*], and even then I'd be fucking worried."'

Sweeney did not include Warren's name in his subsequent report on the Dublin-Irish drug axis. There was a clear feeling that the Cocky Watchman was on the verge of becoming untouchable. In the middle of July, Warren took a chance and returned to Liverpool. He visited his father – then quite ill – in Toxteth and was also spotted 'over the water' on the Wirral. Merseyside detectives, unaware of Operation Crayfish, tried to pinpoint him but failed.

Warren was never noted for violence but clearly the operation was dangerous. Wiretaps revealed discussions about weapons. In one phonetap Warren was caught giving orders to a henchman.

CW   *You'd better get round to that Jamie's after and smash his kipper in.*

TB	*Oh I'm going round there.*
CW	*Don't let him talk his way out of it, you know.*
TB	*Oh I know. He's not going to. I'm going to hammer him.*
CW	*Little faggot.*

'On another occasion we heard Warren saying he has hurt his hand because he had hit someone the day before and it was so hard he'd damaged his hand and he had to go to hospital to get it looked at,' recalls Tom Driessen. 'This was the way he was. He wasn't concerned with the damage he'd done to the other person, just his hand. I think violence for him was a very common thing, he didn't think much about using it. It's not just what he said but the way he said it. It's just like he was talking about the weather.'

Warren's injured hand put him in a bad mood and would cause him problems for days afterwards, as he complained to Tony Bray in a late night phone call to England.

CW	*Oh dear me. Fucking hand's bladdered mate.*
TB	*Is it? How bad?*
CW	*Oh, bad.*
TB	*Be sore that mate for about ten days, I'll tell you.*
CW	*Fucking hell, tell me about it.*
TB	*I bet you it's worse than last night, isn't it?*
CW	*Yeah. You know that aching pain?*
TB	*Oh, like a toothache mate. Fucking horrible.*
CW	*Telling you.*

Warren went for a tetanus jab but his knuckles ballooned. 'Me fucking hand's like Popeye's,' he moaned to Bray. His friend dished out some homespun advice.

TB   *You want to go and buy a bag of frozen peas and put them in the freezer and put them on tonight when you are watching telly.*

CW   *And what happens?*

TB   *It just fucking hurts when you put it on but it sorts it out. It takes all the swelling out of it.*

CW   *What do you do, put your hand in the peas?*

TB   *No, just put the bag on top of your hand when it's freezing.*

Several days later, he was back at the hospital. 'I had to go again this morning, they opened it up again and I've got to go back again tomorrow morning to see how it looks.' Warren punching people in the mouth was not a big concern for the Dutch police. But when his conversations turned more sinister, they had to reconsider their hands-off approach.

'He also talked on the phone about killing people, criminals, business colleagues,' says Tom Driessen. 'They were planning it. It would have been a big problem for us. When someone's life is in danger we have to act. We planned preventative measures but after a day we heard him say, "Oh don't worry, other things have happened now, let's not waste time on that". So nothing happened. It shows you how he thinks, one day he's planning to end someone's life, the next he says it doesn't matter any more. It's very hard to anticipate the next move of someone like this.'

In Holland, however, Warren had become lax. 'He felt so confident that he was, to all intents and purposes, untouchable that he began to break all his own rules,' says a Crayfish officer. 'One conversation was very memorable, Curtis was blowing his top at one of his men back in Liverpool for using his home telephone to make a sensitive call. He lost his rag and was screaming all kinds of abuse at this man. But he was making the call from his home, on his mobile, breaking his most strict rule – and slagging someone off for doing exactly what he was doing.'

In a midnight phone call to his mate Tony Bray on June 24, the name 'Elmore' cropped up in an otherwise routine – for them – chat about friends, enemies and women. Three weeks later, the hunt for Curtis Warren was to take the most extraordinary twist of all.

BENT COP

A corrupt police officer is

the very worst kind of criminal

Sir James Sharples

former Merseyside Chief Constable

THE Venue in Tuebrook, Liverpool, is the kind of nightclub that draws in clientele on off-peak evenings, when clubbers don't want to trek into the city centre. So it was that Philip Glennon Junior arrived there on a sultry Sunday in mid-July 1996. Glennon, a thirty-four-year-old father of three, was a little the worse for drink. First he argued with the doorman over the paltry three pounds entrance fee, then he caused trouble inside. Bottles and punches were thrown and Glennon Jnr was turfed into the street. He produced a gun, pointed it at doorman Joey McCormick and pulled the trigger. The weapon seemed to click but jammed and Glennon ran off, chased by the bouncers. Two police constables issuing parking tickets nearby joined the pursuit and Glennon was brought down and arrested, though not before he had allegedly pointed the gun at one of the officers. Two of the doormen gave statements to the police and Glennon was charged with two counts of attempted murder.

Across the North Sea, a telephone rang. It was an urgent message for Curtis Warren. *Steph's brother has been nicked.* Philip Glennon Jnr was the brother of Cocky's girlfriend, Stephanie, and the son of his friend Phillip Glennon. Without waiting to be asked, Warren took matters into his own hands. At precisely 4.46 PM on Tuesday, 15 July 1996, he palmed his mobile phone, keyed in the international dialling code for the United Kingdom, and set about perverting the course of justice.

The recipient of his call, a go-between named Bobby, was driving through Merseyside. He cradled his car phone against his shoulder as he slowed to the kerb.

CW   *Do us a favour.*
B   *I'm just pulling over to the side here now.*
       Go 'ead.
CW   *Give Philly a ring.*
B   *Who?*
CW   *Ph-ab-illy.* [backslang for Philly]
B   *Yeah?*
CW   *Cos his son's been nicked over something.*
       John Mac's brother has made a statement,
       two of the doormen.
B   *Is he nicked now, is he?*
CW   *Yeah. They've made statements. Just give*
       him a ring, see what he wants.
B   *All right then. I will go to Philly's as soon as*
       I've come from here.
CW   *All right then.*

By early evening, Warren had also located John McCormick, the brother of bouncer Joey. John was clearly unimpressed that his sibling had made a statement to the 'bizzies'. He was anxious to put over his side of the story.

CW   *All right, lad?*

JM   *I've just got hold of him. It's not looking good you know.*

CW   *No?*

JM   *Listen to me for a second. Are you listening to me?*

CW   *Go 'ead lad.*

JM   *You know what I'm like. I've fucking, I've hit the roof on him. He's coming here in ten minutes so I'd like you to phone back. And I'm going to say it to him while you are there. Whatever happens to him after it, if he doesn't drop the charges, is his fault.*

CW   *Yeah, all right lad.*

JM   *Because I mean like, I don't fucking, I don't go for all that, you know that. I said to him, 'Why?' He said, 'They shot at me head and all that.' I said, 'You still don't run to the bizzies' Do you get me?*

CW   *Yeah.*

JM   *I'm wound up on him.*

Warren was tough as teak but also a diplomat. He knew when to soothe sore feelings. Instead of berating McCormick, his tone was placatory.

CW   *Listen, don't even say nothing to him like that, John. It's not like I'm going to fall out with your fucking family, is it?*

JM   *Listen, I don't care. If that's the way his
attitude is, I'm not going to start falling out
with the lads.*

CW   *Well, he's angry, he's angry at the moment,
isn't he?*

JM   *Well he's taken the divvy doormen's side.
I've just got him on the portable and he's
shouting his mouth off. I said, 'Look, you
don't run to the fucking bizzies'… I am
fucking upset at what he's done. I'm not
having it all over the place that one of my
brothers is running to the bizzies.*

Warren laughed. 'I'll ring you back,' he said. Fifteen
minutes later, he called again. The aggrieved Joey
McCormick had arrived and took the phone. Again,
Warren was sympathetic. He had decided to let the
doorman blow off steam.

CW   *What happened?*

Joey   *Basically, he fucking shot me twice like.*
        [NB: in fact the gun was defective and
        could not fire] *Er, put the gun to me head.*

CW   *Yeah?*

Joey   *Shot it. It jammed, whatever, the fucking
thing went off, then he run down the street,
had another go at me but the gun went in
the air. And he tried to fucking kill me.
They got him, they got the gun and
everything.*

CW   *Yeah.*

Joey   *He's a fucking prick. I've made a
statement, yeah. I can't hear with me ears?
The cunt went to kill me twice. John has fell
out with me here but I don't know the cunt*

from Adam. I didn't argue with him or
nothing. What's he want from me?

CW I don't know, mate.

Joey Am I supposed to just drop it now and say,
'You're all right,' and just tap him on the
head?

CW No.

Joey I'm not after big fucking wages and nothing
like that. You know, what am I supposed to
do?

CW Sort it out the fucking way he tried to do it
to you, really. I mean, you know.

Joey I'm forty-three, Curtis. I'm fucking no kid.
This cunt I don't know from fucking Adam
comes in the fucking club. His argument
was all over because he didn't want to pay
the three quid, apparently. He goes upstairs,
smashes two bottles, wants to fight everyone
with the neck of the bottles, so he gets lashed
out. I come round the corner, I'm in the
office and sees all the doormen spread out
everywhere.

CW Joe, I'm not disputing anything you say,
mate.

Joey I need no favours. I'm in no mood for any
fucking favours, Curtis. Here's our John.

With that, Joey McCormick stomped off. John picked
up the phone.

JM I've fell out with him. He can fuck off.

CW No, just let him calm down. All I've just
said to him is, look, just let the plod sort it
out, cos the plod have seen what they've
seen, let them sort it out.

JM	*But I've got my principles. Put it this way, I would have preferred them coming up and saying, 'Let's go and fucking do him'*
CW	*I just said that to Joey, just deal with it however but don't use the plod.*
JM	*You know, he's a divvy doorman who works on the door and he's listening to all the divvy doormen and all the poxy pricks behind the scenes. Do you know? There is no sense in it.*
CW	*The only gain is a bad name, innit?*
JM	*A bad name and probably problems. Because the kid's not going to be happy with it and the kid's old fella's not going to be happy with it.*
CW	*Well, he's not happy, is he? You know what I mean?*
JM	*How is he making sense when he's getting someone nicked and he's got no gains whatsoever? I mean there's no happy ending, is there?*
CW	*Well, he will calm down, won't he?*
JM	*I hope so. But there is no fucking happy ending out of it, is there? I can understand if there was a happy ending. The only end is the blacklist for him.*
CW	*All I just said to him then is that if the plod have seen it, leave the plod with it. You know, no one can sort the plod.*
JM	*He come in here fucking hyped up, saying, 'You're taking their fucking side.'… You know there is no sense in it, Curt, and I feel a cunt.*
CW	*No prob. He will calm down in a few days and talk about it. I'm going to be home this*

> week and I'll come and talk to your Joey
> with you. I'll just calm him down, you
> know what I mean.

JM *Well, I don't think it's nice for you to be*
showing your face on these scenes here cos
half of the things that go off get put down to
you, don't they?

CW *Yeah.*

JM *You have only ever done me favours, you*
have never done me no harm. So I will
always stick with you.

Though his brother was the injured party, John McCormick knew the score. Nobody fucked with Curtis Warren.

The Venue incident was minor in the scheme of things for an international drugs broker with a near stranglehold on the UK cocaine market but Cocky had a fine attention to detail. On July 16, three days after the shooting, Phillip Glennon Snr finally reached him on his mobile in Holland. He said the doormen were dropping the charges against his son.

CW *Oh they will. I said that. I spoke to them*
last night, didn't I.

PG *But do you know what? He* [Joey
McCormick] *is trying to come over as a*
good fella, you know?

CW *Yeah.*

PG *And he wouldn't have gone through with it*
and things like that. But to be honest with
you, if you see what they have got on paper.

CW *Yeah.*

PG *...it was them that held him till the police*
come. Held him down. There was five of

> *them after him and one of them says, 'I*
> *tackled him and held him till the police*
> *come'. You want to read it Curtis,*
> *honestly… But I have got to go along, you*
> *understand… If his one* [charge of
> attempted murder] *goes out the window*
> *then he's only on one, which probably like*
> *halves the sentence. So I'm happy there.*
> *But honestly, what dogs.*

CW   *Well, I know what they are like. Fucking*
      doormen. They're doormen, aren't they?

Even if the doorman had recanted their statements, that still left the problem of the police. Two officers had apprehended the younger Glennon and one of them, Gary Titherington, alleged he had been shot at. Obviously Warren could not persuade them to change their statements. *No one can sort the plod*, he had told John McCormick. Or could they?

A day later, Warren's friend Tony Bray made contact with a mutual acquaintance, 'Big John' Newton. Later described in court as 'a likeable conman, a bit of a rogue', Newton was known to be friendly with a Merseyside Police detective. The officer knew all about Warren and reportedly thought he was 'a nice lad'. Was it possible, asked Bray, that he could help them out?

Late in the evening of July 18, the British customs transcriber known as Jerry picked up on a reference to 'Elly' in one of Warren's phone calls to Tony Bray.

TB   [John Newton] *was saying he's been*
      talking to Elly. He's going to go and see
      Elly. He said I had to try and get in touch
      with you. Do you know [names a White
      Clan member]*?'*

CW   *Yeah.*

TB   *They've bugged his phone and Elly said*
     they heard [him] talking about trying to slot
     [kill] you. They were going to try and slot
     you and it was only about ten days ago.

CW   *Yeah? Daft, aren't they?*

TB   *Fucking dogs mate, aren't they? He's seeing*
     Elly tomorrow and he's going to have a good
     talk to him and find out everything he can.
     He said tell the Cock I'll do anything he
     wants me to do.

Bray said, 'Elmore was asking about you, are you all right and that. No-one knows where you are... Aye, you're liked by the Chief Super, son.'

'Mad that, innit.'

In fact Elly was a detective chief inspector not a chief superintendant. His full name was Elmore Davies and he was not just any DCI but a former deputy head of the drugs squad, with contacts throughout Merseyside Police.

IT TOOK a television documentary to turn Elmore Davies into a minor celebrity, but 'the job' was always his stage. How he played to the gallery, ad-libbing and cracking irreverent asides. Elly, his police colleagues agreed, was good value, a natural centre of attention. But too many disappointments had begun to eat away at him after thirty years in the force, and too many beers and late-night curries had left him bloated. In a barbed profile, the *Observer* newspaper would christen him the Fat Detective and portray him 'a classic copper's copper, a rolypoly Freemason with a medallion, a smudge of a moustache, the belly of a Pygmy hippopotamus and a heart of fool's gold'.

Davies joined Merseyside Police force as a teenage cadet in 1964, became a constable in Birkenhead and within two years was appointed to the CID. As a young detective he helped to trap the legendary Tommy Comerford. He became a detective sergeant in 1985 and a detective chief inspector in 1989, and was selected for a plum secondment to the British West Indies, using his experience to combat the narcotics trade. He spent two years on the Turks and Caicos Islands, a British dependent territory, and came back with the story of how he had arrested Roberto Escobar Gaviera, a close relative of Pablo Escobar, doyen of the Medellin Cartel. Gaviera was given five life sentences in the United States.

On his return, Davies was made deputy head of the Merseyside drugs squad. His final post was as crime manager of Tuebrook police station, in a crime-ridden patch of Liverpool. While he undoubtedly had the respect of many of his colleagues, some among the top brass questioned his methods and doubted his suitability for further advancement. 'Elly had done well in the police force but as a DCI was above his level. I do not mean this to be nasty but that is the way it is. Anyone who knows him knew that from the way he operated,' said one fellow officer.

Two days after the first mention of Davies's name on the wiretaps, Warren instructed Bray to offer him £20,000 to steal the gun seized outside the Venue from the police strongroom. It was the most outrageous suggestion but Warren's tone was matter-of-fact, as though corrupting a senior police officer was no more significant than ordering a takeaway.

By now the listening team in The Hague had figured out who Elly was. They knew the information was dynamite. Det Sgt Steve Kyle knew that by the rules laid down, he was allowed to pass the information only to the liaison officer Cameron Walker who, in turn, would tell the Dutch police. It would then be for the Dutch, if they wished, to relay the news back to Britain. It was a convoluted route but one which had to be followed; if it was breached, it could jeopardise any future prosecution.

Kyle says he alerted Walker on July 19. Defence barristers would later claim that someone also tipped off a senior police officer on the Crayfish team in England. If true, this could have been illegal under Dutch law. Shrouded in public interest immunity, it is impossible to get at the truth. Certainly by July 23, Det Supt Geoff Nicholls from the North West Regional Crime Squad was briefing his colleague Mike Keogh about rumours of high-level corruption within Merseyside Police.

Davies did not steal the gun from the strongroom. It had been sent for forensic tests. On July 22, Bray had more news. He and Cocky would speak six times over the next four hours as the conspiracy thickened.

TB   *Now listen very carefully. That gun was incapable of firing. So what your bird's dad must do today is get onto his solicitors straight away and say you want an independent body to check the gun. Because it's a decommissioned gun. Someone's tried to bore it out to make it like a real one but the bullet's jammed in it. When he pressed the first one, it jammed. When he pressed the second one, it's all jammed up.*

CW   *Yeah.*

TB   *Get an independent body to look at that gun. Then they'll drop the charges on the two attempted murders. They won't do him*

	on it unless he admits he was trying to kill them. They're just trying it on with him… He has to say he bought it as a replica pistol and all he intended to do was frighten them. And they'll have to drop them two charges.
CW	*No problem.*
TB	*But listen, the fella who's in charge of it is an inspector, but Elly's the main man. But he'll want some dough today.*
CW	*How much?*
TB	*Well, I don't know, but if you come across with some dough he can get all the statements on everyone who's said anything. One of the bobbies has fucked up in his statement. It's up to Elly whether they go ahead with it or not. He can fuck it off properly. What shall we give him, Cock?*
CW	*Give him two grand.*
TB	*Yeah?*
CW	*Tell him if the charges get dropped he can have another eighteen grand. And tell him I don't want them opposing bail. I want him out on bail on his next appearance.*

Warren drove a hard bargain. Bray had another important piece of news. 'Tell Steph's dad not to say fuck all on his phone in his house. Special Branch are right on that.' Shortly afterwards, Warren spoke to the elder Glennon on what he thought was a safe line. He explained about the forensic tests and said he had sent a mate to pay £2,000 to 'the plod in charge of the case'. Glennon said he was going to pay £50,000 to the doormen to drop their evidence. Warren exploded.

CW	*No. Don't give it them.*

PG   *Well, I've agreed. And I've got their*
     [statements] *off them.*
CW   *Don't give them it.*

Glennon changed the subject. He was clearly unhappy with his son. 'He's got to be a crank for what he done.'

'It's just the way it is,' said Warren. 'How many fellas have you been arguing with and hit but if you'd had a tool on you, you'd have used it?'

'Yeah, but he's done a ridiculous thing,' said Glennon. 'He knows that. It didn't fire so I'm happy about that, or he'd have had no chance, there were too many witnesses. But things are in motion. I think things are going along well to be honest, better than we thought.'

On July 23, Bray was back on the phone. The police station where the investigation was based had apparently been raided by outside officers. 'The special people went in today. Pulled the inspector… they took all the files and everything.' They had picked up rumours of a plot to 'buy a plod'. It meant that at least one of their phones was bugged.

Warren was furious. 'I keep fucking warning youse and warning youse, don't I? See what I mean about the names, lad? You won't fucking listen, will you?' The irony was not lost on the officers eavesdropping Warren's conversations. Bray told Warren what one of the investigating officers had said about him: 'If he gets his claws in it we are all in shit street. He's got more money than soft Joe, so if he starts wanting to start throwing it around we don't know who the fucking hell to trust.'

They speculated that the tap was on Glennon.

'Be careful son, I'm telling you,' said Warren.

THE INVESTIGATION of Elmore Davies began at a briefing at the Merseyside Police headquarters in Canning Place, overlooking the Albert Dock. Present were Assistant Chief Constable Paul Acres, DCI John Mawer of the Force Intelligence Bureau, Paul Acda and Colin Gurton from HM Customs, DCI Mike Keogh from the North West Regional Crime Squad and Detective Superintendent Philip Jones. It was high-powered and a little awkward.

'We were given details about what Davies had been doing,' DS Jones later testified. 'It was alleged the middleman acting between Davies and Warren was John Newton. Their desire was to get rid of the attempted murder charge. We believed that £2,000 had been paid by John Newton, £8,000 was in the offing and was about to be paid. A further £10,000 was to be paid if Philip Glennon Junior got off the charge and we were also told that Phillip Glennon Senior had agreed to pay £50,000 to the bouncers for them to withdraw their statements. It was described as A1 intelligence, that is to say, a high degree of accuracy at source and of content. The recruitment of an officer of the rank of Davies as far as Merseyside Police was concerned was catastrophic.'

Jones was asked to head a secret inquiry to trap Davies; it would be called Operation Admiral. He handpicked a dozen officers. 'It was stressed that there was presently an on-going operation in Holland into Curtis Warren. They wanted us to be extremely careful and covert. We did things like vehicle checks, what rest days Davies had, what inquiries he was on. Elmore Davies had extensive experience. He had involvement in the management of serious crimes and investigations such as murders.'

Davies was given the codename Nixon after the former American president. No trace was found in his bank accounts of the £2,000 but Jones remained suspicious. He was also concerned about the security of the files and witnesses in the Venue case and about the fact that Davies wanted to make John Newton a registered informant, which would give the two an excuse to meet regularly and possibly collude.

On September 4 came a fresh twist. John Newton was out of the loop; there was a new middleman. The wiretappers picked up a conversation involving Warren, Bray and a man called Mick Ahearne, a close friend and former flatmate of Elly's.

TB   *Mick's here. He wants to have a quick word with you.*

CW   *Hello?*

MA   *Hiya mate*

CW   *All right Mick*

MA   *How are you?*

CW   *Not too bad.*

MA   *Right, listen. I had a meeting last night with you-know-who.*

CW   *Yeah.*

MA   *We will refer to him as Piglet, all right?*

CW   *Yeah, yeah.*

MA   *I've sorted it out after a good hour's deliberation, okay. I've swung him round to, he's looking forward to meeting now. Basically I'd rather talk to you face to face but... what he was frightened of, his words were 'Do you think he's trying to set me up?' I said what the fucking hell would he want to do that for, he doesn't need to do that, you know what I mean?*

CW   *Yeah.*

MA	*So he said what will happen is that he wants to meet you somewhere just into North Wales. Somewhere where it's big, wide, open. He said, 'I'll get out of the car, he can fucking frisk me down as long as I can do the same to him.'*
CW	*Yeah.*
MA	*And then we can go for a walk, chat and talk as long as he wants. And sort things out. How is that?*
CW	*Sound, Mick.*
MA	*So what I am going to do, I am going to make sure everything is kosher and that you are happy and everything. I'm going to pick him up on the day and then ring you and say, 'Hey, look, we are here'. And then come along, okay. But he said you must be on your own.*
CW	*Yeah, yeah, all right.*
MA	*But as far as anyone's concerned there is only you, me and Piglet who knows about it… cos he is fucking paranoid, right. But I've swung it anyway. I was with him two hours last night.*
CW	*Yeah, nice one Mick… I owe you one for that.*
MA	*No, not a problem, don't worry about that. But, er, anyway, that's it, okay.*

Few would have recognised Ahearne's name but millions of British television viewers knew him as Warrior, a star of the popular show *Gladiators*. At 6 ft 5 in and twenty stone, his body honed by workouts, Ahearne cut an impressive figure. He had grown up on a council estate in St Helens. Other youths he knew became petty crooks.

'I refused to go that way,' he once told an interviewer. 'My mum instilled in me that it wasn't the way to go. I did my own thing and it turned out to be right.' He played rugby for England under-19s, was a Mr Universe contestant and worked occasionally as a nightclub bouncer to supplement his income.

He met Elly Davies in 1992, shortly after he had broken into television and the cycle of pantomime appearances and charity events it brought. They were introduced by John Newton, who was acting as Ahearne's driver at the time. After Davies was divorced from his second wife, Ahearne moved into his flat. They could be seen socialising in pubs and clubs. 'Mike came round for a shower and stayed for eleven months because he found out I was a good cook,' joked Davies.

Even his friends called Ahearne 'just a big dope with muscles'. Nevertheless, once Det Supt Jones had been told of the latest development, Warrior joined Davis at the centre of the investigation. Police officers carried out surveillance with a view to installing electronic probes into their homes.

The Dutch phone taps were now more important than ever. They were providing a wealth of intelligence about British crime, though the details were strictly controlled by the Dutch. It emerged, for example, that Johnny Phillips had become uncontrollable. To make matters worse, he was abusing a drug which led to psychosis, as Tony Bray reported:

TB   *He's on the real heavy thing.*
CW   *Charlied up?* [Charlie is a euphemism for cocaine]
TB   *No, the one worse than that.*
CW   *Rocks?*

TB   *Yeah, do you know when you crack
        something?*
CW   *Oh yeah.*
TB   *He's on that. His head's properly gone.*

Phillips on steroids was bad news; Phillips on crack was
a nightmare. Bray said he had been threatening an
acquaintance of theirs who owed money. 'Johnny's doing
his head in. He hasn't been home, he's been sleeping in
his car, Johnny's phoning him up at seven o'clock in the
morning saying, "I'm going to kill you, get my fucking
money."'

Another acquaintance was thinking of checking
himself into a psychiatric unit to escape because Johnny
was after him. His crime was to owe Warren and Phillips
money. Warren had no sympathy. 'He knows he's fucked
up falling out with me, doesn't he? Idiot. He hasn't got
a clue how close he could be to getting hurt.' To owe
Warren and not pay up was a cardinal sin. 'One thing
you never did was piss about with his money,' says
Surveillance Mark. 'And people generally didn't, because
he looked after them well. There was no need to dip
into the till.'

The tapes also revealed that members of the White
Clan were looking for Phillips – and Warren. Towards
the end of July, several of them entered a shop where
some of Warren's friends hung out. One opened his
jacket to reveal a revolver.

'Tell him [*Warren*] he's top of my list,' said the
gunman. 'I'm going to fucking do him.'

Another one chipped in. 'Tell him he's mine. I'm
going to do him.'

When told of the incident, Warren was unruffled.
'[*They*] ain't gonna do nothing. There's no sense
worrying about them. They're just fucking daft cos they

know I'm away. Just in there blowing steam. Well, let them carry on.'

The next update he received suggested matters were getting a little more serious. Bray brought word that the Dingle mob had tried to hire hitmen from Ireland to shoot Warren and one of his Granby friends, nicknamed Boo-Boo. The news apparently came from police phone taps and had been passed on by Elmore Davies. 'They fucking heard on the phone, they know for certain the [*White Clan*] approached the Pads to get you and the Boo-Boo shot,' said Bray. 'He said either they couldn't raise the funds or it was a complete fuck up or it got blocked.'

Warren was planning to get his retaliation in first. It involved guile rather than force. One of the White Clan was holed up in a caravan park. Bray had a suggestion:

TB *Do you know that little caravan place?*
CW *Yeah.*
TB *Big J's mate said, if it can be done, he'll put a jalopy there with some stuff in it. You know what I mean? Squirts [guns].*
CW *Yeah.*
TB *He'll find out what number caravan it is. If he can do that he'll nick them on it, saying it's theirs.*

Later:

TB *The other fella said if you put something in a jalopy...*
CW *Yeah.*
TB *He'll let you know what number the van [caravan?] is and they'll fucking n-ab-ick [nick] them on it.*
CW *Just p-ab-ut [put] it outside like?*

TB   *Yeah, or just put it on the site… he said, well, you know, don't put it outside anywhere on the road they're on. Because he said they wouldn't put it outside their own fucking thing anyway. He said, 'And then we'll nick them on it.'*

CW   *Ask him how many things he wants, though.*

TB   *I'll ask him… You know when he mentioned the, er, the 'Sem' [Semtex].*

CW   *What did he say when you mentioned that?*

TB   *Oh, he's fucking made up. He said, 'Fucking hell, what, as soon as you like on that.'*

CW   *Did he, yeah?*

TB   *He said, 'Bring it on as soon as you like, too soon's never too early,' he was saying and all this… Imagine the pat, the pat on the back he'll get… It's never been found [in Liverpool], never any of that been found. He said his mate's got you down as fucking proper.*

CW   *Yeah?*

TB   *Yeah. He said, 'Oh, they've got you down as proper, proper fucking major.'*

On 24 August, 1996, an ambulance crew was called to a flat on the edge of Toxteth. A loaded gun lay near the entrance. There was blood on the door and carpet and the body of a man on the floor inside. The paramedics tried to revive him, but there was nothing they could do. Detectives arrived soon afterwards, confident from the address that they knew who it was. Someone had finally caught up with Johnny Phillips.

A post mortem examination failed to find the exact cause of death. His family were convinced he had been murdered but it appears that Phillips, body builder and fitness fanatic, had been jogging earlier that day and had suffered a massive cardiac arrest on his return. His heart was grotesquely swollen through steroid abuse and could take no more.

There was no sign of a struggle but the family's solicitor, Robert Broudie, told the *Guardian*, 'This was a suspicious death... A window in the room where he was found was open and there was a large amount of money missing as well as his wedding ring. The interior of the flat appeared to have been ransacked.'

Phillips's funeral was another impressive affair. Two hearses – one for the coffin, one for the masses of wreaths – and nine stretched limousines led the cortège to a private requeim mass at St Bernard's Catholic church in Toxteth. It was monitored by a large police presence, including a helicopter buzzing overhead. Along the way, it passed the site of the now bulldozed Cheers bar.

Warren missed the funeral. It would have been foolish to return to Liverpool. He knew that his unpredictability was a great asset in avoiding capture. His lifestyle was low key for a gangster. He had no interest in territory or petty pride and saw himself as tricky and enigmatic. His new police source had helpfully revealed details of a Merseyside Police operation codenamed Spigot to get him.

TB   *That's on-going, that one.*

CW   *How come? I haven't been home for, fucking how long?*

TB   *I know but it's still on-going – they were aware you were hanging about and then you just fucked off.*

CW   *What did they say?*

TB   *Just that they were aware he was home but don't know where he had been staying and they know he's gone again.*

CW   *Mad, aren't they?*

TB   *Yeah. I was asking about the ordinary plod. He said,*
   'No, they can't they are not allowed to go anywhere near you.' He said they get rollocked if they go near you.

CW   *Mad.*

TB   *That's probably why no-one's pulled you in, like.*

CW   *Innit. It's not allowed, son.*

TB   *Not allowed near you. Oh dear.*

CW   *I must be hard to figure out though, mustn't I?*

TB   *Especially when you are here, there, gone, here, gone, here, gone. They go, 'What the fuck's going on,' don't they?*

CW   *Cos I am quite normal, aren't I?*

TB   *Cos [you're] not hanging around late at night in fucking pubs, clubs, it fucks them up.*

CW   *Do they know I am not a nuisance that way?*

TB   *Oh, they know that, like. Cos he said, didn't he? He said that… he said, 'He's strange. He doesn't go out bevvying, he has no social life and that.'*

CW   *Mad, aren't they?*

TB   *They must be pulling their hair out.*

CW   *Innit – I just mind my own business, don't I, Tone?*

TB   *I can't understand why he [Davies] wants*
     to get on you. I [have been] wracking my
     brains. I can't think why.
CW   *I must be interesting from the outside looking*
     in, though.

There were a lot of people trying to look in. Bray said
that Customs and Excise – the 'cuzzies' – were
particularly keen to find out what Cocky was up to.

TB   *He said if you ever get the paraffin budgie*
     [aeroplane] into Manchester, they're right
     on you. They've all been issued, cuzzies,
     with photos of you. They won't pull you or
     nothing, as soon as they see you they've just
     got to follow you.
CW   *Yeah.*
TB   *He said tell him to come into Birmingham is*
     his best bet. The Manchester bunch of people
     have got special photos of you, all of them.
CW   *They hate me in Manny anyway.*
TB   *They don't know where you are, they know*
     you're abroad but they can't get on you.
     But if you get the budgie into the other
     place, they can't apprehend, they've been
     told not to fucking apprehend, just to look
     the other way, but they'll have a special
     little squad that'll just follow you straight
     away.
CW   *Yeah.*
TB   *He said that's 100 per cent that 'cos they've*
     all been given special little photos of you to
     keep in their fucking wallets and that. Like
     their girlfriends, oh dear.
CW   *Mad, aren't they?*

It had been a long, sweltering summer. Bray complained about the scorching weather. 'Fucking red hot here today. They reckon it's going to get warmer by the weekend. Just too warm, Cock. It's horrible.'

Warren disagreed. He had never felt better.

'It's been the perfect summer,' he said.

Even by the surreal standards of Cocky's

life, it was to be a memorable month.

NOT EVEN the Cocky Watchman could run an empire alone. By the summer of 1996, he had collected an assortment of crooks, chancers and ne'er-do-wells, the criminal equivalent of the The Dirty Dozen. They conversed in thick Scouse or backslang and lived by their wits, hiding behind aliases, lying as a matter of course. Some were hiding out in Holland from the Law, others were there to make their fortunes. And all owed a debt to Cocky.

After Warren, the most formidable was thirty-eight-year-old Stephen Mee, alias Tony Farrell, a burly redhead with an appalling criminal record and a face you could strike matches on. A fugitive from British justice, he was Warren's emissary to the Colombians and a man not taken lightly. Even Cocky had cause to be wary. 'Mee was caught on tape planning Warren's execution,' says a Crayfish boss. 'He had made a deal with the Colombians and wanted to inherit Warren's position as top man.'

The others included:

William Terence Fitzgerald. Aged fifty-five. Alias

Billy Mario. Nicknamed Fitz or Fitzy. A grey-haired, avuncular figure in steel-rimmed glasses, Fitzgerald had been a target five years earlier for the Midlands Regional Crime Squad in its failed Operation Bruise. He had a conviction for fencing stolen antiques and had just emerged from a jail term for drug possession. The Dutch police believed his role in the team was to hold the weapons and guard the drug house.

Stephen Whitehead. Thirty-four. Nicknamed 'Lancashire Steve'. A slim, quiet man from Rochdale area, he made money 'ringing' cars before moving into drug dealing. He was well-connected in Greater Manchester and able to shift large amounts of product, especially heroin, but was not in Cocky's league. 'He was just a gofer, Warren gave the orders,' says a Crayfish officer.

William John 'Billy' Reilly. Forty-seven. A typical Liverpool scallywag with several previous convictions, Reilly had recently arrived in Holland, hiding out – so he said – from reprisals after stabbing a man in a fight.

Ray Nolan. Twenty-eight. Alias Lee Mason. Nicknamed Ray-Ray. An old friend of Warren's and an incorrigible burglar and car thief with a criminal record dating from the age of eleven. 'Years earlier in Toxteth, we'd often get reports of a stolen car being driven around at speed. We used to joke that it would be either Ray-Ray or Billy Whizz. He was always nicking cars and speeding around,' says a Liverpool police officer. By the time he joined Warren in Holland, he was on the run, wanted in connection with Merseyside's biggest-ever robbery, a £1.7 million raid on a Security Express depot in Huyton in which a flat-bed truck had been used to smash through a loading bay and into a vault.

John Anthony Farrell. Thirty-four. Alias Brian or David Chatterley, a name apparently taken from a gravestone. A mystery man from Manchester and a minor figure in the gang.

Javier Atehortua. Alias Michael. Nicknamed No-Neck. A Colombian and Mee's immediate point of contact with the cartels. An unknown quantity.

Several of the gang lived in a house which Warren rented for them in the village of Waverveen, situated between Amsterdam and Utrecht. Nicknamed 'the Shed', it was built on a polder – low-lying land reclaimed for agriculture – and was surrounded for miles by flat, featureless fields, which made it difficult to spy on without being seen. Each man had his story for being there but the Dutch were later to say in court that the reason was drugs.

They were not always the most disciplined outfit. 'It would be easy to paint the picture of a well-organised group run with military precision but it wasn't quite like that,' says a Crayfish officer. 'They were one of the most active drug gangs in Europe yet some mornings they would get up and one would say, "Why don't we go fishing?" And off they would go to spend the day by the canal.'

On one of these trips, Billy Reilly was sitting in a shady spot when another fisherman appeared and sat beside him. As they chatted, Reilly noticed the stranger was using the wrong kind of bait. He later told Warren that he was suspicious of the man but was ignored. It was a sign that Cocky was becoming lax: the mystery fishermen had indeed been an undercover police officer. But with his friends close by and convinced that the British police had no idea where he was, Warren had switched off.

It was a crucial time. By late summer 1996, Mee was finalising a deal for a huge shipment of cocaine. He was believed by Prisma leader Tom Driessen to be acting as Warren's second-in-command and as the conduit to the mysterious Mr L. 'On the wiretaps, Tony was in Bogota, and was heard on the phone telling Warren, "It's okay, Mr L and I have met and I have been to where they are making the cocaine and we are doing business. We need money." Warren said he wouldn't send any money until he saw the dope.' He had a long line of credit in Amsterdam but this deal stretched even his slate.

The cocaine would be in scrap metal ingots again, on a freighter from Santamaria in Venezuela to Rotterdam. Warren often favoured methods he had tried before. 'Once he found something he liked, he would use it again and again,' says Surveillance Mark. Even the choice of freighter was a giveaway: it was named the mv *Colombia*. Such a big deal gave the Dutch an opportunity. 'We like to wait for a big load,' says Commander Driessen, 'because you see a different form of behaviour – the organisers need to be there, they are in a different position when there are big loads of cocaine rather than pieces.'

Cocky being Cocky, it was only the biggest of a number of concurrent deals. 'A problem for us tactically was that we think he was dealing in all sorts of drugs: in cannabis, cocaine, Ecstasy and chemical drugs, automatic weapons and explosives,' says Driessen. 'It was very difficult to separate the different deals. He never talked openly. We had to decipher his conversations. He might be buying property somewhere, but was it because he wanted to use it to store cannabis from north Africa, or heroin, or was it to go there on holiday to be in the sun and for legal activities? It was so hard to separate the information.'

Cocky's position as the undisputed king of the underworld was now not in doubt. Even the Banker had taken a back seat to his protégé. Tony Bray told Warren how the police viewed him in one of their regular late night bull sessions.

TB	*They think you're the leader. They know you're the brains.*
CW	*Who do they say out of me and* [another police target]*?*
TB	*Oh, you. It's you mate. But they don't like you and* [him] *getting together cos they say it's a horrible mix, that.*
CW	*Why?*
TB	*Cos you've both got tank* [money] *and they know you're a slippery sod.*

Warren, who was always keen to know what the police thought of him, returned to the theme in a later conversation:

TB	*He said it's the biggest thing they've ever had in this city.*
CW	*Mad, isn't it.*
TB	[John Newton said] *although they think* [a named individual] *is bad, 'Your mate's the fucking number one.' The full Monty.*
CW	*But they know I'm a bit clever with it, don't they?*
TB	*Oh, they know that, they know that...* *Even the El Fellah* [Elmore Davies] *said, 'I'll give him his fucking due, he covers his fucking tracks.'*
CW	*Innit.*
TB	*Oh aye. I just started laughing.*

> CW   *What was he saying about disappearing and coming?*
>
> TB   *They don't know where you are, do they. They've got an idea now you're not in the country but they don't know where. They said you're fucking hard to keep tabs on.*

Slippery or not, it was difficult for Warren single-handedly to control what had become such a huge enterprise. As he drove around Europe making incessant calls on his portie, it was inevitable there would be foul-ups. One area causing him major concern was his Spanish cannabis subsidiary, according to one of the Crayfish bosses. 'We really forced him out of cannabis. The Spanish Government was getting a rough ride from some of its European partners over its lack of action on drugs and particularly cannabis passing through. So they cracked down on it, increasing patrols and vehicle searches. Warren resorted to getting his gear carried over the Pyrenées by guys with backpacks staying at mountain huts and youth hostels and then loading it up in France on the other side. The problem was that it wasn't arriving in good condition, the wrappings were all messed up. We believe Warren had to go out to a warehouse used by his people to show them what to do, how to wrap it so it would arrive in prime condition.'

He began to distrust some of the people working for him in Spain. 'We also fed false information into his organisation which we knew would get back to him. We wanted him to be unsure about his people. It worked because he started to sack some of his top boys. He felt he couldn't trust them and that started to destabilise his organisation. In the end he decided to cut off his cannabis arm completely. It was just becoming too much aggravation for the return he was getting. Turkish heroin was on the up in the UK and the return was much greater. Heroin was also safer because, from a law enforcement point of view, it was very difficult to infiltrate the source production countries and track the merchandise until it arrived in northern Europe.'

One such heroin order was believed by police to have been placed on behalf of Stan Carnall, the Big Fella, one of Liverpool's top villains. Now a company director and 'security adviser', Carnall was under close observation by the Crayfish team in a linked investigation called Operation Hancock. He was a difficult man to watch, being highly aware of surveillance techniques, and would go to sometimes comical lengths to avoid bugging devices. 'Once, he had to speak to Warren but was very ill with the shits,' says one of the Hancock team. 'We saw him shuffle down the road to a telephone kiosk near his house dressed in pyjamas, a dressing gown and a baseball cap, rather than make a call from his home phone.'

Carnall was believed to have put together a team making mainly cannabis runs. An Irishman called John Kelleher, who worked for a haulage firm, was recruited as the driver and brought in two loads of hash hidden inside metal boxes attached to either side of a tanker. Pleased with its success, the gang decided to increase its profits and bring in one massive groupage load. It would include Ecstasy, amphetamine, cocaine and heroin. Warren was to supply the heroin. When instructed what to do in a meeting at a motorway service station – secretly observed by Crayfish officers – Kelleher became uneasy, concerned he was getting in over his head. But there was no way out. He was scheduled to take his lorry on a legitimate working trip to Spain. On the way back, he was to meet up in France with Guy Nicholson, a convicted armed robber from Doncaster, who would transfer the drugs to Kelleher's lorry and then leave him to drive them back.

Warren was not the only person facing a busy few weeks. Operation Mix was running out of time. Under Dutch law, anyone subject to wire or phone taps must be informed after six months and given transcripts of the tapes. Mix had started at the end of May. If they did not bust him by October at the latest, they would have to spill their hand and Warren would undoubtedly be off.

On Sunday, September 22, Warren told Tony Bray he was looking forward to a long, leisurely evening at the sauna.

TB   *What time are you going up there?*
CW   *About seven. Get a nice scran in there and just relax.*
TB   *Get in that lavender pool and that, can't you?*
CW   *Yeah.*
TB   *Just as nice that.*
CW   *The little jacuzzi.*

He was going to need it. Even by the surreal standards of Cocky's life, it was to be a memorable month.

Thursday, September 26
STEPHEN WHITEHEAD was trailed by Dutch police to a sports shop in Amsterdam. With him was his beautiful Ukrainian girlfriend, Svetlana, a prostitute in the Dam's red light district. Although married with a son, she had travelled to the Netherlands with her husband's knowledge to make enough money to pay for a cataract-removal operation her child needed. Whitehead's relationship with the hooker was a source of annoyance

to Warren. He had deemed that members of his organisation should not bother with girlfriends – 'too much hassle, too dangerous' – and thought Whitehead was growing too fond of her. The young Lancastrian had ignored his advice and begun seeing Svetlana on a regular basis, even during 'business' hours. Warren complained indignantly to Tony Bray.

CW   *In the daytime and everything. His head's gone.*

TB   *No good that, mate.*

CW   *Sitting in a mate of ours the other night, stroking her leg and everything, cuddling each other!*

TB   *Fuck that, mate. Another week or so he will be sick of that, won't he?*

CW   *I don't know, I think he's right into her.*

TB   *It's no good, is it Cock?*

CW   *Mad, innit.*

Whitehead and Svetlana left the shop with two black-and-yellow nylon holdalls and drove in a Mercedes to the house known as 'the Shed'. Parked outside was a white van. Inside was Peter Plumb, another Mancunian drug trafficker known by the nicknames 'Bighead' and 'Cracker' because of his likeness to the character played by Robbie Coltrane in the TV series Cracker. Soon after, Warren arrived in a Volvo estate. He went into the Shed, then emerged with Whitehead. 'We could see them coming out of the house, each of them struggling with these distinctive black-and-yellow bags, trying to load them into the back of the van,' says one of the surveillance team. The two men set off in the Mercedes back to Sassenheim.

The van, now containing the filled bags, was driven away by Plumb. He was tailed to a landmark Chinese pagoda at Breukelen, where he met Yorkshiremen Guy Nicholson in a car. The meeting was photographed by the Dutch. The two vehicles set off south and crossed the Belgian border – in the mistaken belief that any trailing Dutch police would not be able to follow them – before doubling back and driving to the hamlet of Zundert. There, on a remote sports field, the bags were transferred from the van to Nicholson's car. Plumb drove back to the Shed while Nicholson continued south to link up with his lorry driver accomplice.

Friday, September 27
IRISH TRUCKER John Kelleher rendezvoused with Nicholson in the small town of St Quentin in eastern France, conveniently located on a main autoroute to the Channel ports. The get-together was not a happy one. Already nervous, Kelleher was now furious to discover just how many bags he was being expected to carry back. 'I did not want to take them but I was told to,' he later confessed. 'I was afraid of what would happen if I didn't. I was very concerned at the amount of boxes and bags I was expected to transport. My nerve had gone. I was very unsure that I could take it all. I kept protesting but I was afraid to refuse.'

Nicholson said he had even more drugs but had to pick them up from another spot and told the hapless Kelleher to wait until he returned. Almost three hours passed and the lorry driver, nervous, tired and annoyed, took it upon himself to set off for home. After a short distance he stopped to call one of the men he was delivering to in Liverpool.

'Go back and wait for Nicko,' he was told.

He was forced to return. Nicholson finally arrived at midnight, this time with the two black-and-yellow holdalls. They were packed with heroin. So full were the tanker's side compartments already that the only place Kelleher could find to put the bags was behind his seat, barely concealed at all.

Saturday, September 28
AT TWO O'CLOCK in the morning, Kelleher and his drug-packed lorry sailed on a cross-Channel ferry. The Irishman sat down to a full fry-up at a table next to an undercover customs team, even asking to borrow their mustard. At Dover, he drove off the boat and straight into the 'routine check' arranged for him. In the side compartments of the lorry were six kilos of cocaine, forty-nine kilos of amphetamine and 54,000 Ecstasy tablets. A check of the cab uncovered the two holdalls containing fifty-four kilos of heroin, each kilo individually wrapped in red ducting tape, a hallmark of Warren's organisation. The estimated total street value was £8.7 million.

Nicholson had been on the same ship, travelling as a foot passenger. He was observed leaving the vessel at Dover and then hanging around outside the gates to the port's Eastern Docks, anxiously waiting. After seeing three ferries come and go, he went to a car park and got into the stolen Suzuki Baleno he had driven down in. He set off toward the M20 but, in a state of high anxiety, crashed the car. Abandoning it, he jogged to Dover railway station where he was seen making a call. Then he disappeared.

[*Nicholson and another gang member, David Holt Jnr, were not arrested until almost two years later. Holt was jailed for twenty years, Nicholson for seventeen and Kelleher, who confessed, for fourteen. Only afterwards was the reason for the operation being called Hancock revealed. The Crayfish team had been so sure they would catch Holt and Nicholson that one of them recalled the phrase, 'They think it's all over... well it is now.' The same phrase was the title for a BBC TV sports quiz – hosted by comedian Nick Hancock]*

The lifting of the lorry was not Warren's only disaster that weekend. Peter 'Bighead' Plumb, who had driven the white van in Holland two days earlier, was tailed in England by twenty-five officers of the North West Regional Crime Squad. His accomplice, Frances Talmage, a burglar from Manchester, was then secretly filmed storing drugs in a lock-up garage in Heywood, near Rochdale. Officers found 27,000 Ecstasy tablets and more than four kilos of cocaine there, smuggled in from Calais in French wine boxes. Both men were arrested.

Yet news of the losses barely bothered Warren. 'He had had an unbelievably bad weekend,' says a Crayfish officer. 'Yet his response, literally, was: shit happens. He had so much else coming through that he could shrug it off.' In any case, he had not been responsible for the transport or storage of either load. He would get paid no matter what.

Thursday, October 3
ANOTHER BLOW. The Liverpool mafia's money laundering operation [*see Chapter 9*] was busted. Bagman Peter McGuinness was tailed on yet another trip to Ussama El-Kurd's Notting Hill bureau de change. As they sat at a table in the dingy basement counting out £200,000, officers from Customs and Excises's new National Investigation Service burst through the door. 'The table was absolutely covered in cash,' said senior investigating officer Dave Thompson. 'It was spread all over as if a bag had just been tipped onto it.' There was a counting machine and a small safe in once corner.

McGuinness refused to say anything. El-Kurd claimed it was the first time they had met and though he was counting the money he had not decided if he was going to change it because of the vast amount. The pair were led away in handcuffs and the shop was closed. McGuinnness alone had put £10 million from Liverpool's crime gangs through the bureau.

Wednesday, October 9
WARREN AND BRAY had a long phone conversation. 'He had that big house at Sassenheim all to himself and I actually think he was quite lonely,' says Surveillance Mark. 'He couldn't trust people to get that close to him.'

They chattered like typical young men, laughing about the latest video of the *Viz* comic characters 'The Fat Slags', swapping advice on keeping fit and discussing cars and women. Bray said Mick Ahearne had invited them both to see him in pantomime and wanted to take them backstage to 'meet the stars'.

'Fuckin' mad him, isn't he?' commented Warren, who could imagine nothing worse than watching Christmas panto in Kent, starring Stan Boardman and Warrior. He moved on to another slating of Whitehead for his girlfriend, instructed Bray to beat someone up, then said cryptically: 'Just working on that da-da thing lad.'

'Yeah? Slow, innit Cock?' said Bray.

'Well it just takes time sometimes, you know these things,' said Warren. Whatever 'that da-da thing' was, Bray seemed to understand without being told. Cocky said his goodbyes and headed off for a game of squash.

Thursday, October 10
WARREN made a round-trip to Belgium in the daytime. Late that evening, bored in his villa, he had the first of two long chats with Tony Bray. This time the topics

included Neapolitan mastifs – 'if you want something to take down a man they are the best thing' – the funeral of a friend who had his ashes scattered on Everton's Goodison Park football ground, and household improvements to Warren's Wirral residence, including the purchase of new curtains and a wrought iron table and the removal of some 'horrible' pine panelling

They moved on to cars, a subject dear to Warren's heart. 'Nice those Legends, aren't they Tone? You want to get one of them and smoke it.' Cocky advised his pal to splash out on a new motor, telling him he could always re-sell it for the same amount by 'clocking' back the milometer. He himself was 'getting a new Merc this week', a bottle-green four-door. He was also thinking of buying a £100,000 Porsche Turbo.

Cars were Warren's main extravagance. Yet for all his wealth, he could never resist pulling a stroke. He once told friends he had been paying fully comprehensive insurance for seven years on a old Volkswagen Beetle which had not been roadworthy for years. 'I wouldn't mind but there is no such fucking car. Just my imagination, that. It's a good insurance block. I'm covered for any vehicle, motorbike or anything.'

He had been a big fan of motorbikes until the time he was riding a particularly powerful machine around Liverpool, lost control and came off. He suffered no great harm but smashed his mobile phone, which was in his back pocket. It caused him severe problems for several days because he was virtually uncontactable until able to pass on his new phone number to his associates.

Bray had some fresh gossip from an unnamed law enforcement contact. 'He said you earn proper dough, hundreds of millions. Big, big money. He said, "I've got to give him his due, Tone, he's good at going missing... He's like the Scarlet Pimpernel." He can't fathom you out. They are resigned to the fact they won't get you, Cock. "Way out of our league," he said. They know you are the boss.'

Warren was amused. 'They don't like it when you're a bit intelligent, do they?' he said. He went on:

CW	*Oh they don't like it when the Cockle's doing the disappearing act.*
TB	*He* [John Newton or Elmore Davies] *said you earn proper dough.*
CW	*What did he say?*
TB	*Hundreds of millions, they were going.*
CW	*Fuck off!*
TB	*Oh aye, and all that, Cock… He said you were worth big money, proper big money.*
CW	*What did he say?*
TB	*'We can't catch him.'*
CW	*So he said I'm good at it?*
TB	*Yeah. He said, 'He's brilliant at disappearing. I've got to give him his due, Tone, he's good at just going missing.' I just started laughing.*
CW	*What did he say about the goulash* [money]*?*
TB	*He said proper dough mate. Hundreds of millions. He said, 'You wouldn't know half of what he's got.'*
CW	*Mad, aren't they?*
TB	*He can't fathom you out, can he?… Because they can't get on you.*
CW	*Do they know I am alert, like?*
TB	*Oh aye, they know all that. They know you are the slippery brush… I tell you.*
CW	*But they have still got a little bit of respect, haven't they?*

TB   *Oh aye. He knows. He said you are dead*
     slippery.
     'We can't get him,' he said. 'Out of our
     hands, way out of our league,' he said. 'We
     can't catch him.'
CW   *Oh dear me.*

An hour later, shortly before midnight, Warren dialled his mate again. Bray said the police had been laughing about the visit to Liverpool of a female journalist from the Irish Sunday Independent who was trying to track Warren down. 'How can she find him when we can't?' the cops had asked.

Warren launched into another of his pet tirades against Whitehead's girlfriend. 'He's gone daft. He took one of the lads to go and look at some car today down at a garage and he had his bird with him. You take your mates to look at a car.'

'Mad,' agreed Bray. 'You've got to go on your own, haven't you, with your mates to look at it.'

'Fucking hell. I said to him, women are for in the night, you know what I mean. He's backward, anyway.'

The conversation then turned to the arrested Peter Plumb. Warren had little sympathy for him either. 'Stupid, won't fucking listen. That's what's stupid about it. You know what I mean?. Can't listen, won't be told.' [*Plumb would later be jailed for twelve years, his accomplice Talmage for thirteen*]

Wednesday, October 16
THE FATEFUL mv *Colombia* arrived at Rotterdam at the end of a three-week journey from South America. Warren's container, one of 7,000 unloaded at the city's Europort that day, was put in a holding pen.

'Warren had planned to have the ingots transported by train to Bulgaria,' says Paul Acda. 'In the capital, Sofia, he had bought a winery and we believe he was going to break down the coke consignment into much smaller amounts, dissolve it in bottles of red wine and then re-route them back to Holland and eventually to England, where it would be retrieved. He chose Bulgaria because it is a country outside the European Community. It is a classic ploy to mask the original source country of the product you are importing.' The winery would be used not just to mask drugs. Officers believe Warren was also planning to buy fake labels from Africa and cheap wine from India for bottling in Bulgaria, to be sold as fine wine.

As hundreds of containers were craned onto trucks and collected, Warren's remained where it was. The port authorities contacted the freight agents responsible for the crate and they contacted Warren's people in Holland. Within a few hours it became clear to the police officers tapping Warren's lines that something was causing him a major headache. 'Someone at the Venezuelan end had messed up real bad. They had neglected to pay for the onward trip to Bulgaria. That meant that Rotterdam became the end destination. Warren did not want this and got involved. Eventually he sent a fax to the port which connected him directly with the container. At this point we knew we could get him.' says Tom Driessen. It was, of course, possible that the criminals intended to change the destination, something they could do quite legally by submitting new paperwork. It was also possible they were planning to break into the container in the port and rip-off the consignment. The Dutch police watched and waited.

THE SHIPMENT

Monday, October 21

THE START, for Warren, of a long and troublesome week. It was necessary to sort out the paperwork glitch that was delaying the movement of his cocaine. He still found time to see *Independence Day*, the new Hollywood blockbuster, at the cinema.

Tuesday, October 22

A CALL to Tony Bray, who told Warren about a *Cook Report* investigation on television that night revealing failings in security at Manchester Airport. 'They made this home-made bomb, took it to where the cargo goes, the fucking thing goes unchecked on the plane and it could have been a bomb and blew up!'

'Mad, innit,' commented Warren.

Bray also reported the latest improvements on Warren's home. The bathroom had been re-decorated. Tom Driessen had less mundane matters on his mind. 'We put out outward surveillance teams on Warren and we controlled the container. There were fax conversations going on and we were able to intercept those faxes. It took two days but eventually we realised the container really was for Bulgaria. There was no advantage for the investigation to let the container and the cocaine go; we had to make the arrests. We put detailed surveillance on our targets. It was important that we made the arrests all together. 'We planned our operation for the next morning.'

Thursday, October 24

AT FOUR O'CLOCK in the morning, a large number of unshaven, grim-faced men gathered in a conference room at the headquarters of the Prisma team in The Hague. Among them were British Crayfish officers who had flown in the day before, invited along as observers.

Briefings were also taking place in the UK at Fraggle Rock and at the Merseyside Police headquarters. A series of raids in England would be timed to coincide with those in Holland. It was the culmination of the job that had consumed so many lives for so long.

The men who were to apprehend Warren and his co-conspirators were special paramilitary arrest teams. They have a formidable reputation and an awesome armoury, including heat-seeking detectors to locate people inside dark buildings, stun grenades to incapacitate their targets, CS gas and sub-machine guns. Tom Driessen was in charge.

'The district attorney and the prosecuting attorney in the Hague had given their permission for the squad to be used. They always ask what kind of weapons they might confront. It was difficult to say but we knew the kind of people we were up against. One of them, Mee, had escaped from custody in Britain in such a violent way that we knew they probably would be armed and put up strong resistance. No chances were being taken. It was stressful. It was hard to put surveillance on Warren in particular because of his choice of home. He always chose a place where he could look around him. We knew he had a pair off binoculars on a stand at the window.'

Clothed in black, the arrest teams moved stealthily into position around a number of buildings including Bakara and the Shed. 'We got information from our teams on the ground that all the targets were in place, that everyone was where we thought they were and that the cocaine was still in place. At five o'clock, I gave the green light.'

At least ten officers burst into Bakara through several entry points. They ran from room to room, yelling instructions. Warren was asleep in an upstairs bedroom, alone and unarmed. His disorientated state of mind as he was jolted awake by the percussion thump of a stun grenade, to see himself surrounded by hideous armed figures in black, can only be imagined. For once in his life, he showed fear.

'From the moment he opened his eyes the first thing he saw was a gun at his head,' says Driessen. 'I think he was very scared. I hope I never get arrested by those guys. They searched the rest of the house to make sure no-one else was there.'

Arresting his lieutenants at the Shed proved to be more difficult. There were three targets sleeping there and they were all assumed to be armed and dangerous. The arrest team made its silent way through the garden and then, on a signal from the team leader, crashed through the front door with a battering ram. 'They had to move very quickly to get into the rooms of the men. They had to cross at least ten metres and then go upstairs and then move into the bedrooms. We found hand grenades and guns under their pillows. They didn't have time to get to their guns to fire them. I am convinced that if they had had any time at all to react, then they would have used them. Guys like that, they have experienced everything in their lives so there is nothing left that can scare them. They have nothing to lose and that's very scary.'

After the initial elite squad came detectives who began the formal procedure of searching the properties. They were joined by a prosecutor and a judge. Warren was led away in plastic handcuffs in an armoured car. Weapons were found in cupboards and drawers inside the house.

'At two minutes after five, I left for the scene with my prosecutor,' says Driessen. 'After so many months of investigation I always want to experience the feeling of being at the place where my targets have lived, to see how they lived. Warren had been in that house with no weapons. Even despite the world he lived in, he clearly wasn't afraid of staying alone in the house. He didn't fear anything. His house was big but practically empty. It was dull. The image I got was that though these guys had plenty of money, they didn't use it in a luxury way. They are not sophisticated and don't have any idea of luxury in the normal sense.

'Curtis was taken to a jail immediately in a police van, then he was taken to a police station in The Hague. After that he was in one of our special jails, but we didn't know exactly where he was at any one time after that because they kept moving him around. If we wanted to question him, we had to make an application and the jail would make the arrangements because of the special security procedure this kind of suspect is under.'

As the raids were in progress, other officers were moving the Rotterdam container to a large, empty warehouse. One videoed the scene as others unloaded the lead ingots, each about three feet cubed. Lifting gear was brought in, pneumatic drills were acquired and officers began the long and difficult task of drilling through the lead. A few inches in, and the sound of the drill changed – the bit had gone through the lead and hit a steel box. Once a hole had been punctured in the box, white powder flecked the aperture. A square hole was drilled out, allowing the searchers to reach inside and remove the contents. There were hundreds of one kilo blocks, wrapped in brown paper and plastic. It totalled 400 kilos of 90 per cent pure cocaine and filled a small room to the ceiling.

Six houses were raided in the Netherlands and twenty premises searched in the UK. The Dutch searches revealed 1,500 kilos of cannabis resin, sixty kilos of heroin in the garage at the Shed, fifty kilos of Ecstasy, stacked crates containing 960 CS gas canisters, several hand grenades, three firearms, ammunition, false passports and around £370,000-worth of guilders. The total haul, including the cocaine, would have fetched £125 million.

Two personal computers were also recovered from Bakara. It took three days to download all the information on their hard drives and on floppy disks. Someone had been keeping track of the mv *Colombia* on the Internet. The analysts also hoped to find a log of names and amounts detailing Warren's financial dealings. In this they were disappointed; there appeared to be no records anywhere.

A few days after Curtis Warren's arrest, Elmore Davies formally applied for promotion.

15 GUILTY

*'The mythology of British Villainy needs to
be rewritten. The plain fact is that Curtis
Warren is the richest and most successful British
criminal who has ever been caught'*

The Observer

FOR several weeks, Warren was kept incommunicado in solitary confinement. His only contact with others came when guards brought his meals, the police arrived to question him or his lawyer visited. True to form, he gave nothing away. Some of his gang had elaborate cover stories; Warren said nothing. He did not yet know about the wiretaps and the months of surveillance but sensed he was in deep trouble.

Meanwhile his downfall was sending after-shocks through the underworld. There was near-panic in Liverpool, grave concern in Colombia and, according to one Crayfish detective, a body in the former Soviet Union. 'A Russian mafia guy was executed in his driveway a few days after Warren's arrest. He must have been responsible for some of the drugs seized and was blamed for their loss by whoever he worked for. He paid the ultimate penalty.' Warren had nothing to do with the death but it illustrated that people were playing for the highest possible stakes. On the streets of Liverpool, there were many who stood to profit from the Cocky Watchman's misfortune. Dealers who owed him money fancied they might now get away without paying. They were soon disabused. One of Warren's oldest and most feared associates did the rounds, making it clear what the penalties would be for anyone taking liberties. No-one did.

At the same time, an anonymous letter was sent to the *Liverpool Echo*, the city's evening newspaper. It purported to be from underworld figures, contained the names, addresses and detailed movements of senior customs officers and stated £25,000 would be paid for the death of each one. The *Echo* passed the letter to the Crayfish team, which alerted customs bosses and the Chief Constable's office. A directive was put out to tighten security. Police and customs buildings went from the standard black alert to amber, the second highest code below red. Subsequent inquiries revealed the letter was almost certainly a hoax, possibly from a disgruntled law enforcement employee, although the source was never identified. No link has ever been made with Warren.

Cocky's arrest did make one task even more urgent: the conclusion of the Merseyside Police operation against DCI Elmore Davies. Dutch law sets down a time limit after which defendants must be informed of the details of the case against them. Come early December, prosecutors would have to reveal to Warren the transcripts of his telephone conversations over the previous six months. These would show what the police knew of the bid to pervert the Phil Glennon Jnr trial. 'This intelligence would have invariably been passed back into the criminal fraternity within this country and eventually onto Davies himself,' Detective Superintendent Phil Jones later testified. There was no time to waste.

In November 1996, authorisation was given to place bugs in four telephone extensions at Stanley Road police station in Kirkdale, north Liverpool, where Davies was working on a murder inquiry. In December, Jones and his superiors decided to plant an electronic listening device in Davies's home. A piece of the roof was secretly cut out above his flat in Oxton, Wirral, and a probe known as the 'Alabama device' was fitted into the living room ceiling. Less than two millimetres in diameter, it would record everything said in the room and on the telephone for a three-month period. 'We gathered the information on a Sanyo video recorder which recorded all the audio activity in the front room of Davies' flat, twenty-four hours a day,' said Jones.

Plans to insert a similar probe into Warrior's home were halted because of the 'substantial risk of compromise' to the operation; the only way to fit it was through the floor of a flat owned by a third party. Davies remained the focus for the electronic surveillance and a tiny video camera was later hidden behind a smoke detector in his usual office at Tuebrook police station. That a major British police force should bug its own offices was almost unprecedented and was to be a controversial issue at Davies's subsequent trial. Deputy Chief Constable Paul Acres, who gave the authority for the Alabama device, strongly defended his actions: 'The fact that a senior detective with access to our most serious intelligence should have been corrupted posed the most extreme threat to the safety of our community. It was my duty to ensure that whatever method lawfully [*was required*] was carried out to stop him. The threat to order, the scale of treachery in this case, the level of criminality that these people were operating at, meant that what could be done, should be done.'

Bizarrely, this cloak-and-dagger activity was all taking place while Davies and his fellow detectives were being filmed for a BBC fly-on-the-wall documentary series, *Mersey Blues*. The production company, Hart Ryan, spent months with officers investigating serious crimes. Their lenses captured the long hours detectives worked in the face of budget cuts and their brittle morale. Davies was trailed as he investigated the killing of a small-time drugs dealer, a crime for which Les Jackson later admitted manslaughter and was jailed for ten years. Jackson's nasal Scouse rejoinder on being told he was under arrest for murder – '*M-eee-rder?*' – became a minor catchphrase when the series was broadcast in the spring of 1999.

Always outspoken, Davies became even more indiscreet with the camera rolling. When his application for promotion was rejected, it prompted a bitter, tears-of-a-clown soliloquy:

> We're supposed to be targeting criminals and it's going to come to a point where you're going to look at people and go, "It's going to be too hard, too long and too expensive to catch him…" These criminals aren't restricted in budgets. They got more money than Aristotle Onassis, some of them… Well if this is the future of the police force, I feel very, very sorry for people who will succeed me. They say we should be coming into line with industry. I have a lot of friends in industry and I don't know many of them that

work public holidays, weekends and holidays constantly for nothing, believe me.

He paused, then the bile rose in his voice. 'So fuck 'em.'

His disillusionment at missing promotion may have tipped Davies over the edge. The bugging devices caught him passing on details to Warrior about PC Gary Titherington, the officer in the Phil Glennon Junior trial. Davies said Titherington was the key to their attempts to 'fuck up the case' and described the constable's home security, his car and the location of his daughter's nursery. Ahearne received a down-payment of £10,000 to give to Davies for his information. 'You keep it out of the way,' warned Davies. At the same time, he posted an entry in the Force Intelligence Bureau computer which read, 'Phillip Glennon Senior is travelling to Amsterdam to deposit £3 million with the Dutch so Curtis Warren can get bail. Warren will then abscond and go to southern Spain.' The entry was later read out in court, although there is no proof it was more than gossip.

By then, Warren knew the outline of the case against him. What he learned sickened him. The Dutch police had been bugging his phones for months: thousands of calls, hours of tapes. In some he was simply ordering pizza or a taxi. But others were dynamite. There were drug deals, the talk of Semtex and guns, police bribery and discussions of the Gang War back home. It was damning.

In January, the full written evidence was presented at a forty-minute hearing. Warren faced two charges: participating in a criminal organisation and importing and exporting drugs. He declined to attend the hearing on the advice of his Dutch barrister, Han Jahae. 'Mister Warren is okay but he did not feel it necessary to come.

He has to be transferred in a not too pleasant way and he did not want to waste his time. He has too much to do. He is looking forward to the battle,' said Jahae. He also asked the court for some extra time to prepare his case. Jahae was particularly interested in how the British came to tip off the Dutch police about Warren in the first place. 'The co-operation between the Dutch and the British started with information from an on-going British investigation and I want to know who, where, what and how.' All of the defendants were remanded in custody to appear before the court again on 9 April 1997.

Before then, on Thursday, March 13, the police moved against their colleague. Elmore Davies was arrested and put through the same humiliating procedure as the many criminals he had caught, even being subjected to a strip search. Questions were answered with a quiet, 'No comment,' the response he had heard a thousand times himself. Tony Bray was picked up leaving Mick Ahearne's house carrying a piece of paper with the names of police officers written on it. Warrior was also hauled in. 'You can't arrest me, I'm a children's icon,' he protested. In interview, he claimed he had never sought out gangsters but would find them surrounding him in night clubs, eager to bask in reflected charisma. 'You know, it's the Frank Sinatra situation with the Mafia. They have got notoriety in their own little clans and they have got money but they haven't got fame – that is something no amount of money can buy.' Warren, who considered him a buffoon, would not have been amused.

All three were charged with conspiring together and with others to pervert the course of justice in the forthcoming prosecution of Philip Glennon Junior. They appeared in the dock together before magistrates in St Helens; an odd trio, their dress reflecting their very different personalities: Davies wearing a blue, open-necked workshirt, Ahearne in an expensive leather jacket, Bray casual in an Ellesse sports top. Det Supt Phil Jones told the bench:

On July 13, 1996, a young man called Phillip Glennon Junior went to The Venue club. He became involved in a dispute outside. He had a further dispute inside the club. He left the club with the assistance of the doormen. He came back 30 minutes later with a decommissioned handgun. He tried to get back into the club. He was confronted by one of the doormen and attempted to discharge the gun. He ran from the club into Green Lane. Two police saw what was happening and Glennon turned round and pointed the gun at the officer and attempted to discharge it. One officer got behind him and knocked him to the floor. He was arrested and the gun recovered.

This incident, said Jones, had led directly to the corruption of Davies. It was part of a 'much bigger picture which involved the killing of David Ungi and numerous other shootings'. He continued:

The Black Caucus were at war with the Ungis. There were two opposing sides. Two men are sought for the murder of David Ungi. They are Bunji O'Rourke and Darren Jackson. They were part of of a large criminal group at that time which was headed by Curtis Warren. He is currently in custody in Holland. He is there with several other associates... Two days after the [*Venue*] shooting, I became aware that there was an attempt being made to pervert the course of justice. It is quite clear from the evidence that has been gathered that he [*Davies*] was engaged in this conspiracy but also that he was involved in a long-term relationship with these organised criminals.

All three defendants were eventually granted conditional bail. Two weeks later, Warren stood trial. It would be his first glimpse of the outside world for six months.

SEVEN SLEEK black Mercedes shadowed the armoured van which carried Curtis Warren in shackles from a maximum security prison to the Paleis van Justitie in the centre of The Hague. He had first been blindfolded and deliberately disorientated before being helicoptered from his maximum-security prison to a nearby army base to pick up his escort. Special forces troops with machine guns ringed the courthouse, an anonymous building of civil service grey wreathed in scaffolding from an on-going restoration. Armed guards hid in nearby offices, scanning the streets through binoculars. Everyone entering the busy court was obliged to pass through a metal-detecting archway flanked by more gun-toting officers.

Once inside the confines of the court, Warren was brought up to a first-floor courtroom. It had been sealed off for the hearing, with paramilitary officers standing guard. Inside the room stood more kick-ass guards with sub-machine guns. Even the Dutch barristers, accustomed to some of the most powerful criminals in Europe, were impressed. 'This level of security is unprecedented in our country,' said one. 'We never see things like this.'

Warren, for so long anonymous, had suddenly gained notoriety. A few weeks earlier, he had appeared in the well-read Rich List of the *Sunday Times*, an annual compilation of the wealthiest people in Britain. He was listed at number 461 – with an estimated worth of £40 million – alongside the theatre director Trevor Nunn, media tycoon Owen Oyston, the Marquess of Lothian and various landowners and industrialists. 'Warren is a major property player and trader in the North West, particularly the Merseyside area where he is a well known figure in the local community. He also has extensive interests on the continent,' read his entry.

Under the Dutch legal system, three examining magistrates would consider the evidence, led by a chief prosecutor. There was no jury. Warren was not asked to make a formal plea of guilty or not guilty. Proceedings were relaxed. Warren, dressed in a grey sweatshirt, blue jogging bottoms and white training shoes, sat beside Han Jahae and a female interpreter who explained the proceedings as they went on.

The first important development was a new application by the prosecutor: 'I want to bring another charge against Mister Warren: that he was the leader of this organisation. The charge carries a maximum sentence of sixteen years.' For Holland, this was a huge sentence. Warren's barrister immediately countered: he claimed the police raids in Holland were ordered only on the strength of information obtained from illegal phone taps in Britain. The evidence was therefore contaminated. He demanded to know what information had led to Operation Mix.

Warren was asked by the presiding magistrate, Irene de Vries if he had anything to say. He nodded and rose. Purposefully positioning a microphone, he started hesitantly, then his words came out in a rush.

It's important that you investigate how the English got the information and I will state right now that they will all claim public immunity. It was a customs investigation, the customs have agreed. Now they are saying they got the information from NCIS. So now they have put the responsibility on the NCIS to say where they got the information to start the investigation and that is how they came to claim public immunity. Why do they need to claim public immunity if they don't know where it came from?

Asked if he agreed to further investigation, Warren replied, 'Yes.' He went on:

Also I would like to say, when Mister Gurton was questioned by my lawyer he made a reference about if they had wanted to tape my telephones in England he would have been allowed to get the permission. He claimed public immunity but was willing to say the information didn't come from an informant, an electronic probe or a front company. In one breath they are claiming public immunity, in the next they are saying it is not an informer, it is not this, it is not that. My lawyer has got the paper what they sent to him, stating that it is not this or that, but they won't answer the vital question, where it come from. Okay, thank you.

He sat down. Though his words had been unrehearsed and garbled, his looming presence had transfixed the court. The magistrates agreed to further investigation, naming Phil Byrne, a senior customs representative at

NCIS, as someone they still wanted to question. And with that Warren was excused until June 5. He disappeared with his escort back to prison.

THE OTHER DEFENDANTS were trooped into the courtroom one by one. First up was Billy Fitzgerald, grey-haired and wearing steel-rimmed spectacles. He faced charges of being a member of a criminal organisation, trafficking in drugs and holding weapons for a third party. The prosecutor asked for a five-year sentence, saying Fitzgerald was one of the 'guardians' of the house known as the Shed. The phone taps caught him discussing 'minis', which are little pills. She said the house stank of hashish and so Fitzgerald must have known it was there. A pair of his spectacles were found in Billy Reilly's room, which was full of drugs. When shown a photo of Warren by the police, he said, 'Yes, I know him, I've met him, he's Tony Thompson.'

Fitzgerald denied everything. It had all been a terrible misunderstanding. He was involved in legal dealings in wine, bedroom fittings and railway sleepers. He knew Billy Reilly as a mate and had been offered a place on his couch. He did not know there were drugs in the Shed; he never went into the rooms where drugs were found. The spectacles were not his. As for the pervading smell of drugs, he had been injured in a car accident five years earlier and had lost his sense of smell. His counsel, JW Bogaardt, said later: 'He was living there, for he did some trade in Holland. Maybe this is a legal cover for being in a criminal organisation but the prosecution has to prove he is doing other things and all the evidence is circumstantial. He makes telephone calls speaking about completely innocent things but those words, according to the prosecutor, cover criminal actions. He had been in this house for ten days. The house was rented by Curtis Warren. He says he is not a friend of Warren, though he saw him once in the house. He is a very naive man.'

Next came the burly Stephen Mee. His counsel, Jan Schoueveld, took the same tack as Warren's lawyer. 'The problem is that there are doubts about whether the evidence is legal. Regarding the fax from an English liaison officer which started the investigations in Holland, the Dutch court must be able to say that the methods the Dutch and English police officers have used were legal. The time before the fax is not clear. There is a possibility that the evidence from the English police officer is not legal in Holland – maybe wiretaps or he has been observed.'

The case against Stephen Whitehead was also postponed for the same reason: the ongoing debate about English sources of information. The slim, youthful looking Lancastrian was facing serious charges relating to the sixty-seven kilos of heroin found in the garage at the Shed. He was also said to be implicated in the seizure in John Kelleher's lorry at Dover.

Ray Nolan was facing a double whammy: the charges in Holland and extradition to the UK to stand trial for the Security Express depot robbery. He admitted he had come to Holland because he was wanted in England and needed a 'stash'. But he denied any knowledge of a rifle and hand grenades found in the house. He said he had his own money when he arrived and did not need to be part of a criminal organisation. 'They found a lot of drugs in the bedroom where he was sleeping but he said they didn't belong to him, although he knew they were there. He couldn't say they belonged to a criminal organisation because that would have put his life on the line. He was basically a guard, watching on their behalf. He didn't know there were firearms there but one was found under his pillow and there were hand grenades behind his headboard,' said his barrister. 'I never done nottin', added Nolan.

Billy Reilly's story was that he was in Holland hiding out. 'He said someone in Liverpool attacked his wife and so he attacked that person and stabbed him. He was afraid, not of the police but of the person he stabbed and his friends. He said Liverpool was quite a violent environment and he was scared for his life,' said his counsel. 'He was looking for a quiet place to hide and came to Holland. The house was a really deserted place. You come from the highway and it is about thirty minutes drive, green and flat. He knew some guys from Liverpool and had heard about this place. I don't know if he knew Curtis before but he went fishing with him. He loved fishing.'

Reilly denied knowing that various packages in his bedroom contained drugs. Nor did he have much to say about the gun found in his bed. The prosecution said he was caught in a phone call telling his wife he would be getting 'twice as much' as expected. Reilly said this referred to a stolen diamond ring he was trying to sell. The court also heard that when in prison at Rotterdam, Reilly had told one of the guards that if he saw Warren or Fitzgerald he would attack them. His counsel dismissed this. 'I told the judge he wouldn't do it. If you knew Curtis Warren and the background in Liverpool, you would never attack Curtis Warren.'

THROUGHOUT HIS INCARCERATION, Warren maintained his customary cool. 'The only time he got riled in interrogation was when they suggested he only won at squash because his partners let him,' says one officer. He broke silence just once. Journalist Nick Mattingly of Granada Television knocked on Stephanie

Glennon's door in Liverpool and asked if Curtis might be prepared to talk. A message was passed on to Warren in jail and he replied in a fax via his solicitor, Keith Dyson. The fax, dated 18 June 1997, is reproduced here verbatim:

It is my personal belief that the British Police and Her Majesty's Customs and Excise are attempting to pervert the course of justice by malicious propeganda and innuendo. Statements have been made available to the media in the UK with a view to trying to portray me as the following:

1 Target One. Which is self explanatory.

2 Multi millionaire Status. Stories have appeared in the British press that I am one of the wealthiest men in the UK. Even to the extent were I am now on the list of the wealthiest men in the country. This has been put about over the last few months by customs and the British Police it cannot be substantiated in any way, shape or form.

3 Properties home and abroad. It is being said that I own properties all over the world this is not true and the stories are not based on fact. I own a house in the Wirral, I own two very small properties in Liverpool which I rent out. The property I was living at in Holland at the time of

my arrest was rented and not owned
by me. Any other properties at home
in England or abroad that anybody
else wishes to say I own is totally
incorrect and untrue.
4 Anonymous calls and Wispa
campaign. Calls have been made
conveniently to the Dutch
authorities with stories of
elaborate escape plans which I know
nothing about and can know nothing
about because I am in communicado.
The result of these calls has led to
me not being able to communicate
properly with people at home and my
defence team. It has also led to me
being given superstar status which
is not to my convenience and
portrays me in a light which the
prosecution benefit totally.
I feel that the British authorities
are using me to justify asking for
more funding which has become the
norm and I am simply being fattened
up for the kill.

His paranoia could only have been increased when, on
June 5, events took a dramatic turn. On the morning he
was due back at the Paleis van Justitie, the court clerk
announced that Dutch police had been tipped off about
an alleged plan to spring Warren. For the first time in
Dutch legal history, a trial was shifted from a courthouse
to ' a secret location' – the heavily-guarded Alexander
Kazerne military base in The Hague. Judges, legal teams,
interpreters, defendants and security personnel were all

taken to a makeshift courtroom. The proceedings were transmitted via satellite to journalists, each of whom had been vetted by security staff, back at the original courthouse.

Part of the intercepted telephone transcripts were read out by the prosecutor. In one passage Warren was heard to comment about the Ungi family: 'It is very easy for me to throw twenty kilos of Semtex into Park Road. If they touch my brother then I would throw fifty kilos of Semtex into their mother's house.' Such disclosures, and the way the case was being conducted, annoyed Warren. When cross-examined by court president Isaac Holtrop, he snapped, 'There is no point in me saying anything is there? Nothing that I say will make any difference. As far as I am concerned I have already been found guilty. This is a farce. You can guarantee that we will all be convicted.'

Mee was also cross-examined. He admitted flying to Venezuela and then twice piloting private flights from there to Colombia in 1996. But he denied any knowledge of the cocaine shipment. The prosecution asked for a ten-year jail term and a fine. Again the cases of Warren, Mee, Whitehead, Farrell and the Colombian Atehortua were adjourned. In the meantime Nolan, Reilly and Fitzgerald were all convicted. Each was jailed for three years.

Just over two weeks later, on the afternoon of Thursday, June 19, the court reconvened, this time at the Paleis van Justitie, to deliver its verdicts. Warren opted not to attend, waiting instead in his cell for what he believed to be the inevitable result. He was right. After briefly outlining the facts, Isaac Holtrop announced that the remaining five defendants had been found guilty. Mee, Atehourta, and Whitehead each received seven years. Farrell received just twelve months and was due for release two days later because of time spent in custody.

'The setting-up of this operation came from UK telephone taps,' said Mr Holtrop. 'The argument that they could not be presented in a Dutch court has been rejected. Curtis Warren was for a long time the head of a criminal organisation, involved in large-scale importations of Ecstasy, cocaine and hashish. He is the leader of an international criminal group involved in exportation to other countries and importation here and is a dealer in firearms. There is no doubt that he is the leader.' He jailed Warren for twelve years without any chance of parole.

EVERY MAJOR British newspaper ran the story the next day. 'He made it into the richest 500 in the land. Every penny of his fortune came from the misery of drugs' said the *Daily Mail. Observer* Home Affairs editor David Rose went further: 'The mythology of British Villainy needs to be rewritten. Next to Warren, the Krays were pathetic minnows. The Great Train Robbers and Brinks Mat robbers, swaggering highwaymen from the pre-drugs era, were way down the division. The plain fact is that Curtis Warren is the richest and most successful British criminal who has ever been caught.'

Yet in the offices of the Crayfish team, there was a sense of anti-climax. The fact that Warren had been jailed abroad, and not at home, took some of the shine off what would have been the pinnacle of many officers' careers. 'We all had on-going jobs to do and we just got on with them really.' says one officer. 'It was a bit unreal.' We also knew that for the same crime in Britain he would have been looking at twenty years, minimum.

The Dutch, however, were delighted. 'There are so many pieces of the puzzle,' says Prisma leader Tom Driessen. 'These people don't walk around the countryside with suitcases of cocaine waiting to do business. You have to put the puzzle together to make the arrest and the bigger they are, the harder it is to get to them. People like Warren are top level. We are only annoying them. It's the way he faced our court system, like we were annoying him. Guys like that are thinking, okay, a few years in prison, they can do it no problem. They can blank everything.

'The only way we can make a difference is with a top-down philosophy, taking the men at the top and working on them for long periods of time. It's not hard to arrest people or to seize cocaine, we can do that every month. We can make headlines with that, and have to, because people get worried when we don't seize drugs. But if you never go for the bosses you will never solve the problem. And people like Curtis Warren are from the board of directors.'

16

FALL OF A CARTEL

*'These criminal groups dealing in drugs
are the most dangerous threat to the security
of our way of life in Europe'*

Commander Tom Driessen

CURTIS WARREN was imprisoned in the high-security Nieuw Vosseveld prison at Vught, about sixty miles from Amsterdam. There is no other prison in Europe quite like it. A former Nazi prisoner of war camp – with a modern museum commemorating its dead – it is notorious as Holland's toughest jail and defies the popular perception of the Dutch penal system as liberal and lenient. Though each prisoner has his own cell, the regime is harsh, particularly in the special secure unit to which Warren was assigned. 'It is like a prison within a prison,' says Keith Dyson, his solicitor. 'It is very intrusive. They search people several times a day. They listen to phone calls. They are a mixed bunch in there, at the top end of the Dutch criminal spectrum, with a lot of foreign nationals.'

Cocky's fellow inmates, whose number varied between 16 and 23, included terrorists, war criminals, murderers, drug barons and international crooks. Some were on remand awaiting trial or extradition, including Brian Meehan, an Irishman charged with the murder of the journalist Veronica Guerin. He had been the driver of the motorcycle used in the hit; a pillion passenger fired the fatal shots (Meehan would later be jailed for life for the murder). Most were serving sentences of ten years or more. A daily two-hour exercise period was their only chance to breathe fresh air.

Cocky immediately began working on his appeal, ploughing his way diligently through pages of depositions and transcripts. His lawyers believed that if they kept nagging away, they could convince a court that procedural rules had been broken at the start of Operation Mix. Their first port of call would be the Dutch Appeal Court. After that was the option of the Supreme Court, the equivalent of the British House of Lords.

Back in England, the Crayfish team also had work to do. Shortly after Warren's arrest in 1996, Crayfish bosses had privately briefed journalists on the extent of his financial assets. 'We have been heavily involved in asset tracing,' said one. 'So far we have been able to identify two hundred and forty properties that he owns. A large proportion of those have Department of Social Security tenants in them. We managed to get this information from a trawl that the DSS did on our behalf. There are rumours about money in Switzerland and property on the Costa Brava, but they are just rumours. He is not generous with his money and not particularly flash. He had some flashy cars, a Mercedes, a Lexus, but rarely used them and changed or borrowed his vehicles two or three times a day. He dressed in a shell suit, carried a mobile phone and had no outward signs of being very wealthy. He eats well and has quite a good lifestyle but is not flamboyant. He's like a Liverpool lad with a fairly good bank balance, although we can't find his bank accounts.'

A team was put together to find the cash. While conservative estimates put Warren's fortune in the low tens of millions, another Crayfish investigator later admitted they were having difficulties in establishing the truth. 'We acquired a list of over two hundred properties that are supposed to be his but they are all very difficult to prove. There are a couple of office blocks in Liverpool worth about two hundred thousand pounds. We also believe he owned a massage parlour near Piccadilly in central Manchester. It was quite plush inside. The owner admitted he knew him but said only as a customer and wouldn't admit anything else. Warren did go there regularly. It was his only vice. Then there is supposed to be a shopping arcade in Turkey and his share of a winery in Bulgaria. But who knows? We think most of his money was going to Dubai and from there it is a black hole.'

As big a mystery was how Warren kept track of his money and investments. 'We had two stories about his accounts. One came from a source at the prison in Holland. Warren apparently mentioned his accounts were in the boot of a vintage car that he had bought off a Dutch taxi driver and stored in a lock-up garage. Elements of the story checked out but the Dutch have never been able to find it. The other was a piece of intelligence that he kept the information on CD-ROM but again we have not found it.'

Another tantalising line of inquiry sprang from a remark Warren had once made to a helicopter pilot while learning to fly. As they hovered above the non-league Barrow Athletic Football Club on the Cumbrian coast, Warren looked down at the ground and remarked, 'I own that.' It was a throwaway line but would later result in the raiding of the club's offices and the arrest and questioning of Stephen Vaughan, a Liverpool boxing promoter and property developer whose company Northern Improvements Ltd was the club's major shareholder. Mr Vaughan responded in a letter to *Boxing News* magazine in February 1998.

> I am sure you will be aware that I was recently arrested by HM Customs and Excise in relation to the investigation into Curtis Warren. You will be aware that the allegations centre on the laundering of millions of pounds of supposed drug money. This is something I have categorically and strenuously denied and I cannot stress how vehemently any potential prosecution would be defended.
>
> Unfortunately the rumours and stories have reached us through the grapevine and I have heard some fantastic versions of events, most of which are untrue... The investigation surrounds Curtis Warren's reportedly 'missing £185m.' Because I'm a past associate of Mr Warren, the HM Customs have deemed it necessary to investigate matters concerning me and some of my assets, such as the acquisition of an office block, a wine bar, Barrow Football Club's Holker Street Stadium, and to look into my land deals and residential building investments over the past six years. That is all.

Mr Vaughan told the *Sunday Times* that Warren did 'once put £17,500 into my solicitor's account to buy a council house I wanted to sell, but the deal never went through and I gave him his money back. I did buy a Toyota Land Cruiser from him.' He was not charged with any offence but later resigned as club chairman. 'Although I am confident that I will be completely exonerated at the conclusion of this affair, it is possible that the investigation could continue for some time. I have reached the conclusion that my position at the club has become untenable,' he added.

Dutch officers visited England to interview various people. Several were arrested and questioned, including a Greater Manchester police officer whose family were friendly with Warren. There were stories of pubs bought for cash, of businesses set up with unexplained and untraceable offshore loans, of Lancashire farmhouses bought through friends. Proof, however, was hard to come by.

However, the Crayfish team did identify one Liverpool mafia laundering outlet beyond doubt. Ussama El-Kurd's west London bureau de change had processed an estimated £70 million of illicit cash before it was shut down. In late 1998, El-Kurd had the dubious distinction of being the first person in England ever to be prosecuted and convicted solely as a money launderer. In the dock with him was Scouse bagman Peter McGuinness. Knightsbridge Crown Court heard that El-Kurd, aged fifty, had made well over two million pounds, much of it stashed in fifty-one bank accounts across Europe. Judge John Samuels, QC, said it was the most serious case of its kind he could imagine. El-Kurd's shop had been 'open house' to criminals. 'There is a wide range of notorious crime which generates street money in huge quantities,' he said. 'Without important and willing participants in facilitating its conversion…the profits cannot be enjoyed, nor ploughed into further criminal enterprise.'

El-Kurd received the maximum sentence available: fourteen years in prison and a million-pound fine. McGuinness, forty-five, from Dovecot, was sentenced to ten years in prison on two counts of conspiring to launder money. He was not in the dock to receive his sentence. Amazingly, he had been granted bail for part of the trial and had vanished ten days before the end. It is thought he made his way to the Continent where, at the time of writing, he is in hiding. Six others charged with offences relating to transporting the cash were found not guilty after a five-month trial.

FEW OF THE REMAINING Crayfish targets had Warren's sixth sense. Gary and Andrew Murphy, who had pioneered sales of Ecstasy and amphetamine drugs to Australia (see Chapter 11), did themselves no favours when they rented Cocky's white-walled mansion at Meols. The brothers shared the place for many months, together with Gary's fiancé, while Warren was awaiting trial. 'It was like running a flag up a pole outside with the words "Drug Dealer" written on it,' commented one officer. Customs officers estimated that between December 1995 and the end of May 1997 their gang made almost 200 money transfers from Australia to the UK, a total of more than £800,000 made from selling drugs on the club scene.

In May 1997, officers moved in, arresting twelve people and uncovering a batch of powdered amphetamine in a flat, hidden in the heels of ladies' shoes for export. All twelve entered guilty pleas to various charges at Liverpool Crown Court in October 1998. Gary Murphy, twenty-nine, and Andrew, twenty-four, admitted conspiring to export ecstasy and amphetamine and to conceal or transfer the proceeds of drug trafficking. They were each jailed for ten years. It is believed that at least eight members of the ring escaped prosecution and remain at large.

Others among Warren's circle of contacts were taken out. Joseph Noon and Michael Melia - known to Warren as Twit and Twat - were both unemployed, though Melia 'defied the financial odds and lived in a delightful farmhouse on the Lancashire and Merseyside border and drove a Honda Legend', according to the Liverpool *Daily Post*, while Noon ran Three Series BMW. Drugs were brought in on a lorryload of plantains from the Antwerp Fruit Market in Belgium and were transferred to a transit van which was then driven into the West Derby area of Liverpool. Four of the conspirators then stopped at a pub for a celebratory drink. Shortly afterwards they were arrested. Inside the van was a blockbuster groupage load: 110 kilos of ecstasy, ninety-seven kilos of amphetamine, ten kilos of cocaine, three kilos of heroin and forty kilos of cannabis resin. It was, commented one Crayfish officer, probably a week or two's supply for the whole of Merseyside. Seven men were later given long sentences for conspiring to import drugs. Melia received twenty-one years and Noon eighteen, while financial adviser Philip Brown, described by the judge as being at 'the very epicentre' of the plot, received twenty-three years. 'They saw their chance after Warren got nicked. They tend to go kamikaze now,' says one disdainful customs officer. 'Instead of trying to hide the stuff they just bag it up and bring it through. You can make a lot of money very quickly.'

Men like the Murphys, Noon and Melia may have seemed like significant busts. But they were small-fry compared to the biggest catch of them all.

AS THE JET CLIMBED to cruising altitude, Mr Lonzano settled into his club-class seat and glanced through the porthole at the mighty Andes receding below. It was December 17, 1997, and the wealthy businessman was looking forward to an idyllic family Christmas in the Caribbean. That morning he had left his hacienda in the hills above Cali to make the flight to Bogota; there he transferred to a plane heading for Curacao in the Dutch Antilles. A thirty-seven-mile strip of palm-dotted beaches wafted by warm trade winds, Curacao was a tourists' dream, served by elegant restaurants, casinos and shows. Lonzano, a small, dark, neat man with a thin strip of moustache, would be staying at his brother-in-law's mansion on the island. Other members of his large extended family had flown in earlier that week. It would be a merry gathering. He reclined in his chair, took a sip from a glass of champagne and relaxed for the first time in months.

Three thousand miles away, at the Dutch headquarters of the Prisma team, there was a crackle of anticipation. A contact in Colombia had tipped them off that Arnaldo Luis Quiceno Botero – known as Lucho – was heading to Curacao on a fake passport. As the effective head of the European department of a powerful cocaine cartel, he was Prisma's most wanted man. Dutch officers and the US Drug Enforcement Agency privately asserted that he was responsible for eight per cent of the cocaine coming into Europe. He was also, they believed, the mysterious Mr L referred to on the Curtis Warren wiretaps. The man they suspected of being Cocky's supplier. The man they had been after for years. Now he was travelling to an island under Dutch police jurisdiction. At last he was in their sights.

In The Hague, Chief Commissioner Tom Driessen got on a secure telephone link to his team of undercover officers scattered around the airport at Willemstad, the island's capital. Two hours after Botero's plane was due to land, a scheduled KLM 747 would leave for Holland. They wanted their captive on it. But was their intelligence accurate? Was it him or would they arrest an innocent man? Driessen's head whirred.

His confidence picked up when people recognised as Botero's relatives began to gather in the arrivals lounge. It dipped again with the news that the Colombian flight had been delayed by strong headwinds. It finally touched down as the Amsterdam flight was preparing for take-off. There would be no chance of getting Botero on it. That might cause problems. 'It would have been very difficult to take him out inside the airport because of the added security problems we might have encountered. And we certainly didn't want to do it while he was with his family. It would have been a very tricky situation given the limited resources at our disposal on Curacao,' says Driessen.

As the Colombian aircraft touched down and taxied to a halt, officers disguised as baggage handlers made their way on to the tarmac to keep watch. They knew their suspect was incognito. His appearance would probably bear little resemblance to the blurred surveillance photographs they had memorised. They had to ensure that no-one slipped past. A ground support crew pushed the mobile steps up into place and the plane door slid open. Blinking into the sunshine, the passengers clambered down the steps and walked in a single file across the tarmac to the terminal building to clear immigration. None gave any indication of wariness or unease. Radio communications between the snatch squad were relayed back to The Hague and Driessen's office.

'They had only a matter of a few moments to spot the target, confirm his identity and remove him from the line,' says Driessen. 'Then they came up against an unexpected problem; they spotted the man they thought was the target, but the guy walking in front of him looked exactly the same. It was like he had a double with him.'

Despite the confusion, the team leader gave the nod to move in on the man they believed was Botero. He looked startled as he was hustled away from the line and frogmarched quickly across the tarmac to a waiting police van. 'At this point we were very nervous, because from the moment they gave the signal to make the arrest, we heard nothing on the line from Curacao for many minutes. We had to wait while they verified who it was that they had arrested. Of course, he denied being who our officers said he was.'

After an age, the team leader came back on the phone. They had him – at least, they thought they did. He was travelling under the name Lonzano. Botero's relatives became agitated when he failed to appear. Officers also noticed a number of suitcases circling uncollected on the baggage carousel. They contained expensive Christmas presents. At the police station, Lonzano insisted he was an innocent businessman and demanded the presence of a lawyer. It would be several days before the next flight, time enough for a rich man like Botero to stall extradition. As he was questioned at length by the Prisma team officers and Dutch officials, a small delegation formed at the station counter demanding his release. Arguments raged. Voices were raised. The police said he was a member of a drug cartel. The lawyers said he was a businessman. A judge was found. He decreed the officers could take their captive to Holland if they proved it was Botero, but set them a time limit to do it. They had until Christmas Day.

'The deadline was ticking away all the time. In the end we were able to get our hands on Botero's fingerprints from the Drug Enforcement Agency in Washington. They were a perfect match to the man we had in custody.' It was Christmas Eve. Botero was put on the next to Holland, flanked by some quietly triumphant officers. He arrived in handcuffs on Christmas Day. On Boxing Day, senior DEA officials flew in to talk with the Dutch. An order to arrest Botero on suspicion of possessing cocaine had lain on file in their Miami office for some years. The FBI in Los Angeles also had an order to arrest him over a drug conspiracy in 1995. Their visit would be followed by a US Government extradition application. With it was a letter from Thomas Snow, head of the International Criminal Section of the US Justice Department, stating that Botero was 'an important supplier of cocaine for the United States'.

The Prisma team and the prosecutors were not about to give up their prize. 'We scored a very big hit with Botero,' says Driessen. 'From intelligence we know there was a great deal of panic in Cali and Bogota. The information was spreading through the cartels. I really don't think they expected us to be capable of making an arrest like this and it scared them.'

The problem was getting their witness to testify. The only person they had was their snack-bar source (see Chapter 12) – now aged twenty-nine and very nervous, having read about Botero's arrest in the newspapers. Prosecution officials paid him another visit. He wanted money. 'I need it to take safety measures,' he said. His price was 25,000 guilders. Such was the desperation of the public prosecutor's office that they acceded. It had never been done before in Holland, and it is unlikely it will be repeated. Questions were raised in the Dutch

Parliament and a statement was demanded from the Minister of Justice. One of Botero's three lawyers would later call it 'a dramatic lowest point in the Dutch justice'.

Despite this, Botero failed in his attempt to prove his arrest and prosecution was unlawful. On 8 October 1998, he was convicted, fined 100,000 guilders and jailed for six years, joining Warren in the maximum-security prison at Vught. There had been no mention of Warren at his trial; Botero was not even questioned about the Scouser and Warren's lawyer denies he had anything to do with Botero. But the Dutch police are adamant they were linked. For Tom Driessen, a man whose life is devoted to tracking to drug barons, it was the sweetest moment of a notable career. 'He is one of the ten most important criminals inside Colombia. My colleague from the Police Nacional said that at the moment he's the most important Colombian criminal in jail outside Colombia. Cali was worried, the Police Naçional were very congratulatory and the very important people from the DEA were here the next day. It's nice to know that inside that small world, it was a very attractive arrest '

THE TRIAL of Elmore Davies was held well away from Liverpool, at Nottingham Crown Court in the Midlands. Eight people stood accused of a variety of charges relating to perverting the course of justice over the Venue shooting. They included John and Joseph McCormick, John Newton and Phillip Glennon senior. Glennon's secluded luxury home in West Derby had been raided and bags containing around one million pounds in various currencies had been found buried in a flower bed in the garden (at the time of writing, this money is still in the possession of Merseyside Police, its ownership contested). Michael Ahearne and Tony Bray were also charged with corruptly agreeing to give or offer money to Elmore Davies, while Davies was further charged with 'corruptly attempting to obtain money for the supply of information intending to facilitate the subversion of the prosecution of Philip Glennon Junior.' Glennon Junior had been jailed for six years in February 1998 after being convicted of possessing ammunition with intent to endanger life.

The hearing began in May 1998 and immediately became mired in legal argument. During weeks of pre-trial evidence, Glennon's counsel, Tim King QC, argued that the British and Dutch were working together to entrap Warren and illegally swopping information. Judge ruled it would be unfair for Glennon to stand trial with Davies because of procedural errors made in obtaining permission to use the Dutch phone, though not before the sixty-one-year-old had been described in court as 'a very wealthy man as a result of drug-dealing activities from which he amassed a fortune'. The case against him was frozen, not dismissed. He demanded the return of the money found in his garden and compensation for damage caused by the police and their dogs. 'Any property should be returned to the defendant if he hasn't been convicted,' said his solicitor. The cases against the McCormicks and Newton were thrown out and they walked free.

Then Elmore Davies's counsel, Alex Carlile, QC, questioned the legality of the electronic probes planted to trap his client. 'We say the probes were obtained unlawfully, in bad faith and/or dishonestly.' He claimed certain evidence relating to the probe applications had been tampered with or altered, with some entries being removed. But his application to rule the probe evidence inadmissible was rejected.

The court heard that Davies had 'changed sides for money' after being passed over for promotion. In one of the recorded conversations, Davies told Ahearne, 'This is important. Curtis's phone in prison is being recorded. His cell is bugged. There is an undercover policeman in prison with him … This is confidential police information. Dutch police have also tapped the phone of someone Curtis has spoken to … That's top fucking secret. It can only come from one place, and that's me. He won't get it from anybody else.'

Another tape recorded a conversation between the detective and Karl 'Macca' McDonald, a former doorman described by Davies as 'a man heavily involved in selling steroids to bodybuilders'. He had once worked for Ahearne as a driver and bodyguard.

McDonald: 'I'm here to put you on your guard. It's about Warren.'

Davies: 'It's all right. I have had nothing to do with him. They have been at it for months. I've told Warrior to make sure Warren's associates stay away from his house, because it is dangerous. I've never met him. Never spoken to him. Never been in his company. I know that John Newton knows him. I have told everybody, don't talking on the fucking phone. But they never, ever listen to me. That is the way they got Curtis. I guarantee it. I would not take a penny in my life. It has got to be a million pounds because I am not going to take a risk of ten years inside for nothing. Look at Escobar in the Turks and Caicos. All the money in the world is no fucking good to him now. No intelligent person wants to be in jail. They will not find any skeletons in my cupboard.'

The Alabama probe caught Davies asking Warrior about a meeting with Tony Bray:

ED	*What's he bunged you?*
MA	*Ten.*

ED   *You keep it out of the way.*

MA   *Oh, it's gone.*

ED   *We don't mind.*

MA   *It's gone.*

ED   *Leave it.*

MA   *Gone for now, and when it's all sorted...*

ED   *Be a holiday.*

MA   *Oh yeah.*

ED   *Fucking do California.*

There was more and worse. 'Curtis's phone in prison, every call is recorded,' warned Davies. 'His cell is bugged. There's an undercover policeman in prison with him on remand. Curtis thinks he's a criminal but he's not, he's a policeman...'

When Davies, aged fifty, stepped into the witness box, he had a lot of explaining to do. He gave it a good stab. Of course he knew of Curtis Warren, he said. 'In the late Eighties, he established himself in Liverpool as a drug baron of some repute. His fame and reputation grew. In 1995, he left the city and went to Holland. He was the number one drugs baron in Europe and now he is paying the price for that.' But Davies said he had been joking when suggesting he could have advised Warren how to stay out of prison; it was 'bullshit' spoken over a drink in his lounge with Mick Ahearne. He insisted he had turned down Ahearne's request in September 1996 to meet Warren and denied he was a 'bitter' man. He did admit to agreeing to pass on information on the Venue shooting but said it was because the poor disciplinary record of a police witness was being covered up in order to secure the conviction of Glennon as an associate of Warren. 'I felt something nasty was going on,' he said, and was on 'a frolic of my own.'

The jury was unimpressed. Davies, Bray and Ahearne were all found guilty. 'Your motives were sheer greed and anger at not receiving the recognition, by promotion or posting abroad, you felt you deserved,' Mr Justice Curtis told Davies, jailing him for five years. He was the most senior policeman to be convicted of corruption for almost three decades. Ahearne, described even by his own counsel as 'a bit of an oaf', was jailed for fifteen months. The case against Phillip Glennon for perverting the course of justice was dropped on the orders of the judge. Tony Bray, described as the 'go-between and paymaster' to Warren, was jailed for three years. At the time of writing, Davies is pursuing an appeal.

At the conclusion of the case, Phillip Glennon Senior issued a press release through his solicitors:

> On 3 August 1998 Mr Glennon was discharged from the case. Upon being discharged, the Judge made certain observations on the prosecution evidence that, to date, have remained unreported. He observed that the case involved consistent and cynical breaches of law by the investigating officers. He even noted that some of the breaches of law had been incited by very senior officers at an international level and that these breaches had been continuous and over a considerable period of time. These breaches involved investigating offices committing criminal offences on foreign soil and cynically breaching undertakings given to one of this country's European neighbours.
>
> It is hardly surprsing that Mr Glennon feels aggrieved that his name, and that of some members of his family, has been besmirched without any opportunity for redress until now ... My client's only regret is that his son remains in

prison, convicted on the evidence of a police officer who has now been demonstrated to be a liar, and in the face of prosecution evidence that exonerated his son. That case is the subject of an appeal. It is now Mr Glennon's desire to put these matters behind him and there will be no further statement from my client or any member of his family.

Glennon's son was later freed on bail by the Court of Appeal and ordered to be re-tried following revelations at the trial of Elly and Warrior. He agreed to plead guilty to a lesser offence of possessing an imitation firearm with intent to cause fear of violence to persons unknown and the original charge was dropped. His sentence was lowered to three-and-a-half years. Timothy King QC, for Glennon, said it was now accepted that although a crude attempt had been made to restore the gun, it was incapable of firing bullets. It had been placed in Glennon's hand and gone of leaving him 'as shocked as anyone', said Mr King, but the bullet had been jammed.

Warren was pleased for the Glennons, disappointed for Bray, and could not have cared less about Davies or Ahearne. At the same time, he was fighting for his own freedom. In May 1998 the Dutch newspaper *NRC Handelsblad* reported the latest developments in his appeal:

British detectives tapped phone lines of suspects in the Netherlands and bugged their apartments without informing the Dutch authorities. These accusations are dominating the [appeal] in The Hague of suspected drugs trafficker Curtis Warren. For the first time ever, the court ruled that the defence could cross-examine foreign police on their investigative procedure. The allegation that British police used illegal methods in the Netherlands stem from Liverpool police commissioner [sic] Elmore Davies.

In 1996 Merseyside police received permission to tap Davies' phone at the police station and to place a microphone in his apartment in Oxton. The transcripts of the conversations show that Davies regularly warned accomplices of the bugging methods used by the British police. The recordings imply that Cameron Walker, the drugs liaison officer attached to the British embassy in The Hague, co-ordinated the monitoring operations of British suspects by the customs authorities and the police.

Davies further claims that mobile phones are 'cloned' to facilitate tapping by the British police. And, according to Warren's Dutch lawyer H. Jahae, the conversations show that the British police - very likely illegally and without approval from their Dutch colleagues - placed bugging equipment in Warren's apartment in Sassenheim... Last week he obtained documents from the investigation which, he claims, show unequivocally that the British detectives exceeded their authority.'

His appeal failed but he immediately served notice that he would take it to the Supreme Court. By then, Operation Crayfish was over.

'THE JOB took over our lives. I was at McDonalds in Chester with my wife and kids, who I hadn't seen much of, and we were trying to have a family day out together.

We had just sat down with our burgers and fries when my pager and phone both went off. It was a job. There was a run on and I had to go. As I jumped up, grabbed the car keys and started to make my excuses, my wife looked at me and pleaded, "How are we going to get home?" I was taking the car.'

The dedication and sacrifice of the anonymous Crayfish officers was monumental. One had his family Christmas dinner in July because it was the first available opportunity. It had been an unforgettable, rollercoaster ride. 'None of us will ever forget it. The camaraderie and the team a spirit were unforgettable,' is one typical comment. 'Crayfish was a one-off. I don't think it will ever be repeated. It was fantastic,' is another. Though they had a few failures - most notably The Banker, who would escape without so much as a charge - these were massively outweighed by success. By mid-98, more than eighty people had been arrested and the total drug seizures in Crayfish-related jobs were staggering:

Heroin	267	kilos
Cannabis	2600	kilos
Ecstasy	384	kilos
Amphetamine	339	kilos
Cocaine	436	kilos
900 CS gas canisters		
Ten guns		
Three hand grenades		

There were also individual plaudits. Colin Gurton was awarded an MBE. Other officers were rewarded with promotions. Here, surely, was a model for future co-operation between police and customs. Not so. 'By 1996 it was going down a bit, by 97 it was quite bad and by 98 it was all over,' says one officer. 'It went sour over statistics.' The old rivalries over which agency claimed which bust had resurfaced.

In April 1998, the Regional Crime Squads were disbanded and rolled into the new National Crime Squad, with a remit to tackle serious crime wherever it occurred. At its launch, NCS Director-General Barry Penrose made much of the bringing down of Warren. Yet one of the first practical things the NCS did was to effectively withdraw from Operation Crayfish, the most successful joint venture ever undertaken between police and customs officers. 'They came to us one day and said they were pulling out,' says a senior customs officer. 'They offered to leave a token of two officers with us but said they could no longer be involved on a major level.' The offer was declined and Crayfish as an entity was effectively wound up in March 1998, at the end of the financial year, although on-going individual investigations continued.

The police have a different slant on events. According to a senior National Crime Squad officer, 'Crayfish should have become a working concept for operations in the future between customs and police but it didn't for a variety of reasons. First, the NCS was formed. It had to find its feet in the marketplace. It had to be seen to be making an impact and justifying its money and existence. I am also sure there were problems on the ground between police and customs. Another reason for the break was that we differed over the way Crayfish should go. We wanted to use the Dutch Product wiretaps to pursue more targets over here. Customs didn't agree.' The customs officer replies, 'We thought that was a very dangerous route to go down and felt it would be a waste of time. We certainly had different views on how the Product should be used. It was an invaluable intelligence tool but putting it into court was a different matter.'

The arguments coincided with several severe blows to the reputation of HM Customs and Excise. For long immune from the day-to-day flak to which the police are accustomed, the end of the century saw them face unprecedented criticism. Once again their bane, Brian Charrington, was at the heart of it. After a spell in hiding he had turned up in Calpe, an exclusive resort on the Costa del Sol, where he lived in a luxury villa guarded by dogs and electronic security. He had a string of boats, flew a private helicopter and kept crocodiles as pets. In 1995 he was convicted in his absence of involvement in cannabis by a French court after the seizure of a drug-laden yacht but no moves were made to extradite him.

In May 1997, he was arrested by the Spanish at his villa and was later released on £100,000 surety accused of drug-running. He was said to be behind a huge cannabis consignment on a Maltese-registered motor vessel, the Simon de Danser, which was boarded by armed commandos from the Special Boat Squadron 100 miles off the Portuguese coast. Cannabis worth £14.5 million was found on board. Four former Royal Marines were among those arrested. But the subsequent court case collapsed because of what the judge called 'overwhelming' abuse of process by customs officers. The boat had been seized without proper authority. It was 900 miles from Britain, and the defence successfully argued that it was like 'arresting a shoplifter before he got to the checkout'. Extradition proceedings against the Teflon Charrington were dropped. At the time of writing he is still awaiting trial in Spain.

Some police officers expressed quiet glee at what they saw as customs' comeuppance. Wiser heads realised that the spats had to end. At the very least, Operation Crayfish could provide a blueprint for a better way forward. A top-level meeting was called between the two 'sides' and

FALL OF A CARTEL

Steve Rowton, who replaced Paul Acda as Deputy Chief Investigator, was asked to draw up a protocol for joint working practices. 'We spent months going backwards and forward as with drafts of the protocol which would give us a framework. After all, we are on the same side. It is getting the bad guys that we are all interested in,' says Rowton. His ground rules marked out the relationship of HM Customs National Investigation Service and the National Crime Squad. 'Investigators from both organisations are touring the country taking the message to front line officers,' reported the London *Evening Standard*. 'Partnership without duplication' was the buzz phrase. The protocol came into force in the middle of 1999, just as Curtis Warren was awaiting his appeal to the Dutch Supreme Court.

17

DEATH BEHIND BARS

> '*When the guards returned they saw*
> *Curtis Warren standing over the other man,*
> *who was obviously very badly injured...*'
>
> Dutch Justice Ministry spokeswoman

CURTIS WARREN LIKES to keep fit. In his Dutch prison he has lost weight and looks better for it. The fleshy look captured in his mugshot when arrested – the photograph used on the cover of this book – has disappeared. He keeps his mind in shape too and is now almost fluent in Dutch. The energy he previously put into his drug empire is now directed at winning acquittal and fighting other legal actions against him.

'Inside he reads a lot, listens to the radio and trains,' says his solicitor, Keith Dyson. 'He is bright and personable. He helps one or two of the other inmates with their reading and writing. The Dutch are amazed at the loyalty he commands and the way people flock to him, the camaraderie. They don't get that in Holland. If a Dutch national gets jailed, even a real villain, they act as though it's the end of the world, but he takes it all in his stride and they are impressed with that. He knows everything that is going on. He is also very well organised and very intelligent. He only has to read case papers once and he has got it. He is very well up on current affairs.'

There has been a lot to keep tabs on. The boss of a Liverpool security agency was assassinated as he sat at his kitchen table reading a newspaper. Two men were shot dead as they trained at a Liverpool gym. Another former Merseyside Drugs Squad officer faced corruption charges, though he was acquitted. Michael Showers's son Aaron died after drinking rum from a bottle in which cocaine had been suspended. A Scouser was caught driving through Staffordshire with £29 million-worth of cocaine, Ecstasy and amphetamines. Ray-Ray Nolan served two years of his three-year sentence before returning to England to face charges over his involvement in an earlier £1.7 million raid at a Security Express depot. He admitted handling £328,460 of the money and also stealing a Range Rover used in the raid. He was jailed for seven years.

In early 1999 Stan Carnall, the Big Fella, went down. He had been observed the previous summer driving into yet another motorway service station – 'Can't they think of somewhere else?' asked one copper – in Lancashire and handing a package to a woman with two children sitting in a Cavalier. The woman was his sister, Catherine Callaghan. An estate car then parked alongside and its driver, James McGing, removed a rucksack from the Cavalier and drove off. He was trailed and stopped on the M74 motorway in Scotland. The rucksack contained five kilos of heroin.

Carnall was visited at his Liverpool home by Scottish police officers and was told he was under arrest. He began to pack pullovers into a bag, though it was mid-summer.

'Stan, it's not that cold in Scotland,' said one of the officers.

'It is in winter,' came the reply. The Big Fella knew the score. He was going away. At the age of forty-seven, Carnall – described as a 'security firm manager' – was found guilty of drug smuggling and sentenced to six years imprisonment. The Court of Criminal Appeal later increased it to ten years. 'We consider Carnall a significant figure,' a jubilant customs officer told the Liverpool *Daily Post*. 'He is a businessman who has figured on the periphery of many of our investigations in the Merseyside area for some time.'

There was much also speculation among Merseyside detectives about who – if anyone – would 'take Warren's place' in the Liverpool underworld. No-one stood out as having the wherewithal or contacts that Cocky had cultivated, but certain lesser individuals were deemed to be worth investigating. One was Spencer Benjamin. Well-known to the Merseyside Police, he was one of the Granby crowd and a close friend of Mark Osu; the pair had once been arrested together after a high-speed car chase through Liverpool. Benjamin and Osu had also walked free from Manchester Crown Court after being acquitted of attempting to shoot dead Colin Fitzgibbon junior as he walked down a street in 1995, an attack which foreshadowed the Gang War. After Cocky's incarceration, the Merseyside Police Major Crime Unit received information that Benjamin was involved in the movement of large quantities of Class A drugs from London to Merseyside. They decided to put him under surveillance.

THE GRAND NATIONAL is the most famous steeplechase in the world. Every spring the big race meeting it attracts tens of thousands of visitors to the Aintree course and to Merseyside's hotels, bars and restaurants. It is everyman's race, a British institution that draws everyone from high-rollers to housewives. Friday, April 9, 1999, was the eve of the big event and, as usual, Lime Street train station was one of the main points of arrival.

Shortly before 8 PM, the Euston express pulled in at platform seven. Several hundred passengers disembarked and headed for the concourse. Among them was a twenty-four-year-old Toxteth man, Edward Serrano. He clutched a carrier bag bearing the name Wade Smith, an exclusive Liverpool clothes store. The bag contained a shoe box packed with just under four kilos of cocaine, worth around £200,000. Serrano had collected the drugs several hours earlier and was bringing them home for distribution. The crowds arriving for the National offered perfect cover. Or so he thought.

Serrano was a friend of Spencer Benjamin, and tailing him were officers from the Major Crime Unit. They had been conducting a lengthy investigation which revealed that Benjamin travelled often to London, there meeting several individuals not known either to the MCU or their colleagues from the National Crime Squad. The main contact was a man of Latin American origin whom he met regularly in the Pizza Hut restaurant close to the Queensway tube station in Bayswater. At around midnight on a Wednesday in March, 1999, the duo had been observed near the tube station. Benjamin was carrying a black satchel, which he passed to the Latino before stepping off the pavement to hail a cab. Police would later conclude that this handover was the first part of a down payment on a large shipment of cocaine.

A week later, Benjamin and Edward Serrano were back at the Pizza Hut, where they were joined at a table by the South American. Serrano was carrying his Wade Smith bag. They spoke briefly, then the South American left, taking with him the bag, which contained the second instalment of cash for the cocaine. The following morning Benjamin returned home, while Serrano waited outside a telephone kiosk on Queensway. Again the South American arrived, carrying the same Wade Smith bag, which he handed back to Serrano. The Liverpudlian then headed off to catch the train from Euston, mingling with commuters and with Londoners bound for the Grand National.

The detectives on his tail planned to follow Serrano out of Lime Street station; they wanted to know where the drugs were bound. Sometimes, however, things go wrong. Two British Transport Police officers, unaware of the undercover surveillance operation, decided there was something suspicious about Serrano and stopped him before he could leave the station. A search revealed the cocaine. The two officers could scarcely believe their luck, but to the watching MCU team it was nothing short of calamitous, potentially putting the entire job in jeopardy.

And it was no ordinary drug job. The police had scored a major breakthrough when they named the mystery Latin. He was Ivan Mendoza di Giorgio and he hailed from Venezuela. Intelligence identified him as the highest-ranking UK representative of the Cali Cartel. His job was to hand over the coke, pick up the payment and ensure the money was sent safely back to his paymasters in South America. He had established an ingenious method of moving large quantities of cash from one place to another. He would wait outside a unit on an industrial estate close to Gatwick Airport, where a security van made a regular tour to pick up money from companies on site. The guard would collect around £100,000 a time from him and then take it to his firm's headquarters, from where it would be dispatched to a bank in The Netherlands. It is estimated that around £1.5 million was laundered, this way thanks to the unwitting help of the legitimate security company.

Back on Merseyside, the non-arrival of Serrano spooked Benjamin. It was later alleged in court that in just eighty-five minutes he called his associate's mobile phone eleven times to try to locate him. 'After Serrano's arrest a decision was taken not to arrest Benjamin or di Giorgio at once but to continue surveillance on them,' says Det Supt John Kerruish, who headed the investigation. Patience paid off. When Benjamin's home was finally raided a month later, police recovered almost forty kilos of cocaine, along with eight mobile phones and around £75,000 in cash.

Benjamin was arrested later that afternoon at a flat on Lodge Lane in Toxteth which he had occupied following Serrano's arrest. Sparsely furnished, it contained only a television, video and hi-fi system, for which Benjamin had paid £2,500 in cash.

Benjamin denied that he was heavily involved in organised crime, claiming that he was just an 'area manager' paid only £70 a week. His lifestyle told a different story. The previous December he had taken his girlfriend and their two young children to the Mexican resort of Cancun, paying £1,742 cash for the trip and then a further £75 for use of the exclusive first-class lounge at Manchester Airport. The couple shared a £120,000 house on south Merseyside and Benjamin wore a £10,000 Ebel wristwatch.

Benjamin later pleaded guilty to his role in the plot but claimed to be only a courier. He was jailed for ten years. Serrano, who also admitted guilt, was jailed for nine years. The biggest sentence went to di Giorgio, who got twenty years.

Yet the successes failed to dent the flow of drugs. Recently one of the most violent Black Caucus members has been spending time in southern Spain, getting to know his new friends in the Russian Mafia. Another leading Granby figure is reported to have spent several months in the Near East. The fact that it is a major staging post for Afghan heroin is surely a coincidence. Not to be outdone, the White Clan sent a two-man delegation to Colombia in a bid to contact the cartels. An informant told a Liverpool detective that they tried to meet the Ochoa organisation. 'They wanted to establish direct links to Colombia as Curtis Warren had done and have access to as much heroin and cocaine as they wanted,' he said. They were unsuccessful.

In May 1999, 300 heavily-armed police, backed by ten helicopters, raided a cocaine factory the size of a village in the Colombian jungle. Guarded by a paramilitary warlord, the plant had three laboratories up to four storeys high, sleeping facilities for more than 200 workers and was capable of producing eight tonnes of cocaine a month. In October, law enforcement officials arrested thirty people in Bogota, Cali and Medellin, including Fabio Ochoa junior, forty-two, the former Medellin cartel kingpin. 'It is as if we had removed the CEOs of several major corporations who had joined together in a major conspiracy,' bragged US Attorney-General Janet Reno. Yet a report to Congress suggested that the US was losing its battle to stop the flow of illegal drugs from South America, and estimated that Colombia would export 250 tonnes of cocaine to the States by 2001.

There was also been interesting news closer to home. Stephen Whitehead, described as Warren's 'first lieutenant' at their trial, escaped. The prison authorities had decided, without consulting the Dutch police, to de-categorise Whitehead from a high risk to a lower-risk inmate and moved him to a jail near Gröningen. He had a maximum of only eighteen months left to serve of his seven-year term. But on 10 June 1999 he locked himself in a workroom after others had left, then broke a window, slipped through and swam across a moat to a waiting car. 'When we catch him we will have to look for a more secure prison,' a fatuous Ministry of Justice spokesman observed. Whitehead was recaptured six months later, hiding out in central Holland.

WEDNESDAY, SEPTEMBER 15, 1999. It was late afternoon and Warren had been allocated one of the last exercise periods of the day. The rules within his secure unit dictate that only four prisoners at a time are allowed into the yard, for a maximum of two hours a day each. The prisoners are always under the intense gaze of the watching guards and of CCTV cameras. Warren and his three companions stepped out as the sun was beginning to fall.

They made quite a quartet. H.Baybasin, a Turk of Kurdish descent, was regarded by the Dutch authorities as one of the biggest heroin barons in Europe. He had been arrested in 1998 by a Dutch police team specialising in heroin trafficking, similar to the Prisma Team that targeted Warren and the cocaine cartels. His trial caused a sensation, with allegations that he operated with the collusion of the Turkish government. Voluminous wiretap evidence revealed him planning murders and kidnappings in Turkey, the USA and Canada. Jailed for twenty years, he was likely to serve the entire sentence at Vught.

With him was a Dutchman, Henk Ebben, who had been in Nieuw Vosseveld since 1994. Described by one source as 'a psychopath from Rotterdam,' Ebben had run a gang exporting Ecstasy and cannabis. He was caught after killing a courier who had defected from his organisation, taking some of Ebben's clients with him. He was expected to serve eighteen years.

Finally they were joined by Cemal Guclu, another Turk serving twenty years. Guclu was, quite simply, a maniac. In the 1980s, he served a jail sentence in Spain for drugs offences: while incarcerated, he strangled a fellow inmate. He was examined by a Spanish psychiatrist who ruled that Guclu was so crazy there was no point trying him for the killing. On his release, he moved to Holland and set up an operation smuggling Turkish heroin to Denmark. He soon suspected one of his lackeys of stealing money: in May, 1991, Guclu and an accomplice walked into a Dutch snack bar armed with a machine gun and two pistols and opened fire on the man. He was badly injured; his Polish girlfriend was killed. Guclu was arrested and was again assessed by a psychiatrist. This time the doctor ruled that Guclu faked his madness and was in fact perfectly normal, and so he was tried and convicted.

In prison he soon earned a reputation for impulsive and uncontrollable bouts of violence. He slashed one fellow prisoner with a craft knife, leaving wounds so serious that a plastic surgeon was unable to repair the damage. Had he been serving his sentence in the United Kingdom, Guclu would probably have been moved to a secure hospital, but in Holland he was sent to Nieuw Vosseveld. There he was several times put into isolation for attacking other inmates.

'I knew from the beginning that he was a very strange man,' Curtis Warren would later say. 'He used to call people names, shouting out all the time, and there had been several incidents in the jail with him involving either other prisoners or prison staff. ' Other inmates shunned

Guclu; only the personable Warren and a Colombian drug dealer ever gave him the time of day. The Turk was unpredictable at the best of times, but that afternoon in the yard he had a grievance. The previous evening, Henk Ebben had been watching his beloved Feyenoord football team on television and infuriated Guclu with his vociferous shouting. When the Rotterdam-based side scored a goal, prompting prolonged cheering from Ebben, matters came to a head. Order was subsequently restored but it seems Guclu remained incensed.

That may explain why, as the four men gathered in the exercise area, Guclu picked a fight. He approached Warren and began to berate him. In the pressure-cooker environment of the maximum security unit, things soon boiled over. 'I tried to calm him down but he hit me in the chest,' Warren later said. 'I hit him back and he fell down and hit his head against the wall. But he came at me again, so I hit and kicked him and he went to the ground. I kicked him three or four times in the face but he came back at me again so I hit him and he fell to the floor, again hitting is head on the floor.'

The fight was spotted almost immediately by guards monitoring the exercise yard but the strict regulations at Vught stated that they could not intervene in an incident within the yard until extra officers could be alerted. By the time they rushed in, Guclu was unconscious. He was rushed to hospital and put on a life support machine. The next day he died of a brain haemorrhage.

As the news broke, a Dutch Justice Ministry spokeswoman gave a statement which was quoted in the *Independent* newspaper:

We are trying to find out the cause [of the fight] but guards saw the Turkish man head-butting Warren. They don't know the reason or what was behind the apparent vendetta. Curtis punched him back and within seconds they were hitting out and kicking each other and rolling over on the ground. Because of security fears, the guards' priority was to get the other prisoners out of there as quickly as possible. They felt it would be too dangerous to separate the men fighting while other prisoners were in the immediate vicinity. When the guards returned they saw Curtis Warren standing over the other man, who was obviously very badly injured.

As soon as he heard the news, Keith Dyson, Warren's solicitor, rang journalists to put his client's side of the story:

> From what I gather, Curtis was attacked by the Turk. The guy headbutted him. I have never butted Curtis myself but I would imagine it's like slamming your head against a brick wall. Whatever happened, Curtis was only defending himself. The Turk came off worse and tragically died from his injuries. Whilst at Vught, Curtis has not got himself into any trouble of any sort. There will be an inquiry and we will have to wait and see. Although this is now a murder inquiry, I believe the facts that I have heard dispute that it was murder.

At first it was believed the fight had been caught on the prison's security camera system and Warren and his legal team were confident this would support his claim of self-defence. They were soon to be disappointed when it was discovered that, mysteriously, the cameras covering that part of the yard were not working at the time of the incident. It did not take long before conspiracy theories began to surface. One even suggested that the incident had been stage-managed by the prison authorities to deal with the troublesome Guclu. During subsequent police interviews, Warren insisted that he had been attacked first and had acted only in self-defence. In a statement, he said, 'I am terribly sorry that he died. I never meant to kill him. He was a pitiful character and I felt sorry for him. He was so lonely. But I got angry when he kept coming back at me.'

Warren was put into solitary confinement and allowed to see only his lawyer and the prison chaplain. Even this was to cause controversy. After several weeks, the chaplain publicly complained that the conditions in the prison were inhuman; he likened them to a concentration camp. He was particularly critical of the treatment of Warren, even claiming he had been pressured to 'spy' on the Liverpudlian and divulge any information he was told to the authorities. After his outburst, the chaplain was relieved of his position.

This was not the first time that the regime at Nieuw Vosseveld had attracted condemnation. Prisoners routinely claimed that they were denied basic prison rights such as visits and phone calls and some even alleged they had been woken by the guards every two hours during the night, preventing proper sleep. According to one informed source, 'In 1995, a group of priests wrote a report saying that the regime made people go crazy. And the European Committee Against Torture has in the past said that the conditions in which inmates are kept amounts to inhumane treatment. One governor was even moved because he was deemed to be too severe. Some prisoners are on the edge of paranoia. It is very grey and depressing and there have been major outbreaks of violence there in the past. Curtis Warren is one of the few who can cope.'

Within a fortnight of Guclu's death, Cocky was summoned to appear before an examining magistrate for a preliminary hearing into the attack. A court in the southern Dutch medieval town of s'Hertogenbosch, a twenty-minute car ride from Nieuw Vosseveld, was to be the venue. Then the Dutch authorities made another unprecedented decision. Concerned, they said, that Warren might try to escape with outside help, they set up a courtroom inside the confines of the prison itself. A convoy of unmarked Mercedes cars tore down the tree-lined country road leading from the nearby village of Vught, bringing the prosecutor, magistrate and clerk to hear the case opening.

Although it would be more than a year of examination and legal procrastination before the authorities decided what action to take over Guclu's death, the publicity could not have come at a worse time for Cocky. His appeal against conviction for the drugs conspiracy was at that moment being considered by the Hoge Raad, the highest court in Holland. He had launched it on twelve grounds. 'One of the main ones is that he was inhibited from asking questions of the English police officers involved in the Dutch investigation. They were citing diplomatic immunity to avoid giving evidence. He was unable to receive a fair trial. He was stopped from cross-examining witnesses over what precisely the facts were,' said Mr Dyson.

Like so much in Warren's story, his appeal was no run-of-the-mill event; Cocky seemed incapable of doing anything ordinary. It threatened to have major ramifications for international co-operation and the Dutch legal system. 'There are special lawyers who argue these things before the Supreme Court. They call them causation hearings. If it went against him he would certainly take it to the European Court quite quickly. Also it is not necessarily the end of the road in Holland. The Dutch Supreme Court can only review the law as it applies to his trial. The Dutch court refused to look at the English evidence other than to say that they were going to operate on a 'principle of trust' and accept what the English had told them to be correct. They wouldn't let any questions be asked.'

On 16 November 1999, the Supreme Court rejected Warren's appeal. He vowed to fight on and, at the time of writing, is taking his fight to the European Court of Human Rights. Even drug barons have rights. He continues to claim that Operation Mix was initiated on the basis of evidence from wiretaps that were 'illegal' and breached his rights as a European citizen. The case has been lodged but no date set for a hearing.

On Millennium Eve, when the rest of the world was celebrating, a large detachment of soldiers ringed Nieuw Vosseveld. Armoured cars and troop carriers blocked the gates. No-one was allowed in or out. The Ministry of Justice claimed it was merely a precautionary measure in case the Millennium Bug caused the failure of locking systems on the doors. But inside sources told Dutch radio that the authorities had received reports of a planned breakout. Chief suspects were hard-core members of the Yugoslavian mafia: at least one of their number, a major gun-runner named Popovic, is in the prison. The evening passed without incident.

IN THE SPRING of 2000, the Dutch public prosecutor finally made a formal application to seize Warren's criminal assets. He wanted a staggering 63 million guilders – around £18 million. It was way, way more than any similar claim ever against a British criminal;

indeed it was the second-highest such application made in Holland under the country's new 'stripped to the bone' legislation aimed at depriving criminals of their illegal loot (the most was 77 million guilders sought from convicted hash dealer Charles Zwolsman).

Details of how the figure was arrived at have remained elusive, as the matter has never been aired in open court. Information supplied to the present authors suggests it includes 270 mainly terraced properties in the North West of England, worth an average of between £18-25,000 each and providing regular rental income; a number of pubs in Liverpool; the funding for a housing development on Merseyside; a number of apartments and hotels in Turkey; and a large number of commercial properties on a Liverpool city centre street.

The action was contested by Warren and the figure sought gradually fell, first to 36 million guilders, then to 15 million, less than a quarter of the original claim. There was also the a small matter of the £3.1 million found in Brian Charrington's loft in June 1992 (see page 112). It had been sitting in a police bank account ever since, earning interest. Who did it belong to? In January 2001, the British press reported that Warren had struck a deal with the Dutch authorities to pay around £5 million, to include the money from the loft. 'If it is not accepted then we will not reach an agreement,' said his barrister, Han Jahae. The deal was expected to be finalised in May 2001.

On February 13, 2001, after months of pre-trial hearings, Warren was finally due in court for final submissions over the killing of Cemal Guclu. He was to present his own account of what happened and to answer any questions put by either the prosecutor or the panel of three judges who would decide his fate. The location was the Palais van Justitie in s'Hertogenbosch: this time there was no last-minute switch but security around the courthouse was at a level never seen before in the town. Just as proceedings were due to start, however, word came that there was a problem. Warren was refusing to wear a bullet-proof vest on his journey to the court: he argued that he had no fears for his personal safety and that turning up in body armour would prejudice his case by making him appear to be a dangerous criminal. The guards insisted that he wear the vest. With stalemate between them, Warren stayed in his cell.

'Mr Warren definitely wants to come to tell his story,' Han Jahae told the court. 'In fact, he has a message for you today. He has asked me to say, Tell the president [of the court] that I am desperate to come. He does not have any problem with the handcuffs, the hood they want to put on his head, the disorientation by the guards or the helicopter shadowing the escort to the court. Just the vest. He understands that they want to prevent him from escaping but he thinks it is a bit hypocritical and cynical to want to protect him now because the authorities should have protected him in September 1999. This is the first time they have wanted him to wear a hood. He has a fundamental right to be present and I shall be doing all I can to try and persuade him to come after all. Because it is an argument of self-defence it is essential that he comes and makes his case in front of the court.'

Proceedings were adjourned for an hour but there was no resolution to the problem and the hearing resumed without the only man who really knew what happened that day. Prosecutor Maria van Thiel demanded a five-year sentence for the charge of manslaughter. She said Warren was bigger, heavier and stronger than his victim. The fact that Guclu went down on several occasions should have told Warren he was gaining the upper hand. She added that the kicks to the face were of particular relevance.

Mr Jahae's drew attention to Guclu's history of violence and said his client was known to have tried to help the Turk in the past. The pathologist's report also seemed to favour Warren. It stated the kicks to the face were of small significance to the death of Guclu, as they left little if any impression on the deceased's face. Even Guclu's family, who were present at the hearing, blamed the prison reghime and not Warren. After listening to the arguments, the judges adjourned and decided to reconvene to announce their verdict a week later.

Again they met in s'Hertogenbosch. Again, Warren was absent. The court took less than a minute to return its verdict. Shortly before 10.30 AM on Friday, February 23, 2001, the presiding judge read out the decision he and his two colleagues had reached: 'Guilty.' While they partly accepted the self-defence line, they ruled that 'the level of violence used by the defendant during the incident had been excessive.' The penalty: four years in jail, to be served consecutive to his existing sentence.

The announcement was a hammer blow to Warren. It meant the chances of him being freed before the end of the decade were now remote. Han Jahae announced an immediate appeal against the conviction, stating his 'astonishment' at the outcome. He had been quietly confident after addressing the judges for almost an hour on behalf of his client the previous week. At the time of writing, a full re-trial was expected to be held within twelve months.

THE LIVERPOOL MAFIA continues with new blood and fresh contacts. In November 1999, four more men received long jail terms for smuggling heroin. One was a former associate of both Delroy Showers and Stan Carnall, though there was no evidence to link either of them to the case. National Crime Squad investigators believe the gang could have been bringing in up to fifty kilos a month for almost eighteen months, a frightening statistic even by Liverpool standards. One of the group lived in Curacao and was described as 'a travelling salesman arranging drug deals' on behalf of a Turkish syndicate in the Netherlands.

In July 2000, Merseyside drugs baron Eddie Gray was jailed for twenty-four years for the supply of more than £2.5 million of heroin and Ecstasy. Gray, aged thirty-eight, a seventeen-stone bear of a man, was worth an estimated £20 million and was notorious for rolling up at his local Aldi supermarket in a £100,000 Ferrari Spyder convertible. His house in West Derby was furnished in garish opulence, with a swimming pool housed in an enormous conservatory. 'I hope you die of Aids,' he shouted at the jury as he was sentenced.

And in February 2001, gangster John Haase, aged fifty-one, who had figured prominently in Liverpool's 'Turkish Connection' (see page 173), was jailed for thirteen years after admitting selling guns to crime gangs in Glasgow. The weapons included an Uzi sub-machine gun and a .357 Magnum revolver, immortalised in Clint Eastwood's *Dirty Harry* movies as 'the most powerful handgun in the world'. Haase, who was much feared within the Merseyside underworld, also ran a security firm called Big Brother.

There is, however, no indication of a new 'Mr Big', a man with the influence and respect Warren commanded from so many quarters. The Banker is in retirement abroad, latterly on the Spanish coast, though he doesn't much like the heat. No-one knows how much he made from crime. Despite one or to claims in the

British tabloids, there is no evidence that Warren has tried to continue his activities from inside. The conditions in which he is held would prevent that, even if he wanted to. Links with the outside world are severely limited. In 2000, Warren's father, Curtis Senior, died after a long illness, aged sixty-five. The funeral mass was held at a Catholic church in Kingsley Road, Toxteth. There was no chance of Warren being allowed to attend.

So what does the future hold for Curtis Francis Warren, the Cocky Watchman? Some senior police officers would dearly love to see him facing an English court over the Elmore Davies corruption case (Davies himself was due for release in March 2001: incredibly, he will come out to a £92,000 lump sum in addition to a £22,000 police pension for life). Police say he could be charged with a similar offence or with conspiracy to pervert the course of justice. Yet while the sight of him back before a British judge would delight many in law enforcement, others believe a line should be drawn under the Warren affair. They fear that extraditing him back to England would open a Pandora's Box of problems best kept sealed. Warren and his legal team on both sides of the North Sea have long claimed to know secrets about collusion, corruption and illegal practices relating not just to their case but to other high-profiles investigations involving both HM Customs and Excise and various police forces over the years. What they claim may be irrelevant or incorrect but not everyone is prepared to take the risk.

In the meantime, Warren will spend his days in a claustrophobic nightmare. While the Dutch penal regime is generally regarded as liberal, Nieuw Vosseveld is an anomaly. It has been criticised by human rights groups and its regulations likened to mental torture. His fellow inmates still include men like Colombian kingpin Lucho

Botero, Henk Ebben, the Turk Baybasin, Popovic the Yugoslav, Khalid Salah, an insanely violent Moroccan armed robber, and Menk Kok, a Dutch double-dealer awaiting trail on serious arms offences and who is said to have links with intelligence services all over Europe. One can only speculate on the nature of their recreation-room conversations.

Warren's lawyers say he will continue to pursue his appeal, based on alleged violations of his human rights. His case was put into the European Court timetable in early 2000 but there is as yet no date for a hearing. Could he win his freedom? Stranger things have happened. Meanwhile his notoriety grows rather than diminishes. In the final month of the twentieth century he was the subject of a national television documentary in a series called *Godfathers* – 'a new six-part series for ITV that pulls no punches' – which gave a brisk overview of his career. True to form, he had declined an interview for the programme.

Perhaps one day he will give his side of the story. The cannabis smuggler Howard Marks did, reinventing himself in the process as a charming rake. Until then, others can only make informed guesses about his character, his personality and his motivations. As he sits in his cell and keeps his own counsel, it is impossible to penetrate his multi-layered mind or to say how he feels about what he has done and where he is going. Surely he imagines the day of his freedom. Maybe he plans to find a positive outlet for his enormous energy and ambition. But it will be his burden to be forever remembered as the Cocky Watchman, the drug baron *par excellence*. It was a burden he chose.

Where will he go when released? Would he ever return home?

'Why not?' says his solicitor. 'He likes Liverpool.'

GUVNORS

THE BEST-SELLING AUTOBIOGRAPHY OF A SOCCER HOOLIGAN GANG LEADER

BY MICKEY FRANCIS WITH PETER WALSH

FOR FIFTEEN YEARS, Mickey Francis and his brothers led a violent gang following one of Britain's biggest football clubs: Manchester City. They fought scores of battles with rival 'firms' until their bloody reign was brought to an end by the police Omega Squad in the most successful undercover operation of its kind.

'I have had hundreds of fights, on the terraces and in shopping centres, in pubs and night clubs, in motorway cafes and train stations. I have been stabbed, hit with iron bars and beer glasses, kicked unconscious, punched and butted. I have been threatened with death by people who meant it. I have been chased alone through dark alleys, hunted like a dog, and suffered cracked ribs and broken hands and black eyes. I have dodged bricks, coins, rocks, cans, distress flares, planks of wood and bottles filled with piss. I have been beaten by policemen, arrested, fined and thrown in jail. And I have dished it out. In spades.'

GUVNORS tells it like it was in the heyday of the soccer hooligan culture.

'Compulsive reading... riveting stuff.' – *INSIDE SPORT*

'The most explosive book about soccer violence... EVER!' – *SUNDAY SPORT*

AVAILABLE AT ALL MAJOR BOOKSTORES PRICED £6.99